The Seven Secrets of
CRYSTAL TALISMANS

Photograph by Gallery Photo

About the Author

Hailing from a family of gemologists and gem cutters, Henry M. Mason is a gemologist, lapidary, gem cutter, and amateur mineralogist. He is certified by the Gemological Institute of America and holds an MBA and a bachelor of science from the United States Air Force Academy. Henry is the owner of the Crystal Vaults, www.crystalvaults.com, a website devoted to producing the best in crystals and crystal knowlege.

The Seven Secrets of
CRYSTAL TALISMANS

How to Use Their Power for
Attraction, Protection
& Transformation

Henry M. Mason

Llewellyn Publications
Woodbury, Minnesota

First Edition
First Printing, 2008

Cover design and insert design by Gavin Dayton Duffy
Interior book design by Joanna Willis
Interior illustrations by Llewellyn art department
Insert photography on pages A-27 and A-28 (except carved horse) by Bob Dube, Roshard Minerals;
    page A-1 and carved horse on page A-28 by Llewellyn art department

Llewellyn is a registered trademark of Llewellyn Worldwide, Ltd.

Library of Congress Cataloging-in-Publication Data
Mason, Henry M., 1949–
    The seven secrets of crystal talismans : how to use their power for attraction, protection & transformation / Henry M. Mason.—1st ed.
        p. cm.
    Includes bibliographical references and index.
    ISBN 978-0-7387-1144-7
    1. Crystals—Psychic aspects. 2. Talismans. I. Title.
    BF1442.C78.M38 2008
    133'.2548—dc22
                            2007049607

Llewellyn Publications
A Division of Llewellyn Worldwide, Ltd.
2143 Wooddale Drive, Dept. 978-0-7387-1144-7
Woodbury, MN 55125-2989, U.S.A.
www.llewellyn.com

Printed in the United States of America

CONTENTS

Color plate gallery follows page 228

INTRODUCTION

Do you seek prosperity, love, or happiness? Do you want to increase your fortune, rid yourself of a bad habit, or protect yourself from harm? Does someone you know want to create a better life, find true love, or gain financial success? Are your needs for friendship, security, safety, growth, wisdom, and spirituality unfulfilled? Is joy, faith, or peace missing in your life? If so, you need a talisman. Made and used correctly, a talisman can focus and magnify your abilities by connecting you with the Universal Life Force and the Life Force of the planet Earth. The correct talisman can lead you to riches, happiness, love, growth, wisdom, or whatever you seek. It can enhance your abilities, help protect you from harm, and show you the path to free yourself from afflictions.

Talismans are wondrous objects having what in the past appeared to be mystical powers. They can focus energy to accomplish the seemingly impossible. They can magnify our abilities, enhance our power, and protect us from harm. However, for virtually all of history, their secrets have been undiscovered. Their powers have been hidden. But now, through the efforts of scientists and researchers, their secrets have been revealed. We understand now what was previously thought to be magic. We know how to make talismans that actually work! We have discovered the Seven Secrets of Talismans.

Throughout history, and surely before recorded history, people used all manner of things to make lucky charms, amulets, and talismans to aid in their quests and in achieving their desires. In this book we focus on the use of gems, crystals, and minerals. Our reason is simple: as you will discover shortly, the First Secret of Talismans reveals that only natural minerals actually work reliably as talismans. Of course, not knowing the Seven Secrets of Talismans, many people in many cultures have attempted to use animal bones, herbs, cabalistic runes, and complex astrological signs and numbers to somehow aid them in achieving their desires. Certainly some of these efforts were successful and some were not. The problem has always been to know how talismans actually work so that they can be made and used dependably. Applying the knowledge revealed in these Seven Secrets will enable you to quickly and easily use the power of talismans and amulets.

After reading this book, you will discover the Seven Secrets of Talismans. You will master the art and science of making, selecting, and using talismans successfully. You will be delighted and amazed; but more importantly, you will become successful in your endeavors. You will learn how to help others achieve what they desire through the capabilities of the human mind magnified by the Universal Life Force.

What are these wondrous things, these talismans? A talisman is an object, often a crystal or gemstone, that serves to focus and amplify people's personal power to get what they want, protect what they have, and help guard and defend them from harm and trouble.

In this book, you will learn about talismans and gain an understanding of how they can work effectively to focus and amplify energy. Then, as we explore their mysteries, you will discover why a talisman must be a natural object like a gem, crystal, or mineral. You will come to know the secrets of the inner crystal energy grids and the deeper mysteries of the natural earth power structures that science has discovered only recently, which give each talisman its special and unique power. You will explore and master the mystery of the color rays and gain greater understanding of the color spectrum and its central role in choosing the right talisman. In later chapters, the proper methods for preparing, selecting, and activating a talisman will be clearly explained. Finally, in the last chapter, the proper use of a talisman will be examined. In all, the Seven Secrets will be revealed, allowing you to fully realize the power inherent in these mysterious but powerful objects.

How to Use This Book

To understand how to make and use talismans and amulets, you need to master each of the Seven Secrets explained in this book. In the discussion of most Secrets, there are charts that can be used to apply the Secret in your efforts to select, make, and use talismans and amulets. These charts will provide detailed references to the talismanic properties of many commonly available minerals.

Read through each chapter to become familiar with the material. Once you have done so, you will see that the book is organized so that it serves easily as a reference book. Each Secret explains a key step and provides detailed listings for quick reference. The book concludes with a summary example that will lead you through the use of each chapter. Use it for quick reference and as a refresher.

Appendices and inserts provide detailed summary listings of commonly available minerals suitable for making talismans and amulets. Be aware, however, that there are over six thousand valid mineral species, and many have a dozen or more common names. The charts are a beginning. Mastering the Seven Secrets will give you the knowledge to go beyond the charts to use any mineral or combination of minerals to fashion a powerful talisman or amulet for virtually any purpose.

Within the text, all mineral names are in lowercase for ease in reading. In the tables, valid mineral names are in BLOCK CAPITALS, and trade names or synonyms are in small letters and cross-referenced to their proper species. This effectively provides a valuable glossary of common minerals that will be useful in searching for the necessary raw material for fashioning effective talismans and amulets.

Introducing
Talismans
and Amulets

The stories of talismans and amulets go back to the very beginnings of recorded history and reveal a long tradition of seemingly magical artifacts used by kings, queens, bishops, popes, sultans, and ordinary folk to improve luck or prosperity, or to cure diseases. The history of these objects, made by alchemists, priests, magicians, magi, shamans, and witches, goes back as far as we have records. George Kunz reports that Pliny wrote in the first century about some of their uses and that poems and epics of the third and fourth centuries paint a rich pattern of the uses of elixirs, potions, talismans, and amulets.[1] Albertus Magnus, writing in the thirteenth century, elaborated on the uses of herbs, plants, and minerals for both protection and health.[2] All through history, curative, protective, and divination powers have been attributed to rubies, sapphires, emeralds, and virtually every other precious stone. The records of virtually all Western and Eastern civilizations provide extensive reports on the use of all kinds of talismans for a seemingly inexhaustible list of needs.

But history is confusing at best. History gives us thousands of years of prescriptions for the use of minerals in making talismans and in healing. The ancient Greeks used amber to cure deafness. The Romans believed a topaz could stanch the flow of blood from a wound, and they used lodestones to cure blindness. In 1320, for example, Nostradamus reported that diamonds would render one invisible, that an amethyst would prevent intoxication, and that wearing a carnelian would dissipate anger. Medieval writers reported that opals strengthened the eyes. The Romans associated emeralds with sexual passion and reproduction. In later times, other cultures believed they improved memory and eliminated depression.

---

1 George Fredrick Kunz, *The Curious Lore of Precious Stones* (New York: Dover Publications, 1971), 13.
2 Ibid., 17.

However, we also know that in the Baltics, amber was used to cure not deafness but toothaches. And whereas the Romans believed a topaz would stop the flow of blood, the ancient Hebrews believed a carnelian would do so. And although the Romans used lode-stones to cure blindness, other cultures have used silver or rubies.

You may have read somewhere that an emerald will protect a person from harm, yet in another source you find that it is the stone of happiness. As reported by Kunz,[3] a Chinese encyclopedia dating to the Ming Dynasty prescribes that jade be ingested in a powdered form to strengthen the lungs, the heart, and the vocal organs. Kunz, however, also reports that Arnoldus Saxo wrote in 1220 that the emerald will render one unconquerable and cure one of laziness.[4] And, adding to the confusion, *The Catholic Encyclopedia* tells us that in the Middle Ages, the emerald was considered to have the power to heal blindness.[5]

The history of amulets is similar and intermixed with that of talismans. Generally, an amulet was a device worn to protect the wearer from some specific evil or malady. The term *amulet* seems to be derived from the Latin word *amuletum*, a "means of defense." Differing from talismans, amulets were generally worn as ornaments. The wearing of an amulet was believed to endow the wearer with the magical properties represented by the shape and inscriptions. To add to their power (and durability, if not value), amulets were often made from precious and semiprecious stones, usually the medium-hard ones. These were not too difficult to carve, yet retained their shape in use. Virtually all amulets were culturally and religiously based.

Most amulets were carved or inscribed with figures and symbols whose meanings were often considered magical.[6] Often the protection was derived from the shape, not the material. The Egyptians, Assyrians, Arabs, and virtually all other cultures employed them. The Egyptians were prolific users. They carved frogs to protect fertility, ankhs to provide for protection from death, and scarabs (dung beetles) as the symbol of new life. Animal shapes have been popular in many cultures. Carved bears gave strength to protect from physical harm, carved bulls endowed virility and protected from impotence, and lions bestowed courage, protecting the wearer from injury in battle.

---

3 Ibid., 385.

4 Ibid., 59.

5 Charles L. Souvay, "Precious Stones in the Bible," *The Catholic Encyclopedia, Volume XIV* (New York: Robert Appleton Company, 1912), http://www.newadvent.org/cathen/14304c.htm (accessed May 28, 2007).

6 Nick Farrell, *Making Talismans: Living Entities of Power* (St. Paul, MN: Llewellyn Worldwide, 2001). This book serves as an excellent reference for the history and uses of inscribed talismans and amulets.

In addition to the shape of an amulet, in many cultures the protection was based on the inscriptions on the amulet. The variety of runes, languages, signs, symbols, and meanings is staggering. While it is certainly possible to catalog many of them, and many such catalogs exist, there is no Rosetta stone that will allow us to find the universal powers of runes, signs, and symbols. With the exception of depictions of plants, animals, and natural landscape formations, there is no relationship between nature, runes, and symbols. Runes and symbols are purely products of the human mind, and, for the most part, they are completely cultural in meaning.

However, as we will discover in our exploration of the Seven Secrets of Talismans, there is a natural basis for the power of amulets. We will discover that there are indeed protective talismans. We will discover the basis for their powers and learn how to use them effectively.

After reading through the numerous new and old texts that report on the uses of minerals as talismans and amulets throughout the ages, you certainly could not be blamed for being bewildered. You would end up confused and honestly wondering, for example, what power a moonstone really has for someone seeking inner peace, or doubting the ability of a blue tourmaline to really protect you on a sea voyage. You may have wondered, in total exasperation, if you need to inscribe some cabalistic, ancient mystical symbols on a pure gold tablet and wear it over your heart during the full moon to find true love! The record of the use of minerals for talismans and amulets is certainly confusing.

The history of the uses of herbs and other plants as talismans and amulets, and for healing, is also as old as recorded history and just as confusing and conflicting. For centuries, herbs were really the only medicines. The lore and legends of their uses were passed down from healer to healer. Preparations of flowers, petals, roots, and bark from virtually every growing plant were tried for almost every ailment.

It is certainly probable that the power in the plant kingdom, particularly in the herbs, can be used for talismanic purposes as well as for healing. However, the lore and legend of such uses, like that of the crystals, gems, and minerals, is contradictory. Jasmine is cited in one source as useful for protection, yet another says it helps in acquiring love and money. One source says lemon grass repels snakes, a second says it draws a new lover to the user, and a third says it can bring a sense of stability to life. The Celts are reported in some sources to have believed that they would be invincible in battle if they passed some St. John's wort through the smoke of the summer solstice fire, and then wore it into battle. The people of Scotland wore it as a charm against the influence of fairies. Another source tells us it is useful for love, strength, and happiness. Verbena has long been believed to protect against witches, but so has rue. Ancient Greeks believed thyme would give a person strength, but the English once were convinced you used it to see fairies. The Greeks used agrimony to relieve eye troubles, and the Anglo-Saxons believed it was a talisman against goblins.[7]

The conflicts are caused by lack of knowledge and understanding. Early civilizations did not have the tools and science to learn nature's secrets. The priests, sorcerers, and magicians of previous times did their best, but any success was hit or miss. Even if they stumbled on the correct talisman for a particular use, they had no way to know if they were right. Unfortunately, even today the knowledge needed to sort fact from fiction in the use of herbs and plants as talismans does not exist.

We know nature's herbs and plants have life-giving power. Their uses in the healing arts are well documented. *Plant Talk* magazine reports that plants are the origin of over thirty medicinal drugs whose efficiency has been proven in therapeutic trials.[8] One example is colchicine. Colchicine is derived from the autumn crocus, also known as the "meadow saffron." It is approved by the U.S. Food and Drug Administration for the treatment of gout and also for familial Mediterranean fever.[9] Science is doing a good job in determining the medical uses for plants, but so far has had little success in determining their talismanic uses. We simply as yet have no way to understand which ones have what powers and why.

However, in the mineral kingdom, this is not the case. Science has discovered the basis of talismanic uses for minerals. This knowledge is revealed here in the Seven Secrets of Talismans. This book recognizes the power and healing energy of herbs and plants, but focuses on the verifiable talismanic uses of the earth's minerals.

Due to recent scientific discoveries, we now have the ability and knowledge to unravel mysteries that have been hidden to this day. We can now answer such questions as: "What exactly is a talisman?" "What is an amulet?" "How do they work?" "How do I select the right talisman or amulet for a particular purpose?" "How do I use it properly?" It is time to start answering these questions.

---

7 Gretchen Scoble and Ann Field, *The Meaning of Herbs, Myth, Language, and Lore* (San Francisco, CA: Chronicle Books, 2001).

8 Arthur Hollman, "Plants in Western Medicine Plant Fact 82," http://www.plant-talk.org/Pages/Pfacts11.html (accessed April 28, 2007).

9 RxList, "Colchicine: Indications & Dosage," http://www.rxlist.com/cgi/generic/colch_ids.htm (accessed April 28, 2007). Part of WebMD, this site states that "RxList is an online medical resource dedicated to offering detailed and current pharmaceutical information on brand and generic drugs. Founded by pharmacists in 1995, RxList is the premier Internet Drug Index resource."

What Is a Talisman?

A talisman is an object, often a crystal or gemstone, that has a specific ability to aid a person in focusing and amplifying his or her power. A talisman is not a lucky rock. The power of a talisman is its ability to aid us in achieving the future we desire. Modern studies of psychology have taught us a powerful lesson:

> Our feelings become our thoughts
> Our thoughts drive us to action
> Our actions solidify and become our habits
> And our habits lead us to our future[10]

A talisman is both a focus and a natural amplifier. As a focus, it serves to control our feelings to lead us to the right thoughts. It serves to focus our thoughts to lead us to performing the actions we need to take. It focuses our actions, creating important new habits. It is through these new habits that our desired destiny is achieved. As an amplifier, a talisman brings us the ability to join with the power and energy of the Life Force of this planet. This power and energy serve to multiply our own individual efforts when they are properly applied. A talisman is, in a way, similar to a flashlight.

Imagine you have to walk on a dark, dangerous mountain trail one night. For many people, it would seem foolhardy to just pocket a lucky rock, then head down the trail and hope they don't fall. A wiser person, first having a desire to be safe and feel secure on the journey, would think about the problem and determine that maybe a flashlight with charged batteries would be good to take along. He or she would procure a flashlight, turn it on, focus it on the ground ahead, and follow the light. The flashlight would help the person focus his or her feelings and thoughts on being safe on the trail, and through the light it emitted from the power in the batteries, it would amplify his or her efforts to see effectively on the dangerous trail and be safe on the journey.

---

10 Ramses Seleem, *The Illustrated Egyptian Book of the Dead* (New York: Sterling Publishing Co., 2001), 64.

What Is an Amulet?

An amulet is a special talisman that is used for defense and protection. Certain crystals and minerals form in crystal structures that focus their power to defend and protect. The discussions of the Second Secret of Talismans will teach you how to identify and use amulets. For the rest of this book, the term "talisman" will be inclusive of both talismans and the specialized talismans called "amulets."

So, Now, How Does a Talisman Work?

A talisman works in two ways. First of all, it focuses your feelings, thoughts, actions, and habits so they serve to help you achieve the destiny you desire. Secondly, a talisman is a natural energy and power source. When properly connected to a human mind, it can channel the Universal Life Force to that mind to amplify its power.

How Do I Select the Right Talisman for My Needs?

Selecting the right talisman requires understanding two things: how to determine the proper material for a particular talisman, and how to fashion and empower that material successfully. The first four Secrets of Talismans explain how to select the right material from which to fashion a talisman for a particular purpose. The First Secret explains the necessity of using only natural things to make effective talismans. The Second Secret reveals the crystal energy structures of talismans and explains how the six structures are aligned with human needs. The Third Secret teaches us how to align the color rays of influence of a talisman to our needs. Finally, the Fourth Secret delves deep into the heart of a talisman and explains the fundamental earth power of every talisman.

Understanding the first four Secrets of Talismans will ensure we select the right talisman for our needs. The next two Secrets of Talismans explain how to correctly fashion a talisman for a particular use and how to ensure it is as powerful as it can be. Only an understanding of these six Secrets will allow the successful selection of a powerful talisman.

Knowing I Have the Right Talisman, How Do I Use It Effectively?

Using a talisman is not particularly difficult. The Seventh Secret of Talismans teaches us how to master the use of talismans in our lives through the principle of Causal Duality. Once you understand what this principle involves, and you know how to apply it, you will be able to use talismans effectively. While the concept is explained in detail in the Seventh Secret, applying the principle of Causal Duality is very similar to using that flashlight we just described. Causal Duality teaches us that once you understand what you desire (in our flashlight example, safe travel), you use that understanding to focus on your feelings (in this case, alleviating the sense of danger coming from the dark trail) to result in the thought to take a flashlight. This thought leads to the action (again, in our example, taking the flashlight, turning it on, and focusing it on the trail), and that action leads to the habit of being safe while traveling. That habit leads us to the desired result of safe travel. Using a talisman effectively involves not doing certain things as well, but we will leave the details for the Seventh Secret discussion.

Summary

The long history of talismans and amulets is confusing and contradictory. Different cultures have ascribed different capabilities to the same gem and crystal. The ancients did not have a scientific way to determine the talismanic properties of minerals or plants. While we are still seeking the knowledge to understand the talismanic uses of plants, we now have the knowledge of the mineral kingdom we need to make effective talismans and amulets. We need only understand the Seven Secrets of Talismans to begin to use the powers of these wondrous creations.

THE
FIRST SECRET
OF TALISMANS

The power of a talisman comes from the natural energy
of the sun, the moon, and the planet Earth.

To discover the Secrets of Talismans and understand their power to help us achieve our desires, we first need to understand ourselves as humans, and as children of this Earth. The reason is revealed in the First Secret of Talismans.

We all know that we are a part of this Earth. Our bodies are made of the atoms of this planet. Our physical attributes are those that allow us to survive and prosper here on Earth. Our lives and fates are linked to the fate of the planet. As children of Earth, physically, we have a natural affinity for Earth things. We can breathe the atmosphere, walk on the surface of the planet, and tolerate the extremes of heat and cold found here. We can drink the water, gain sustenance from the plants and animals, and use the minerals for energy and heat. That affinity has made us a part of the earth's ecosystem. We are part and parcel of this place. We are, as the Native Americans know well, children of the earth. We draw our life's energy from this place we call Earth.

The Life Force of the planet Earth is a layer of the Universal Life Force that underlies and powers the universe. All cultures and civilizations have recognized this force. The Taoists call Life Force energy *chi (qi)*. It is *mana* in Polynesia, *prana* in India, *ruach* in Hebrew, *baraka* in Islamic countries, *ch'i* in China, and *ki* in Japan. Whatever it is called, the Universal Life Force is the power of the mutual replenishment, transformation, and renewal of all things in the universe.

The universe started with the big bang, a release of unfathomable energy. The Universal Life Force springs from the big bang that created the universe, and, at the same time, is the source of that energy release. Colleen Deatsman describes this Universal Life Force exquisitely as "the formless pervasive, causal undercurrent of all that is . . . the divine intelligence, the engine of creation, the cosmic grid upon which and from which the universe springs."[1] As the universe expanded after the big bang, this Life Force energy expanded

---

1 Colleen Deatsman, *Energy for Life* (Woodbury, MN: Llewellyn Worldwide, 2006), xiii.

and transformed into multiple forms and layers, some light and some dense. The lighter forms of the Universal Life Force are elements of the spirit world; the denser ones are elements of the physical world. The Life Force of the planet Earth is a lighter form. The earth itself, and its material elements, are denser forms of that energy. Before we can understand the Life Force of the planet Earth, we need to understand that we and our planet are energy layers of the Universal Life Force.

As you know, matter is just coalesced energy. Albert Einstein's famous formula $E=mc^2$ gives us the relationship: energy is matter times the speed of light squared. Energy can become matter, as it did in forming the sun and the earth, and matter can be converted back into energy. The thermonuclear fires of the sun and our atomic energy plants bear testimony to the power of this conversion. Matter is energy.

So, the universe is energy. That energy is the universe, and the source of everything manifested in our universe: the stars, our sun in particular, our planet, our lives, and ourselves. We are part and parcel of the universe. We are dense, self-aware energy beings. We are a part of the Universal Life Force, and we live on a planet that is a part of the Universal Life Force. We came from the same place. We are made of the same elements, coalesced from the same energy.

As parts of the universe, we are composed of energy. We take in energy for life and give off energy as we exist. We consume dense matter as food and convert it to chemical energy to nourish our physical bodies. We consume spiritual energy, and use it to nourish our minds and our souls. To some, this spiritual energy comes from prayer; for others, it comes from meditation. Still others find it in solitude, in the laughter of a child, or in the stillness of a winter night. These are some of the bountiful sources of the lighter, spiritual forms of the Universal Life Force.

In absorbing energy, we not only consume it, but we also convert it and transmit it. We use our bodies to transmit physical energy, as when we exert great physical force or lift heavy weights. In a similar vein, we use spiritual energy to conquer great issues like fear, uncertainty, and loss. As we use our physical and spiritual energy, we again seek to replenish it from the physical and spiritual energy sources of the universe.

The life energy we use comes from the Universal Life Force manifested in three sources:

- The sun, which radiates energy on the surface of the earth in tremendous quantities each day

- The moon, which reflects the energy of the sun onto the earth and also, through its revolutions around the earth, causes cycles in the earth's energy rhythms

- The earth, with its molten core of magma, a powerful storehouse of energy that makes up most of the planet

None of this is in any way a religious issue. Many religions have different notions of where the sun, the moon, and the earth got this energy and power. The Universal Life Force in some cultures and religions is considered to be the manifestation of God's will and power, making it divine. In others it is viewed as a natural phenomenon. But the devotedly religious of all faiths, the agnostics, and the pagans do agree that the Life Force energy in the sun, the moon, and the earth does actually exist—they just differ on the nature of its origin.

We all agree that the sun produces energy that is transmitted through heat and light to the earth. It has been estimated that about every three weeks, the sun transmits the same amount of energy to the earth as is contained in all our reserves of coal, oil, and natural gas. Averaged over a year, the sun transmits enough energy to light three 100-watt light bulbs to every square meter of the earth! It would take well over a billion average power plants to come close to the energy of sunlight on the earth.[2]

In a like manner, the sun projects tremendous spiritual energy to the earth. Virtually all cultures with recorded history have a sun god or goddess or the equivalent that embodied their understanding of that spiritual strength and power. He is Tonatiuh to the Aztecs, Horus to the ancient Egyptians, Apollo to the Romans, Tsohanoai to the Navaho, and Freyr to some Norse. She is Sol in Norse mythology, and Sunna to the Germans. But whatever the name and whatever the culture, we instinctively understand the sun as the source of spiritual strength.

We all also know that the moon provides us light it gets from the sun, but it does more than simply reflect it. It transmutes that light, moves it toward the cool end of the spectrum (the blue end), and changes the energy in subtle ways. We all are affected to a degree by light. Everyone can sense the eerie elements of moonlight, and we inherently know the differences. Sunlight is bright, warm, and physically energizing. Moonlight is dim, cool, and much more metaphysical in its energy effect. We also know life on Earth, like the tides, seems to be regulated by the moon. But it might well be that life on Earth was made possible by the moon. The moon stabilizes the tilt of the earth on its axis, allowing for a variety of climates on the earth, preventing the Iceball Earth scenario. It would have

---

2 National Aeronautics and Space Administration, "Why Isn't Earth Hot as an Oven," http://Earth observatory.nasa.gov/Library/Oven/ (accessed May 2, 2007).

been hard for human beings to evolve on Earth without the moon exerting its influence to make the planet hospitable to life as we know it.[3]

Like the sun, the moon is also a source of spiritual strength to Earth. The moon has been worshiped, like the sun, since recorded time. While in some cultures the moon was a god, in many it takes the feminine form. For example, to the Chinese she is Shing Moon, to the Celts she is Morgana. Again, different names in different cultures, but a universal recognition that the moon is a power in the affairs of men and women, and one that should be respected and honored.

The earth is, as we are, a construct of the Universal Life Force, a manifestation of it in dense matter. The earth absorbs energy from the Universal Life Force, uses it, and transmits it in the same ways we do. It gets physical energy from the heat and light of the sun. For example, it uses that energy, and the energy from its molten core, to warm the ground, keeping it just a few feet from the surface at about 50 degrees Fahrenheit. In fact, the deeper you go, the warmer it gets. For every 100 meters you go down, the temperature goes up 3 degrees Celsius.[4] Animals have burrowed into the ground since the beginning of time to take advantage of this heat energy. People use it too. The United States produces over 2000 megawatts of electricity from geothermal energy. That is the same amount of heat as we would get from four large nuclear power plants. Magma (for the most part) is our friend. It helps warm the ground, and lets us live on this Earth.[5]

The earth also absorbs the Universal Life Force from the sun and the moon, uses it, and transmits it to the wind, the waves, and the life-giving atmosphere we need. In a like manner, it absorbs the spiritual energy of the Universal Life Force from the sun and the moon, uses it to nourish itself, and transmits that spiritual energy through its elements and compounds into the plants and animals that absorb it to sustain life. The Life Force of the planet Earth is the transmuted, transmitted spiritual energy of the planet Earth, drawn from the Universal Life Force. It is real.

We all feel and use the Life Force of this planet. Different religions and cultures have different beliefs about its origins, but we humans know deep in our consciousness that it is real. We experience it in the green of the new leaves of spring. We feel it in the warmth

3 Paul J. Henney, "How the Earth and the Moon Interact," Astronomy Today, http://www.astronomy today.com/astronomy/earthmoon.html (accessed May 2, 2007).

4 California Energy Commission, "Geothermal Energy," http://www.energyquest.ca.gov/story/chapter11 .html (accessed May 2, 2007).

5 Oregon Institute of Technology, Geo-Heat Center, "What Is Geothermal?," http://geoheat.oit.edu/what geo.htm (accessed June 23, 2007).

of the summer sun. We feed on it through the autumn harvests, and we sense its mystical elements in the cold light of a winter full moon. The Life Force of this planet nourishes us, body and soul, warms us, clothes us, and provides for our needs in this universe of mostly cold, empty space. The earth, like the sun and the moon, is a source of great spiritual strength. Mother Earth has many names. In Syria and Palestine she appeared as Astarte; in ancient Greece she was variously worshiped as Hera, Gaea, and Demeter. Even today, the concerns for global warming, the ecology movement, and the concerns for the ozone layer are tributes to the dawning understanding of the dependency we humans have on the health of Mother Earth. Her power to nurture us has always been understood. Our responsibility in return is slowly being learned. As we gain strength and power both physically and spiritually from the earth, we are learning that we must also be a source of strength and power for her.

The Universal Life Force that is transmitted to us through the power and energy of the sun, the moon, and the earth is real, tangible, and life giving. It is found in the rocks, minerals, plants, animals, water, air, and soil of the planet. It is found in us, as we are made of these things. It is powerful energy. It is our lifeblood, both physically and spiritually.

We all know that much of that energy is contained in the rocks and minerals of the planet. For example, we have split the uranium atom to harness its power, and we burn coal to heat our houses and produce electricity. The rocks and minerals give us the energy we need to survive and prosper physically. But there is more to the power and energy in the mineral kingdom than just producing heat and electricity. There is power and energy to help us in most human desires. Sometimes we use the power directly. We seek shelter; granite makes good walls. We seek heat; so we burn coal. We seek protection; and we learn that iron makes good shields.

However, this energy is not only the dense, physical kind; it also contains all the lighter, spiritual elements of the Universal Life Force manifest in the Life Force of the planet Earth. It can not only be used directly, but it can help us in other important ways as well. A talisman can draw on the spiritual power it contains to focus and amplify our abilities through channeling the Life Force to our minds. It can use the Universal Life Force flowing through the energy of the sun, the moon, and the earth to focus and amplify our feelings to lead us to the right thoughts, drive us to the necessary actions, prompt us to form the right habits, and guide us to the future we desire. Humankind has known this for millennia. History records the multiple uses of rubies, diamonds, emeralds, and all matter of crystals in human efforts to magnify our abilities, increase our powers, and protect ourselves from harm. We know the power is there; we just haven't been able to really understand how to use it. The secrets have been hidden from us—until now.

Now we know the First Secret of Talismans. It tells us that a talisman's power doesn't come from inscriptions or runes. It doesn't come from magic or mystery. A talisman's power comes from the sun, the moon, and the earth. Only natural things have this power. We need natural materials. In making and using talismans, we need to begin with natural elements if we seek to harness the power of nature, because only natural, pure things can function as talismans. This Secret tells us that all natural things, including the traditional talismans like herbs and other plants, natural crystals, minerals, and rocks are all candidates for talismanic uses. However, this book restricts itself to talismans that are made from the mineral kingdom. The mineral talismans are durable and widely available, and now with the Seven Secrets of Talismans revealed, their powers are finally understood. Another reason we focus on the mineral-based talismans is because they are by far the most prevalent. Their popularity is based partly on their appearance and partly on our instinctive attraction to their hidden powers.

Many popular minerals form attractive crystals, and our minds have a great affinity for these bright, colorful objects. They somehow resonate within our consciousness. Even tiny babies are attracted to shiny, colorful things like beads and gems. The jewelry industry thrives on this natural, inborn affinity our species has for the bright gems and natural crystals of the mineral kingdom. That affinity is embedded deep in the psyche of the human mind and is as old as time. Colorful gemstones and crystals have been prized throughout human history for their mystery and seemingly magical powers as well as their beauty. To a large degree, the affinity is based on a simple attraction for the pretty colors of beads and crystals. But in the case of nature's treasures—gems and minerals—the attraction is much stronger. We instinctively seek their power and energy. We seem to long for their presence. We actually need them in our lives. Part of this attraction is the energy they possess from the Life Force of the planet Earth. The Second Secret of Talismans explains that energy. While it isn't magic, it is certainly powerful.

THE
SECOND SECRET
OF TALISMANS

Nature has hidden crystal energy structures in
virtually all minerals. Each mineral has a specific
crystal energy structure that controls its power.
These crystal energy structures are completely
aligned with basic human needs.

The people of early civilizations had great difficulty in using talismans effectively because they could not see the secrets deep within the stones. Ancient makers of talismans were limited to hit-and-miss when trying to determine which mineral would produce crystals with a desired ability. Certainly they could see some external attributes like the color of the crystal and its shape, but many minerals form in complex combinations of colors and shapes. Sorting out all the combinations was an insurmountable task. There are just too many minerals, too many combinations of external shapes, and too many colors. Relying on the external cues of a crystal's shape and color wasn't sufficient to really understand what power the crystal had.

What has always been needed is to see into the heart of the crystal, to see the very energy structure that powers the crystal. However, until modern scientific instruments and processes were discovered, the molecular structures of minerals—their hidden crystal energy structures—could not be known. There was no understanding of how the molecules were arranged, how they held energy in their unique alignments, or how the energy was bonded within the very structure of a crystal or stone.

The hidden crystal energy structures of minerals have long been suspected. The external shapes of many mineral crystals offer good hints. Some look like cubes, some like pyramids. Some look like rectangles, and some have strange contorted shapes seemingly without any rhyme or reason. These external shapes were not enough to help unfold the crystals' inner mysteries, and they often led to confusion. Nevertheless, they were enough to give modern scientists the clues to look deeper. And look they did.

With the invention of modern scientific tools such as x-ray diffraction, scientists now can see the actual internal crystal structures of all minerals and crystals. Through instruments, we can now see the very crystal energy lattices that define their core power. With modern capabilities we can now understand how the crystal energy lattices work to charge and power talismans. Through modern science, we have unlocked the secret. We can finally see the six secret energy structures and unravel their mysteries. Fortunately for us, these crystal energies align with the basic needs of humans. But then again, why wouldn't they? We are from this world, this Earth. We have adapted to survive and prosper here. We are made of the same energy as this world. We evolved to prosper on this planet. We are a part of this planet and its life environment. It would be more surprising to discover that we were somehow misaligned with nature!

Once we understand our basic human needs, and understand how they match the hidden crystal energy structures of this world's minerals, we will readily see how those crystal energy structures that power gems, crystals, and minerals with the Life Force of the planet Earth can help us find what we seek, guard what we value, and protect us from adversity and harm.

Human needs and desires fall primarily into five basic categories. The first three relate to acquiring and protecting things we value, and the other two are related to keeping away that which we do not desire. These five needs are universal, timeless, and independent of culture, religion, sex, age, intelligence, and each other. We have more than one need at a time.

- We seek that which we do not have, yet desire. We all seek food, shelter, love, companionship, victory, health, and ten thousand other things. Life is a constant quest. We seek adventure, security, companionship, success, fortune, fame, possessions, well-being, and friendship. We seek stimulation, relaxation, knowledge, wisdom, peace, prosperity, and meaning to our lives. Humankind is unique in our constant search for elements in our lives that are missing. Everyone is looking for something or someone.

- We strive to enhance that which we possess and value. If we have some success, we want more. If we have some talent, we want to make it grow. If we have a small fortune, we want a bigger one. If we win a minor golf tournament, we want to win a big one. One of the strengths of humankind is that we have a constant desire to improve. Civilization is possible because of this valuable human trait. We develop new drugs to enhance medical care, new tools to enhance our productivity, and new social structures to enhance our quality of life. Each of us wants to improve on our lot, and improve ourselves. We all want to enhance our abilities, our lives, and our accomplishments. We want to be better.

- Third, we wish to guard that which we do possess and value. Once we find food, shelter, love, and other objects of our desire, it becomes important to protect these things. We exercise to protect our health, build fences and raise armies to protect our property, and act civilly to protect our reputations and relationships. Defending ourselves, our property, our culture, our way of life, and our loved ones is a constant battle. Nature has no compassion. Nature provides us with resources to use, but constant vigilance against the loss of that which we possess and desire is required.

- Our fourth need is to dispel that which we possess yet do not want. We get sick and we want to get well. We have bad habits we want to break. We have relationships from which we want to escape. We have worries we want to be rid of.

- Finally, we need barriers. We often wish to protect ourselves from that which we do not have but which we do not want. Famine, disease, war, accidents, natural disasters, and unpleasantness of all kinds are the afflictions against which we seek to protect ourselves. There is a lot on this planet from which we would very much desire protection.

Understanding hidden crystal energy structures and seeing how they are aligned with these basic human needs will lead us to the understanding of how to use the minerals of each structure to aid us in our efforts to survive and succeed in our endeavors. Knowing how these energy structures match human needs will help us to understand which minerals, crystals, and gems have certain powers. We will finally know what the ancients could only guess. We will master the Second Secret of Talismans.

As you would expect, crystalline structures have scientific names. After all, scientists discovered them. While these scientific names can be found in modern mineral textbooks, those descriptions just recount the basic geometric shapes of the crystal lattices. In seeking to unravel the mystery of how these hidden structures can help us focus our energies through our natural affinities for the stones, we have to look at these structures a bit differently and go beyond the basic descriptive information found in the textbooks.

As a note, the study of talismans and the minerals from which they are made is still not an exact science. The field is dynamic. For example, mineralogists have not agreed on a completely standard crystal classification system. Some books separate out the trigonal crystals as a separate system, others include it as a class within the hexagonal. This book follows the latter approach.

Seekers and Simplifiers
(HEXAGONAL CRYSTAL SYSTEM)

The first crystal structure is the hexagonal crystal system that includes the minerals that form with their molecules arranged in triangular structures, one of nature's simplest forms. The minerals of the hexagonal crystal system often form crystals with an external shape that mirrors their internal arrangement, appearing like an arrow or pointer. With this alignment of the visible external structure and the internal one providing directions and focus, these crystals and minerals can be made into powerful talismans to aid us by pointing out the way when we desire to acquire that which we do not yet possess. These crystals' energy structure will focus and multiply our desires and efforts to point to a path to that which we seek. These are the Seeker talismans.

The Seekers are powerful, numerous, and very useful talismans for aiding us in successfully starting a new effort. The Seeker talismans help us to discover new opportunities and to set out to achieve new goals. These are the fresh-start talismans, the talismans of new beginnings and new discoveries. These are the talismans of the scientist, the adventurer, the hunter, the wanderer, and the explorer. They are also the talismans of the student and the researcher.

Seeker talismans are pointers, directors, and compasses. They help us align our feelings for new beginnings into thoughts that are focused on discovery. Those thoughts lead to actions that result in the discovery of the new approaches, new angles, and new beginnings we seek. Those actions, as they become habits, develop into the new lives we

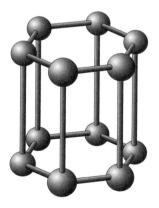

Hexagonal crystal system

seek. Later, as we unravel more of the Secrets of the Talismans, we will discover which of the Seeker talismans are useful for achieving which types of goals.

Seekers are probably the most popular type of talisman. When we need help to find new relationships, new love, new capabilities, new experiences, or new ways of living, Seekers empower us to focus and amplify our abilities to seek out the new elements we desire in our lives. Seeker talismans contain the crystal energy structure that aligns the natural energy of the crystal to the natural power of the human mind to find our way to new horizons and new capabilities.

In addition to their uses as Seekers, these crystals, gems, and minerals are excellent talismans when the need is to simplify a life or situation. From their triangular crystal energy matrix they bring us the attributes of simplicity, tranquility, minimal effort, mastery of the path of least resistance, pragmatism, practicality, indulgence, rest, relaxation, and peace.

This use of these crystals and minerals to make Simplifier talismans is very important and very valuable in today's fast-paced world. It seems everyone is looking for an oasis in his or her life. Spas are springing up everywhere. Massage therapy is a rapidly growing industry. Cruise ships are full. The high-stress world takes its toll on our bodies and our souls. We all seem to seek some rest, some relaxation, and some peace in our lives. The Seeker and Simplifier talismans are extremely useful in achieving these goals. When you or someone you know needs to simplify, to find tranquility, or to just find some time to relax and recharge, use a Simplifier.

Seeker and Simplifier talismans include rubies, sapphires, cinnabar, hematite, calcite, rhodochrosite, dioptase, tourmaline, beryl (aquamarine and emerald), and many others. Each of these minerals can be fashioned into a particularly effective talisman for use in seeking new desires and in simplifying our lives.

Common Seeker and Simplifier Talismans

Common Name (MINERAL)	MINERAL
Abraciated Jasper	Jasper QUARTZ
Achroite	ELBAITE TOURMALINE
AFGHANITE	
African Queen Picture Jasper	Jasper QUARTZ
AGARDITE	
Agate	Chalcedony QUARTZ
Agate Jasper	Jasper QUARTZ
Agatized Coral	Agate Chalcedony QUARTZ
Almandine Spar	EUDIALYTE
Aluminilite	ALUNITE
ALUNITE	
Amberine	Agate Chalcedony QUARTZ
Amethyst	QUARTZ
Amethyst Sage Agate	Agate Chalcedony QUARTZ
Ametrine	QUARTZ
ANKERITE	
ANTIMONY	
APATITE	
Aphrizite	TOURMALINE
Aquamarine	BERYL
Arroyo Picture Jasper	Jasper QUARTZ
Australian Jasper	Red/White Chalcedony QUARTZ
Aventurine	QUARTZ
Azeztulite	QUARTZ
Azurlite	Turquoise Chalcedony QUARTZ
Band (or Banded) Jasper	Jasper QUARTZ
Basanite	Jasper Chalcedony QUARTZ
Basinite	Chalcedony QUARTZ
BASTNASITE	
Bayate	Jasper QUARTZ
BENITOITE	
BERYL	
Beta Quartz	QUARTZ
Bi-color Quartz	QUARTZ
Bi-color Sapphire	CORUNDUM

Continued on next page

Common Seeker and Simplifier Talismans (continued)

Common Name (MINERAL)	MINERAL
Bi-color Tourmaline	TOURMALINE
Biggs Jasper	Jasper QUARTZ
Biggs Picture Jasper	Jasper QUARTZ
Binghamite	Hawk's Eye Chalcedony QUARTZ
Bird of Paradise	Brown Jasper QUARTZ
Black Lead	CARBON (Graphite)
Black Onyx	DYED Chalcedony QUARTZ
Black Skin Agate	Agate Chalcedony QUARTZ
Black Star Sapphire	CORUNDUM
Black Tourmaline	TOURMALINE
Black Zebra Agate	Agate Chalcedony QUARTZ
Blood Agate	Agate Chalcedony QUARTZ
Blood Jasper	Bloodstone Chalcedony QUARTZ
Bloodstone	Chalcedony QUARTZ
Blue Chalcedony Quartz	Chalcedony QUARTZ
Blue Chrysoprase	Chalcedony QUARTZ
Blue Lace Agate	Chalcedony QUARTZ
Blue Mist Chalcedony Quartz	Chalcedony QUARTZ
Blue Mountain Picture Jasper	Jasper QUARTZ
Blue Sapphire	CORUNDUM
Blue Star Sapphire	CORUNDUM
Bonamite	SMITHSONITE
Botswana Agate	Chalcedony QUARTZ
Brazil Agate	Agate Chalcedony QUARTZ
Breccia	Agate Chalcedony QUARTZ
Brecciated Jasper	Jasper QUARTZ
Breithauptite	NICKELINE
Brown Spar	CALCITE
Bruneau Jasper	Brown/White Chalcedony QUARTZ
Bruno Canyon Jasper	Jasper QUARTZ
Buchanan Thundereggs	Agate Chalcedony QUARTZ
BUERGERITE	TOURMALINE
Burrow Creek Jasper	Jasper QUARTZ
Cactus Quartz	QUARTZ
Calamine	SMITHSONITE
CALCITE	

Common Seeker and Simplifier Talismans (continued)

Common Name (MINERAL)	MINERAL
California Moonstone	Chalcedony QUARTZ
Cambay	Carnelian Chalcedony QUARTZ
Cameo (Agate)	Agate Chalcedony QUARTZ
Campylite	MIMETITE
Canadian Ocean Rock	Jasper QUARTZ
Canary Stone	Yellow Chalcedony QUARTZ
Candy Rock	Jasper QUARTZ
Caribbean Blue Chalcedony	Chalcedony QUARTZ
Carnelian	Chalcedony QUARTZ
Carnelian Onyx	Sardonyx Chalcedony QUARTZ
Carrie Plume Agate	Agate Chalcedony QUARTZ
Catalinaite	Jasper QUARTZ
Cathedral Agate	Agate Chalcedony QUARTZ
Cat's Eye Apatite	APATITE
Cat's Eye Tourmaline	ELBAITE
Cave Creek Jasper	Red Jasper QUARTZ
Caviar Agate	Chert QUARTZ
Ceragate	Yellow Chalcedony QUARTZ
CHABAZITE	
Chalcedony	QUARTZ
CHALCOPHYLLITE	
Champagne Citrine	QUARTZ
Chapinite	Jasper QUARTZ
Chicken Track Picture Jasper	Jasper QUARTZ
Chinese Opal	White Chalcedony QUARTZ
Chlorapatite	APATITE
Chrome Chalcedony	Green Chalcedony QUARTZ
Chrome Tourmaline	TOURMALINE
Chrysojasper	Green Jasper QUARTZ
Chrysoprase	Chalcedony QUARTZ
CINNABAR	
Cinnabar Matrix	Red Jasper QUARTZ
Citrine	QUARTZ
Clay Ironstone	SIDERITE
Cloud Agate	Agate Chalcedony QUARTZ
Cobaltian Calcite	CALCITE

Continued on next page

Common Seeker and Simplifier Talismans (continued)

Common Name (MINERAL)	MINERAL
Cobaltian Dolomite	DOLOMITE
CONNELLITE	
Copper Nickel	NICKELINE
CORUNDUM	
COVELLITE	
Crazy Lace Agate	Agate Chalcedony QUARTZ
Creolite	Red/White Jasper QUARTZ
Cripple Creek Picture Jasper	Jasper QUARTZ
Cuyunite	Chalcedony QUARTZ
Dallasite	Green/White Jasper QUARTZ
Dalmatian Jasper	White/Black Jasper QUARTZ
Damsonite	Lilac Chalcedony QUARTZ
Dark Blue Beryl	Irradiated BERYL
Dark Ruby Silver	PYRARGYRITE
Demion	Carnelian Chalcedony QUARTZ
Dendritic Agate	Agate QUARTZ
Denio Dendritic Agate	Agate Chalcedony QUARTZ
Depalite	Olive Chert QUARTZ
Deschutes	Jasper QUARTZ
Desolation Canyon Thundereggs	Agate Chalcedony QUARTZ
DIOPTASE	
DOLOMITE	
Donnybrook Thundereggs	Agate Chalcedony QUARTZ
Dougway Thundereggs	Agate Chalcedony QUARTZ
DRAVITE	TOURMALINE
Drusy Quartz	QUARTZ
Dumortierite Quartz	Blue QUARTZ
Dyed Agate	Dyed Agate Chalcedony QUARTZ
Eagle Rock Plume Agate	Agate Chalcedony QUARTZ
Edinite	Prase Chalcedony QUARTZ
Egyptian Jasper	Brown Jasper QUARTZ
ELBAITE TOURMALINE	
Eldoradoite	Blue Chalcedony QUARTZ
Elephant Jasper	Brown/Black Jasper QUARTZ
Ellensburg Blue Agate	Agate Chalcedony QUARTZ
Emerald	BERYL

Common Seeker and Simplifier Talismans (continued)

Common Name (MINERAL)	MINERAL
ETTRINGITE	
EUDIALYTE	
Ezteri	Bloodstone Chalcedony QUARTZ
Fallen Tree Thundereggs	Agate Chalcedony QUARTZ
Ferruginous Quartz	Red QUARTZ
Fire Agate	Agate Chalcedony QUARTZ
Flame Agate	Agate Chalcedony QUARTZ
Flint	White Black Chert QUARTZ
FLUORAPATITE	
Fred Bed Thundereggs	Agate Chalcedony QUARTZ
Frieda Thundereggs	Agate Chalcedony QUARTZ
Friend Ranch Thundereggs	Agate Chalcedony QUARTZ
Frogskin Jasper	Tan/Green Jasper QUARTZ
Frost Agate	Gray Chalcedony QUARTZ
Fryite Picture Jasper	Jasper QUARTZ
GASPEITE	
Glory Blue	Blue Chalcedony QUARTZ
GMELINITE	
Gold Included Quartz	QUARTZ
Golden Beryl	BERYL
Golden Sapphire	CORUNDUM
Goshenite	BERYL
Graveyard Point Plume Agate	Agate Chalcedony QUARTZ
Green Beryl	BERYL
Green Gold Quartz	Irradiated QUARTZ
Green Moss Agate	Agate Chalcedony QUARTZ
Green Onyx	Chrysoprase Chalcedony QUARTZ
Green Sapphire	CORUNDUM
Green Tourmaline	ELBAITE TOURMALINE
Gray Quartz	QUARTZ
Gray Star Sapphire	CORUNDUM
Hampton Butte Moss Agate	Agate Chalcedony QUARTZ
HANKSITE	
Hawk's Eye	QUARTZ polymorph of Crocidolite
Heliodor	BERYL
Heliotrope	Bloodstone Chalcedony QUARTZ

Continued on next page

Common Seeker and Simplifier Talismans (continued)

Common Name (MINERAL)	MINERAL
Hemachate	Red Jasper Chalcedony QUARTZ
HEMATITE	
Holly Blue	Chalcedony QUARTZ
Holly Blue Agate	Agate Chalcedony QUARTZ
Hornstone	Chert QUARTZ
Hydroxylapatite	APATITE
Ice Stone	White Chert QUARTZ
Iceland Spar (Calcite)	CALCITE
ILMENITE	
Imperial Jasper	Green/Yellow Jasper QUARTZ
Indian Star Ruby	CORUNDUM
Indicolite Tourmaline	Blue ELBAITE
Indigolite	TOURMALINE
Iolanthite	Banded Red Jasper QUARTZ
Iris Agate	Agate Chalcedony QUARTZ
JAROSITE	
Jasp-Agate	Jasper QUARTZ
Jasper	Jasper QUARTZ
Jasper Breccia	Jasper QUARTZ
Jasperine	Jasper QUARTZ
Jasponyx	Agate Chalcedony QUARTZ
Joshua Tree Agate	Agate Chalcedony QUARTZ
Kidney Ore	HEMATITE
Kinradite	Jasper QUARTZ
Lantana	Agate Chalcedony QUARTZ
Larimar	PECTOLITE
Lazurquartz	Blue Chalcedony QUARTZ
LEIFITE	
Lemon Chrysoprase	Chrysoprase Chalcedony QUARTZ
Lemon Yellow Citrine	QUARTZ
Leolite	Agate Chalcedony QUARTZ
Leopard Jasper	Jasper Chalcedony QUARTZ
Leopardskin Jasper	Orange/Tan Jasper QUARTZ
Light Ruby Silver	PROUSTITE
Lingam	Jasper QUARTZ
Lorimar	PECTOLITE

Common Seeker and Simplifier Talismans *(continued)*

Common Name (MINERAL)	MINERAL
Lucky Strike Thundereggs	Agate Chalcedony QUARTZ
Lydian Stone	BASANITE
Madagascar Mariposite	Yellow Chalcedony QUARTZ
Madeira Citrine	QUARTZ
MAGNESITE	
Man Yü	Red Carnelian Chalcedony QUARTZ
Marra Mamba	Jasper QUARTZ (Tiger Iron)
Maury Mt. Moss Agate	Agate Chalcedony QUARTZ
McDermitt Thundereggs	Agate Chalcedony QUARTZ
Mecca Stone	Carnelian Chalcedony QUARTZ
MIMETITE	
Mohave Blue	Violet Chalcedony QUARTZ
Mojave Moonstone	Blue Chalcedony QUARTZ
Montana Moss Agate	Agate Chalcedony QUARTZ
Morganite	BERYL
Morlop	Jasper QUARTZ
Morrisonite	Jasper QUARTZ
Mosaic Agate	Agate Chalcedony QUARTZ
Moss Agate	Agate Chalcedony QUARTZ
Moss Jasper	Jasper QUARTZ
Moukaite	Pink Jasper QUARTZ
Mozarkite	Multicolored Chert QUARTZ
Mtorolite	Dark Green Jasper QUARTZ
Munjina Stone	Agate Chalcedony QUARTZ
Myrickite	Red Chalcedony QUARTZ with CINNABAR
Neon Quartz	Irradiated QUARTZ
Niccolite	NICKELINE
NICKELINE	
Novaculite	White Chert QUARTZ
Nunderite	EPIDOTE in QUARTZ
Nunkirchner Jasper	Brown Jasper QUARTZ
Ocean Jasper	Jasper QUARTZ
OLIVINE (usually FORSTERITE)	a mineral group
Onyx	Jasper QUARTZ
Oolitic Chert	Chert QUARTZ
Oolitic Hematite	HEMATITE

Continued on next page

Common Seeker and Simplifier Talismans (continued)

Common Name (MINERAL)	MINERAL
Oolitic Jasper	Jasper QUARTZ
Opal Butte Thundereggs	Agate Chalcedony QUARTZ
Ora Verde Quartz	Irradiated QUARTZ
Orange Beryl	BERYL
Orange Chalcedony	Chalcedony QUARTZ
Orange Sapphire	CORUNDUM
Orange Tourmaline	TOURMALINE
Orbicular Jasper	Jasper QUARTZ
Oregon Jade	Plasma Chalcedony QUARTZ
Oregonite	Jasper Chalcedony QUARTZ
Owyhee Picture Jasper	Jasper QUARTZ
Padparadscha Sapphire	CORUNDUM
Paradise Jasper	Red Jasper QUARTZ
Paraiba Tourmaline	TOURMALINE
Pastelite	Pink/Green Jasper QUARTZ
Peach Aventurine	QUARTZ
Peach Beryl	BERYL
PECTOLITE	
Petersite	QUARTZ
Petrified Wood	Jasper QUARTZ
PHENAKITE	
Picture Jasper	Jasper QUARTZ
Pietersite	Hawk's Eye Chalcedony QUARTZ
Pigeon Blood Agate	Carnelian Chalcedony QUARTZ
Pink Sapphire	CORUNDUM
Pink Tourmaline	TOURMALINE
Pisolitic Chert	Chert QUARTZ
Plasma	Chalcedony QUARTZ
PLUMBOGUMMITE	
Polka-dot Agate	Agate Chalcedony QUARTZ
Polka-dot Jasper	Jasper QUARTZ
Pony Butte Thundereggs	Agate Chalcedony QUARTZ
Poppy	Red/Orange/Yellow Jasper QUARTZ
Poppy Jasper	Jasper QUARTZ
Poppy Stone	Jasper QUARTZ
Prase	Green QUARTZ

Common Seeker and Simplifier Talismans (continued)

Common Name (MINERAL)	MINERAL
Prase Malachite	Green Chalcedony QUARTZ
Prasiolite	QUARTZ
Priday Plume Agate	Agate Chalcedony QUARTZ
Priday Thundereggs	Agate Chalcedony QUARTZ
PROUSTITE	
PYRARGYRITE	
PYROMORPHITE	
QUARTZ	
Rainforest Jasper	Jasper QUARTZ
Red Beryl	BERYL
Red Jasper	Jasper QUARTZ
RHODOCHROSITE	
Riband Jasper	Banded Jasper QUARTZ
Richardson's Thundereggs	Agate Chalcedony QUARTZ
ROCK CRYSTAL	QUARTZ
Rocky Butte Picture Jasper	Jasper QUARTZ
Rogueite	Green Jasper QUARTZ
Rose Cat's Eye Quartz	QUARTZ
Rose de France Amethyst	QUARTZ
Rose Quartz	QUARTZ
Rubellite	ELBAITE TOURMALINE
Ruby	CORUNDUM
Ruin Agate	Agate Chalcedony QUARTZ
Russian Agate	Agate Chalcedony QUARTZ
Russian Jasper	Red-Flecked Jasper QUARTZ
Rutilated Quartz	QUARTZ
Saddle Mountain Fire Agate	Agate Chalcedony QUARTZ
Sagenite	QUARTZ
Saint Stephen's Stone	Bloodstone Chalcedony QUARTZ
Sapphire	CORUNDUM
Sapphirine	Blue Chalcedony QUARTZ
Sard	Brown Chalcedony QUARTZ
Sardonyx	Chalcedony QUARTZ
Scenic Jasper	Tan Jasper QUARTZ
Schizolite	PECTOLITE
SCHORL	Black TOURMALINE

Continued on next page

Common Seeker and Simplifier Talismans *(continued)*

Common Name (MINERAL)	MINERAL
Sea Jasper	Jasper QUARTZ
Seftonite	Green Chalcedony QUARTZ
Serandite	PECTOLITE
SIDERITE	
Sioux Falls Jasper	Jasper QUARTZ
SMITHSONITE	
Smoky Quartz	QUARTZ
SPANGOLITE	
Specularite	HEMATITE
SPHAEROCOBALTITE	
Spirit Quartz	QUARTZ
Star Malachite	Green Chalcedony QUARTZ
Star Quartz	QUARTZ
Star Ruby	CORUNDUM
STAUROLITE	
Steins Pillar Thundereggs	Agate Chalcedony QUARTZ
STICHTITE	
Stinking Water Plume Agate	Agate Chalcedony QUARTZ
Stone Yard	Jasper QUARTZ
STURMANITE	
Succor Creek Thundereggs	Agate Chalcedony QUARTZ
SUGILITE	
Sunset Agate	Agate Chalcedony QUARTZ
Swiss Lapis	Dyed Blue Chalcedony QUARTZ
TAAFFEITE	
Teanaway Agate	Agate Chalcedony QUARTZ
THAUMASITE	
Tiger's Eye	Jasper QUARTZ
Tourmalinated Quartz	QUARTZ
TOURMALINE	a mineral group
Tree Agate	Agate Chalcedony QUARTZ
Turgite	HEMATITE
Turritella Agate	Agate Chalcedony QUARTZ
Utica Jewelstone	White-Banded Chert QUARTZ
UVITE	TOURMALINE
Vabanite	Red/Yellow Jasper QUARTZ

Common Seeker and Simplifier Talismans (continued)

Common Name (MINERAL)	MINERAL
Valley View Thundereggs	Agate Chalcedony QUARTZ
VANADINITE	
Variegated Jasper	Jasper QUARTZ
VERDELITE	TOURMALINE
Violet Sapphire	CORUNDUM
Violite	Violet Chalcedony QUARTZ
Watermelon Tourmaline	TOURMALINE
Whistler Springs Thundereggs	Agate Chalcedony QUARTZ
White Fir Springs Thundereggs	Jasper QUARTZ
White Sapphire	CORUNDUM
Whiteskins	Agate Chalcedony QUARTZ
Wild Horse Jasper	Jasper QUARTZ
Wilkite	Multicolored Jasper QUARTZ
WILLEMITE	
Willow Creek Jasper	Jasper QUARTZ
Xyloid Jasper	Jasper QUARTZ
Yellow Sapphire	CORUNDUM
Yellow Tourmaline	TOURMALINE
Zebra Jasper	Jasper QUARTZ
ZINKENITE	
Zonite	Jasper QUARTZ

Enhancers and Arrangers
(ISOMETRIC CRYSTAL SYSTEM)

Enhancers and Arrangers are minerals and crystals with internal crystal lattices of perfect cubic symmetry and internal harmony. They form perfect building blocks internally, and often this internal structure of equal and exact right angles produces crystals of equally perfect external shapes: cubes!

These are the "building block" talismans. The internal structure of blocks builds up perfect crystal lattices that can help us focus our efforts to build on our successes and enhance our lives. Whereas the Seekers and Simplifiers system produces crystals and minerals that aid in new beginnings, the Enhancers and Arrangers of the isometric system aid us in building on our successes and achievements.

Many of the uses of these crystals are focused on self-improvement. Both physically and mentally, we all seem to be trying to get better at something. We want to be able to run faster, jump higher, shoot more accurately, serve a tennis ball faster, or just jog all the way to the corner. We want a lower golf score, a lower personal best time in a 10K race, or a higher batting average. We want to bench press 220 pounds, or just bend over and put our palms on the floor without bending our knees. We want to learn new languages, get a better grade on the next test, or finally understand algebra. As Enhancers, these talismans are perfect for such purposes. They can focus and enhance our energy on the feelings of improvement we desire and help turn them to the thoughts that will produce the actions we need to improve. Those actions, little by little, will develop into the habits that will solidify our improvements and lead to greater accomplishments.

Among others, diamonds, gold, and silver form in this crystal system. The uses of diamond in engagement rings is certainly due to its external beauty, but we now know its power goes beyond that external beauty down into its perfect internal crystal lattice. From this lattice, it draws power to extend, enhance, and build the perfect love the diamond represents. Gold and silver are used to enhance the beauty of many gems in the jewelry trade. Again, the external beauty is certainly an important factor in this use, but like the diamond, these minerals have a deep, previously hidden perfection in their crystal energy structure that gives them "hidden enhancing power" only suspected in the past. Copper, spinel, fluorite, pyrite, and lapis lazuli are also minerals that form in this crystal energy system. These minerals and crystals have wide applications in making talismans.

This crystal system, with its internal structure so perfectly arranged, also holds the energy we need to help us arrange our lives in a more orderly manner. When there is a

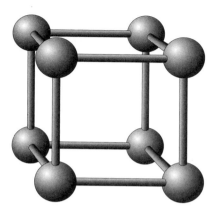

Isometric crystal system

need for arranging our paths through life, establishing equality or equilibrium, reducing chaos, aligning priorities, or just "squaring" things away, talismans made from crystals from this system are very powerful Arrangers. This crystal system produces excellent talismans of order, rule, law, constancy, higher ideals, patterns, simple connections, fitting into a social order, linking, learning, growing consistently, and acting logically.

Some of the common uses in which these talismans are particularly valuable as Arrangers include finding common ground with others, aiding in negotiations, organizing people and activities, and setting priorities in daily life. I suppose they could even help you get that closet under control.

Common Enhancer and Arranger Talismans

Common Name (MINERAL)	MINERAL
Acanthite	ARGENTITE
African Jade	GROSSULAR
ALMANDINE (Garnet)	
Almandite (Garnet)	ALMANDINE
ANDRADITE	
ARGENTITE	
Ballas	CARBON (Sphere Diamond)
Binnite	TENNANTITE
Black Diamond	CARBON (Diamond)
Black Spinel	SPINEL
Blackjack	SPHALERITE
BLENDE	SPHALERITE
Blue Spinel	SPINEL
BORNITE	
BOULANGERITE	
Bravoite	PYRITE
CACHEMIRINE Garnet	
Carbuncle	ALMANDINE Garnet
Chalcotrichite	CUPRITE
Chloanthite	SKUTTERUDITE
Cinnamon Stone	GROSSULAR
COPPER (Cu)	
Copper Blooms	COPPER
CUPRITE	
Demantoid Garnet	ANDRADITE
Desmine	STILBITE
Diamond	CARBON
FLUORITE	
Fool's Gold	PYRITE
FRANKLINITE	
GAHNITE	
GALENA	
Garnet	a mineral group
GERSDORFFITE	
GOLD (Au)	
Grandite Garnet	ALMANDINE (mostly)

Common Enhancer and Arranger Talismans (continued)

Common Name (MINERAL)	MINERAL
GRAPHITE (Carbon)	
GROSSULAR	
Grossular Garnet	GROSSULAR
Hackmanite	SODALITE
HALITE	
HAUERITE	
Hessonite (Garnet)	
Imperial Garnet	SPESSARTINE
IRON	
Iron Pyrite	PYRITE
Lapis Lazuli	LAZURITE (mostly), PYRITE, CALCITE
LAZURITE	
LEUCITE	
MAGNETITE (Iron Oxide)	
Malaya Garnet	Mixed GARNET
Mandarin Garnet	Mixed GARNET
MARCASITE	
Melanite	ANDRADITE
Merelani Mint Garnet	ALMANDINE (mostly)
Mozambique Garnet	Mixed GARNET
Peacock Copper	BORNITE
Peacock Ore	BORNITE
PERICLASE	
Pink Spinel	SPINEL
PLATINUM	
Psilomelane	ROMANECHITE
Purple Garnet	ALMANDINE-PYROPE
PYRITE	
Pyrite Dollars	PYRITE
Pyrite Suns	PYRITE
Pyrope Garnet	PYROPE
Pyrope-Almandine Garnet	ALMANDINE-PYROPE
PYRRHOTITE	
Queensland Garnet	ALMANDINE-PYROPE
Red Spinel	SPINEL
RHODIZITE	

Continued on next page

Common Enhancer and Arranger Talismans (continued)

Common Name (MINERAL)	MINERAL
Rhodolite	ALMANDINE-PYROPE
ROMANECHITE	
SAL AMMONIAC	
SENARMONTITE	
SILVER (Ag)	
SKUTTERUDITE	
SODALITE	
SPESSARTINE	
Spessartite	SPESSARTINE
SPHALERITE	
SPINEL	
STIBICONITE	
STILBITE	
SULFUR (S)	
Sylvine	SYLVITE
SYLVITE	
TENNANTITE	
TETRAHEDRITE	
Thai Garnet	ALMANDINE
Topazolite	ANDRADITE
Tsavorite	GROSSULAR
Umbalite Garnet	ALMANDINE-PYROPE
UVAROVITE	
VILLIAUMITE	
Violet Spinel	SPINEL
White Spinel	SPINEL

Guardians and Dreamholders
(MONOCLINIC CRYSTAL SYSTEM)

When we possess that which we value, and desire to protect it from harm or loss, we need Guardian talismans. The minerals of the monoclinic crystal system have an internal structure that is composed of parallelograms. The parallel structure of their crystalline lattice gives these talismans their power to protect us in the physical world and in the spiritual one. Physically, some of these Guardian minerals have legendary strength. Jade is tough. Malachite is tough. At the same time, the legendary spiritual strength of moonstone is undisputed. Another famous Guardian, Preseli bluestone, from which the inner circle of Stonehenge is constructed, is even harder than granite.

The Guardian talismans do not reveal their inner strength. These stones rarely, if ever, form transparent crystals. Rather, they hide their strength behind an opaque mask, obscuring the power they possess. They guard their secrets well. When we have a need to protect valuable possessions, the Guardians are the talismans of choice. They can help us focus our energies effectively in protecting that which we hold dear.

The Guardian talismans have a wide spectrum of uses. In the physical world, they are excellent aids in protecting our loved ones, our possessions, our physical security, and ourselves. They are very useful in protecting houses and homes, property, and valuables. If you have prized possessions you want to guard and protect, use a Guardian talisman. They can make excellent "home stones" when the purpose is protection. They are also useful for travelers and adventurers to take with them on their travels as insurance against harm. They

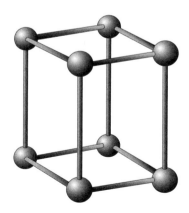

Monoclinic crystal system

are useful for emergency workers, soldiers, sailors, and airmen in the performance of their dangerous duties.

In the spiritual world, the Guardian talismans have several special uses. They first serve to guard our beliefs against doubt. Everyone at some point begins to doubt some of his or her most cherished beliefs. That doubt can grow and affect our lives. A Guardian talisman can help us keep true to our ideals and beliefs, offering us strength of character. The Guardian talismans can also protect our spirits. If we anticipate a trying and difficult, even stressful future, a Guardian can be very effective in aiding our efforts to maintain our disposition, sense of humor, and respect for others.

The minerals that form in this monoclinic system are also known as the Dreamholders. They often appear to have a hazy surface as if there is something veiled from our sight just beneath the surface. This is best observed in the moonstone. This stone, being a Dreamholder talisman, is a particularly powerful talisman when used to aid us in focusing our energy to hold on to our dreams.

Everyone has dreams. Holding on to those dreams as life unfolds takes tenacity, perseverance, and patience. We all know the power of following a dream, but at times life puts obstacles in the way. It can seem overwhelming, and anyone's will can waver. A Dreamholder talisman can be a tremendous help in such situations. It has the ability to help us focus on our dream, to hold on to it, and to feel, think, and act in the ways our dreams require.

Other Guardians and Dreamholders include kunzite and azurite.

Common Guardian and Dreamholder Talismans

Common Name (MINERAL)	MINERAL
Acmite	AEGIRINE
ACTINOLITE	
Adularia	ORTHOCLASE
AEGIRINE	
Agalmatolite	PYROPHYLLITE
Alabaster	GYPSUM
ALLANITE	
ANNABERGITE	
ANTIGORITE	Serpentine
ARFVEDSONITE	
ARROJADITE	
ARSENOPYRITE	
ARTHURITE	
ARTINITE	
ATELESTITE	
Atlantisite	Serpentine with STICHTITE
AUGITE	
Azulicite	SANIDINE
AZURITE	
Azurite-Malachite	mixed minerals
BAKERITE	
BAYLDONITE	
BERYLLONITE	
BIOTITE	
Biotite Lens	BIOTITE
Black Star Diopside	DIOPSIDE
Blue Asbestos	Crocidolite RIEBECKITE
Blue Moonstone	ORTHOCLASE
Bluebird	AZURITE with CUPRITE
BOLTWOODITE	
BORAX	
Bowenite	ANTIGORITE (Serpentine)
BRAZILIANITE	
BROCHANTITE	
CARNOTITE	

Continued on next page

Common Guardian and Dreamholder Talismans (continued)

Common Name (MINERAL)	MINERAL
Cat's Eye Diopside	DIOPSIDE
CHAROITE	
CHENEVIXITE	
Chessylite	AZURITE
Chlorastrolite	PUMPELLYITE
Chrome Diopside	DIOPSIDE
CHRYSOBERYL	
Chrysotile	Serpentine
CLINOCHLORE	
CLINOCLASE	
CLINOHUMITE	
Cobalt Bloom	ERYTHRITE
COLEMANITE	
CREEDITE	
Crocidolite	RIEBECKITE
CROCOITE	
Cryptoperthite	ORTHOCLASE
DATOLITE	
DIOPSIDE	
DUFRENITE	
Eakleite	XONOTLITE
EDENITE	
EPIDOTE	
EPISTILBITE	
ERYTHRITE	
EUCLASE	
EUDIDYMITE	
FERBERITE	
FLUORRICHTERITE	
Fuchsite	MUSCOVITE
GADOLINITE	
GAYLUSSITE	
GIBBSITE	
GLAUBERITE	
GOOSECREEKITE	
Green Moonstone	ORTHOCLASE

Common Guardian and Dreamholder Talismans (continued)

Common Name (MINERAL)	MINERAL
Green Starstone	Chlorastrolite PUMPELLYITE
Greenstone	Chlorastrolite PUMPELLYITE
Gray Moonstone	ORTHOCLASE
GUANACOITE	
GYPSUM	
HEDENBERGITE	
HEULANDITE	
Hiddenite	SPODUMENE
HORNBLENDE	
HOWLITE	
HUBNERITE	
HUREAULITE	
HYDROBORACITE	
HYDROMAGNESITE	
HYDROZINCITE	
Infinite	Serpentine (ANTIGORITE)
Jade	Nephrite ACTINOLITE, or JADEITE
JADEITE	
JAMESONITE	
JORDANITE	
Kämmererite	CLINOCHLORE
KAOLINITE	
KERNITE	
Kidney Stones	JADEITE
KINOITE	
Knaufite	VOLBORTHITE
Kunzite	SPODUMENE
Lavenderine	LEPIDOLITE
LAZULITE	
LEGRANDITE	
Lemon Jade	Serpentine
LEPIDOLITE	
LINARITE	
Linerite	LINARITE
LUDLAMITE	
MALACHITE	

Continued on next page

Common Guardian and Dreamholder Talismans (continued)

Common Name (MINERAL)	MINERAL
MANGANITE	
MESOLITE	
MONAZITE	
Moonstone	ORTHOCLASE
MUSCOVITE	
Nephrite (Jade)	ACTINOLITE
NEPTUNITE	
Nickel Bloom	ANNABERGITE
ORPIMENT	
ORTHOCLASE	
PALYGORSKITE	
PAPAGOITE	
Peach Moonstone	ORTHOCLASE
PETALITE	
PHILLIPSITE	
PHLOGOPITE	
PHOSPHOPHYLLITE	
PIEDMONTITE	
POLYBASITE	
POLYLITHIONITE	
Preseli Bluestone	AUGITE (with feldspar)
PSEUDOMALACHITE	
PUMPELLYITE	Chlorastrolite PUMPELLYITE
PYROPHYLLITE	
REALGAR	
RICHTERITE	
Ricolite	Serpentine and TALC
RIEBECKITE	
ROSASITE	
ROSELITE	
SANIDINE	
Satin Spar	GYPSUM
SCOLECITE	
SCORZALITE	
Selenite	GYPSUM
Seraphinite	CLINOCHLORE

Common Guardian and Dreamholder Talismans (continued)

Common Name (MINERAL)	MINERAL
Serpentine	CLINOCHLORE
Soapstone	TALC
Sphene	TITANITE
SPODUMENE	
STELLERITE	
TALC	
Tawmawite	EPIDOTE
THOMSENOLITE	
TINCALCONITE	
TITANITE	
TREMOLITE	
TRONA	
TSUMEBITE	
Turtleback	Chlorastrolite PUMPELLYITE
Uigite	Chlorastrolite PUMPELLYITE
VESZELYITE	
Violan	Blue DIOPSIDE
VOLBORTHITE	
WENDWILSONITE	
WHITEITE	
Withamite	Red EPIDOTE
WOLFEITE	
WOLFRAMITE	
XONOTLITE	

Barriers
(TRICLINIC CRYSTAL SYSTEM)

With the inner form of a trapezium, a geometric figure with no right angles, a triclinic crystalline structure gives a talisman strength in all directions, allowing it to provide barriers to attack from all directions simultaneously. This crystal structure forms an effective amulet that can aid us in defending ourselves from the misfortunes of this world.

It can be a dangerous world. Disease, war, famine, heartbreak, accidents, and misfortunes of all kinds can await us. Ships founder, cars crash, the flu spreads. The Barrier talismans are useful when we desire to protect ourselves from such misadventures. They can aid us in our efforts to prevent mishaps and keep us from harm. The minerals that form in the triclinic, Barrier crystal structure are the true protection talismans. As a note, while most of European history relates the use of rubies and sapphires, for protecting against illness and injury, the fact is that those minerals really don't have such power. They are actually formed in the Seeker crystal structure, which gives them the ability to help us on quests to find new capabilities and lives, but not the power to protect us on those journeys.

The Barrier talismans are similar to the Guardian talismans previously discussed; the difference is the focus. The Guardians are talismans that help us focus on protecting something we value—an inward focus in a way. In contrast, the Barrier talismans are externally focused—on keeping us from undesirable environments and free from harm. Many efforts can be successful using either type of talisman. We can use a Guardian talisman to guard our health or a Barrier to keep from becoming sick. The choice is an individual one that

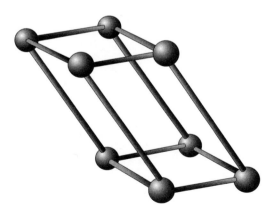

Triclinic crystal system

mostly depends on the focus of a specific need or desire. Often these talismans are used together.

However, even used individually, the Barrier talismans have incredible abilities to help us focus and amplify our efforts to keep undesirable elements out of our lives. One particularly powerful Barrier, turquoise, has a long history of success as a protective talisman. Native American cultures have long recognized the power of this talisman and still use it extensively to protect themselves and their ways of life.

Many early uses of talismans centered on protection from various misfortunes. Unfortunately, history records few effective uses. The reason is now known. There are actually only a few common minerals that form in the shape of Barrier crystals. Barrier talismans such as turquoise and labradorite are the best talismans for safe travel. Travelers are constantly venturing into new and unfamiliar environments. Protecting ourselves from accidents and misfortunes is tough enough, but it is much more difficult when we are away from our homes. One particular crystal, kyanite, makes an excellent Barrier talisman. Kyanite is a blue crystal that is particularly well suited to be a protection stone for travelers, especially those who travel by sea or air.

Common Barrier Talismans

Common Name (MINERAL)	MINERAL
AJOITE	
ALBITE	
Amazonite	MICROCLINE
AMBLYGONITE	
ANALCIME	
Analcite	ANALCIME
ANDESINE	
ASTROPHYLLITE	
AXINITE	
BABINGTONITE	
BULTFONTEINITE	
BUSTAMITE	
BYTOWNITE	
CERULÉITE	
CHALCANTHITE	
Chinese Turquoise	TURQUOISE
Cleavelandite	ALBITE
Cotton Balls	ULEXITE
Cyanite	KYANITE
EMMONSITE	
GORMANITE	
GYROLITE	
HENMILITE	
HUBEITE	
INESITE	
JENNITE	
KYANITE	
LABRADORITE	
MICROCLINE	
MONTEBRASITE	
OKENITE	
OLIGOCLASE	
PARADAMITE	
PARAVAUXITE	
Peristerite	ALBITE
Perthite	MICROCLINE

Common Barrier Talismans (continued)

Common Name (MINERAL)	MINERAL
POLYHALITE	
Rainbow Moonstone	LABRADORITE
RHODONITE	
Spectrolite	LABRADORITE
STRUNZITE	
Sunstone	OLIGOCLASE Feldspar
SUOLUNITE	
Television Stone	ULEXITE
TUNDRITE	
TURQUOISE	
ULEXITE	
VAUXITE	
WOLLASTONITE	

Dispellers and Restorers
(ORTHORHOMBIC CRYSTAL SYSTEM)

Sometimes in our lives we need to rid ourselves of things we have but no longer want. We want to get rid of pains, sickness, worry, and a host of unpleasant things. For these needs, the Dispeller talismans that form in the orthorhombic system are needed. Peridots, topazes, and aragonite are some of the minerals that form in the orthorhombic crystal system. These "diamond-shaped" internal crystal arrangements are similar to those of the cubic system, but have one elongated axis. They often appear as multiple diamond-shaped crystals like a multitude of arrowheads or pyramids—the diamond shape of their crystal lattice acts like a radiator, with sharp points from which the energy can flow easily outward. This outward flow of energy can carry with it the undesirable elements in our lives.

Dispellers are a good choice when we wish to rid our lives of physical pain, discomfort, injury, illness, or disease. However, a note of caution is needed. Remember, talismans have the ability to focus and magnify our power. They are not magic rocks. Seek professional medical advice for physical ailments.

Dispellers are very helpful talismans for mental and spiritual problems. All of us have problems. Some are physical, some mental. Certainly our lives would be more enjoyable and more productive if we could rid ourselves of them. Worry, anxiety, fear, and doubt can literally cripple us and make our lives miserable. Again, for serious mental disorders, the care of a licensed professional is required. Use the Dispeller talismans to aid you in the recovery plan prescribed. For relieving everyday concerns, the Dispeller talismans are superb.

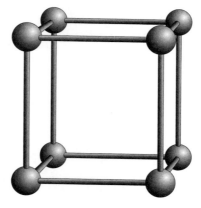

Orthorhombic crystal system

The Dispellers are also known as the Restorers. These crystals are used to put things right again after they are out of balance. If we are worry free, then become plagued by doubt, these crystals help us to focus and magnify our energy to rid ourselves of the doubt and restore ourselves to the worry-free state. If we are working in a great job, then lose it for some reason, these crystals and minerals can help us restore our lives as productive members of the working community. Usually we want to rid ourselves of something because it has caused an unwelcome change we would like to undo. The Dispeller and Restorer crystals of the orthorhombic system have the crystal energy to aid us in such endeavors.

The Third Secret of the Talismans will reveal the power of the color rays of influence, but a point is important here. Dispellers and Restorers can be, and usually are, used as complements to Seekers and should be of the same color when used so. For example, as we shall learn, scarlet is the color ray of strength. If we desire to rid ourselves of a feeling of powerlessness and grow our power in some way, we could use either a scarlet Seeker or a scarlet Dispeller. This might seem odd, but the reason will be made clear in the Third Secret of the Talismans.

Common Dispeller and Restorer Talismans

Common Name (MINERAL)	MINERAL
ADAMITE	
ALEXANDRITE	CHRYSOBERYL
ANDALUSITE	
Angelsite	ANHYDRITE
ANGLESITE	
ANHYDRITE	
ANTHOPHYLLITE	
ANTLERITE	
Anyolite	ZOISITE
ARAGONITE	
ATACAMITE	
AURICHALCITE	
BARITE	
Basalt Bomb	FORSTERITE
BERTHIERITE	
BERTRANDITE	
Blue Topaz	TOPAZ
Bog Iron Ore	GOETHITE
Bologna Stone	BARITE
BORACITE	usually artificial
BOURNONITE	
Breislakite	ILVAITE
Bronzite	ENSTATITE
BROOKITE	
CALEDONITE	
CARMINITE	
Cat's Eye	CHRYSOBERYL
Cat's Eye Enstatite	ENSTATITE
Cat's Eye Kornerupine	KORNERUPINE
CAVANSITE	
CELESTINE	
Celestite	CELESTINE
CERUSSITE	
Cervantite	STIBNITE
Chiastolite	ANDALUSITE
CHILDRENITE	

Common Dispeller and Restorer Talismans (continued)

Common Name (MINERAL)	MINERAL
CHRYSOCOLLA	
Chrysolite	FAYALITE
COBALTITE	
Cog Wheel Ore	BOURNONITE
COLUMBITE	
CONICHALCITE	
CORDIERITE	
CORNETITE	
Cuproadamite	ADAMITE
Cymophane	CHRYSOBERYL (Cat's Eye)
DANBURITE	
DESCLOIZITE	
Desert Rose	BARITE
DUFTITE	
DUMORTIERITE	
ELPIDITE	
ENARGITE	
ENSTATITE	
EOSPHORITE	
EPIDIDYMITE	
Evening Emerald (Peridot)	FORSTERITE
FAYALITE	
Fibrolite	SILLIMANITE
FORSTERITE	
Garnierite	NÉPOUITE
GOETHITE	
Green Topaz	TOPAZ
HAMBERGITE	
HEMIMORPHITE	
Heterosite	PURPURITE
HOPEITE	
Hot Pink Topaz	Heat-Treated TOPAZ
HUMITE	
Hypersthene	ENSTATITE
ILVAITE	
Iolite	CORDIERITE

Continued on next page

Common Dispeller and Restorer Talismans (continued)

Common Name (MINERAL)	MINERAL
KORNERUPINE	
LEPIDACHROSITE	found in QUARTZ
LIBETHENITE	
London Blue Topaz	Irradiated TOPAZ
MANGANOTANTALITE	
MOTTRAMITE	
NATROLITE	
NÉPOUITE	
Nuumite	ANTHOPHYLLITE
Peacock Topaz	TOPAZ
PENTAGONITE	
Peridot	FORSTERITE
PEROVSKITE	
PLANCHÉITE	
Precious Topaz	TOPAZ
PREHNITE	
PURPURITE	
SANBORNITE	
SCHOLZITE	
SCORODITE	
SHATTUCKITE	
SILLIMANITE	
Silver Topaz	TOPAZ
SINHALITE	
Sky Blue Topaz	TOPAZ
STEPHANITE	
STIBNITE	
STRENGITE	
Swiss Blue Topaz	Irradiated TOPAZ
Tanganyika Artstone	ZOISITE, with Ruby
TANTALITE	
Tanzanite	ZOISITE
Tanzanite Topaz	TOPAZ
Tarnowitzite	ARAGONITE
Teal Topaz	TOPAZ

Common Dispeller and Restorer Talismans (continued)

Common Name (MINERAL)	MINERAL
TEPHROITE	
THENARDITE	
THOMSONITE	
TOPAZ	
VALENTINITE	
VARISCITE	
Water Sapphire (Iolite)	CORDIERITE
WAVELLITE	
White Topaz	TOPAZ

Attractors
(TETRAGONAL CRYSTAL SYSTEM)

There is an additional crystalline structure. While it is not directly related to a fundamental human need, it provides us with a very desirable and valuable capability to augment the power of other talismans. Attractors have an internal structure built on the rectangle, which often manifests itself by producing minerals with a surface sheen that seems to catch your eye and attract you to the crystal or even the rough mineral specimen. These crystals, like rutile, stand out and are noticed by the play of light over their surfaces. These crystals are perfect talismans when your purpose is to attract someone or something to you.

Attractors help us focus on being attractive so that what we are seeking will actually seek us. Gaining recognition, winning friends, or attracting wealth are all needs that Attractors can help us fulfill. Used in conjunction with Seekers, the Attractor talismans can provide us with very potent and focused energy.

Be aware, however, that the Attractors seem to have a passive energy, like a magnet. When nothing is around to attract, the energy of a magnet seems to be gone. It is only energized when something is around to attract. Then suddenly a magnet's power is apparent. So, too, the Attractors seem to have a waiting element to their energy. If nothing comes along, Attractors don't seem to have much power. That is why they are used with Seekers. The Seekers help us get out and find what we need. Then the Attractors power can be applied. Avoid reliance on Attractors alone. You might someday get what you desire, but it could be a very long wait.

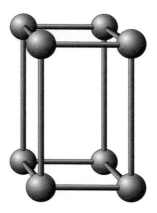

Tetragonal crystal system

Common Attractor Talismans

Common Name (MINERAL)	MINERAL
ANATASE	
APOPHYLLITE	
BOLEITE	
Californite	VESUVIANITE
CARLETONITE	
CASSITERITE (Tin Oxide)	
Cerian	VESUVIANITE
CHALCOPYRITE	
DIABOLEITE	
HARDYSTONITE	
HAUSMANNITE	
Idocrase	VESUVIANITE
PHOSGENITE	
PLATTNERITE	
Polianite	PYROLUSITE
POWELLITE	
PYROLUSITE	
RUTILE	
SCAPOLITE	
SCHEELITE	
VESUVIANITE	
WARDITE	
WERNERITE	SCAPOLITE

The Amulets

An amulet is a protective talisman. With the Second Secret of Talismans revealed, we can now understand amulets. Much of the history of talismans is focused on using them to ward off danger and protect people from harm, disease, and injury. The Second Secret tells us clearly which talismans are useful in such efforts. The Guardian talismans, with their parallel crystal lattices, have the power to protect us in both the physical and spiritual planes of existence. The Barrier talismans, with their triclinic crystalline structure that gives strength in all directions, provide barriers to attack from all directions simultaneously. These two types of talismans, the Guardians and the Barriers, are the only effective amulets. Other types like Attractors, Seekers, and Enhancers don't have the crystal energy matrix that is necessary. The history of rubies and emeralds includes their use for protection in battle, and to ward off illness. We know now why these efforts were unsuccessful. Rubies and emeralds are Seekers. Jade, being a Guardian, would have been a much better choice.

Summary

Understanding the Second Secret of Talismans allows us to very quickly sort out which minerals, gems, and crystals are useful for which general purposes based on their crystal energy matrices. If we are preparing a talisman to help protect someone on a dangerous sea crossing, we can start our search with minerals and crystals that form in the Guardian and Dreamholder (monoclinic) crystal system. We certainly wouldn't want to consider using a zircon, for example. It forms in the Attractor (tetragonal) structure, and its powers to attract would be counterproductive in our effort to ward off danger! If we were seeking help in attracting a mate for love and companionship, we would begin our search with the Seekers and perhaps also use an Attractor for a little extra help. Should our desire be to rid ourselves of a particularly bad habit, we now know we would begin with a crystal like a topaz or a peridot because it forms in the Dispeller crystalline structure.

As you now understand, using talismans effectively requires that you actually use the right talisman for the right purpose. Talismans are specific in their uses and applications. They are individual artifacts that are made and used for specific purposes in specific ways. Understanding and using the Second Secret of Talismans will ensure that you start with the right crystalline energy for your purpose.

Crystal Energy Structures

Primary Crystal Energy	Secondary Crystal Energy	Crystal System	Human Need
Seekers		Hexagonal/Trigonal	Gain what we lack
	Simplifiers		Add tranquility to our lives
Enhancers		Isometric	Improve on our lives
	Arrangers		Add order
Guardians		Monoclinic	Protect valuables from loss
	Dreamholders		Keep our dreams alive
Barriers		Triclinic	Keep harm away
Dispellers		Orthorhombic	Rid ourselves of undesirable elements in our lives
	Restorers		Restore our fortunes after loss
Attractors		Tetragonal	Bring what we desire to us

Understanding this Secret unlocks a great deal of the mystery about the real power of talismans. However, there are additional Secrets that will help us even more with our desire to understand the mysteries of talismans. The Third Secret of Talismans will show us how the influence of the color rays augments the crystal energy structures to provide talismans of great power.

THE
THIRD SECRET
OF TALISMANS

The color influence rays of talismans align the power of
the crystals to the power of our minds.

The previous Secret, in which the alignment of crystal energy structures with human needs was discovered, was virtually impossible for ancient peoples to completely understand. Without the ability to see deep into the crystals, early civilizations had no real way to learn and use the crystal energy matrices correctly. They did, however, have a better understanding of the Third Secret. They realized that color has influence over the human mind. They had a fundamental understanding that color is visible energy, that color is an element of the Universal Life Force, and that color is a special part of that Life Force that, through our optic nerve, allows direct connections between the Life Force and our minds. What was difficult for them, and frankly even for modern cultures, was separating out the differences between the natural meanings of the colors of this planet, and the superficial cultural and religious meanings that served to confuse and obscure the pure natural influence of the spectrum on the human mind.

For example, in American culture, black is often associated with death, but in the Orient, white is the traditional color of mourning. In Catholicism, purple is the color of mourning, and in Iran, blue is used for mourning dress.[1] In Western cultures, white is the color of purity and used for wedding dresses, but in the Zulu culture, black is the color for a bride to wear.[2] But the natural crystals and minerals have no culture and no religion. They are a part of the earth. Their natural color influence rays stay the same.

With the research of today's practitioners of biology, biochemistry, and physics, we can sort truth from fiction. Based on extensive research in both the history and tradition of talismans, and the more modern psychological studies of the fundamental effects of color on human bodies and minds, we now know the real, natural effects of gemstone, crystal,

---

1 Sibagraphics, "The Meaning of Colours," http://www.sibagraphics.com/colour.php (accessed May 26, 2007).

2 Ontario School Board, "An African Valentine: The Bead Code of the Zulus," http://www.edunet connect.com/cat/soccult/afrval.html (accessed May 26, 2007).

and mineral color influence rays. This wisdom is captured in the Great Talismanic Color Wheel of Influence.

The Great Talismanic Color Wheel of Influence

The Great Talismanic Color Wheel of Influence (featured on page A-26 of the color insert) combines the concepts of time and color in a circular context. This might seem unusual, because we are often more used to viewing both time and color as linear ideas. However, both time and color can be experienced linearly or cyclically. To many of us in the modern world, time seems to just run on and on, day after day, year after year. We measure how much of it we use in certain activities, bemoan being delayed in traffic as a "waste of time," and count birthdays as monuments to our passage through time. We mark days, months, years, decades, and centuries. We have major celebrations at the millennium. We see things as having a start, a duration, and a finish. We see a life as a sequence of events that stretches from birth to death. We measure our existence by the stages of our lives. We have the Judeo-Christian viewpoint that we are the center of events. We see time through the lens of a historian. We see a sequence of events pertaining to our species. We measure the intervals to gain perspective. We are just points on a timeline extending backward.

But there is another way to see time. It is a cosmic view, an Earth-centric view, and a circular view. Time is a great circle. Galaxies rotate around their galactic cores. The earth circles the sun. The moon circles the earth. The earth rotates on its axis. We are living a dance—a gyrating, pulsing, rotating, spinning dance through space and time. We circle and circle. The sky changes and changes back. The seasons change, and then change back. We circle from colder to warmer and back to colder. The ice thaws to water, and then refreezes to ice. The sun rises and sets. The moon is new, full, and new again. Time on Earth is a cycle of repeating dawns and sunsets, days and nights, and winters, springs, summers, and autumns.

Like time, color can be viewed in both a linear and cyclical manner. The color spectrum humans can see starts at violet and extends through the colors of the rainbow to red. The wavelengths are well known. The colors we see extend from about 400 nm to about 700 nm. This spectrum is often depicted as a linear bar graph showing the colors' change as the wavelengths change. But imagine bending that bar around into a circle, melding the infrared with the ultraviolet, producing a red-violet color. Now you have a circle where the colors continually merge into the next, going round and round without beginning or end.

Why would we want to depict colors as circular? We do so because that is how we, as humans, relate to color. We, as children of this Earth, are aligned with the cyclic nature of color because we are aligned with the cyclic nature of life on Earth, and our planet cycles through the colors as it traces out the cycle of the year. This cycle is shown in the Great Talismanic Color Wheel of Influence.[3] It depicts the fundamental alignment of nature's color with life itself. It depicts the cyclic nature of time and color on Earth, revealing their natural meanings.

On the Great Wheel, the colors flow from the dark violets and blues of the winter sky through the promise of spring in the melting turquoise waters of the brooks and lakes as they are freed of ice. The colors change to the greens of spring grass as the vernal equinox passes, then quickly to the bright yellows of the hot summer sun. As the colors darken, first to the oranges, then to the reds of the autumn leaves, the earth approaches the autumnal equinox. Then the colors darken further, and the earth moves into winter. The amethyst skies darken into the violets and indigos, reflecting the now-barren landscapes and the darkening natural earth tones of the shortened days. Then at the vernal equinox, the cycle begins again with the indigos and blues of the winter sky slowly giving way to the transitional greens of spring.

The influence rays of the natural minerals, crystals, and gemstones affect our deepest mind based on this natural cycle. We, as humans, are aligned with the earth and its cycles. We are aligned with its natural colors. We respond to the vibrations from deep within our natural selves. We feel color. We interpret color. In our brains, color triggers emotions and feelings.[4] Colors have meaning to our natural selves.[5] We feel the growth of the spring green. The reds of autumn excite our passions, and we all respond to the sense of dreamlike wonder that violet transmits.

Not only is the Great Talismanic Color Wheel of Influence a depiction of the natural progression of the year, but it is also a depiction of the natural order of human life.

---

3 Phillip Ball, *Bright Earth: Art and the Invention of Color* (Chicago: University of Chicago Press, 2001), 38. Phillip Ball, in this work, shows us the color wheel of Isaac Newton from his book *Optics* (1706). Newton seems to be the first to use such a color wheel, in which the rainbow is folded back on itself by connecting the violet end to the red end using a red-violet color to combine them into a circle.

4 Johann Wolfgang von Goethe, *Theory of Colours*, trans. Charles Eastlake (Cambridge, MA: MIT Press, 1970), paragraphs 761 and 915. The concept of colors having specific, unchanging meanings to humans is presented in these paragraphs specifically.

5 John Gage, *Color and Meaning: Art, Science, and Symbolism* (Berkeley, CA: University of California Press, 1999), 22.

While the year technically starts as the days begin to lengthen at the winter solstice, life is still enshrouded in the oncoming winter. The seeds of new life lie dormant, awaiting spring. But like the earth, our older generations are preparing for spring when the life of new generations will burst forth in all its vibrancy once more. Like the earth, the cycle of human life spins around as generations create new ones. The cycle of birth, death, and renewal is natural. Like other parts of nature, in our springtime of life we experience a period of rapid growth as we find our way to adulthood and maturity. For us it is a time of physical, spiritual, and mental growth. And, just like other life on Earth, a high summer period of young adulthood occurs when we have the physical vigor of youth. For us it is a time of enthusiasm, success, and joy. We then have usually found our mates and paths and, as we mature into full adulthood, the time of passion arrives. We have found our loves, both physical and spiritual. As we mature and gather experience, our lives turn inward with reflection, and we see things for their real value. In the autumn of our lives, our insights into and understanding of our place in the cosmos grows. Often at this point we are freed of many worldly demands, and a time to pursue dreams arrives. Finally, through our discoveries, growth, passions, and introspection, we become wise in the ways of the world, and we are able to see what truly is important. As the winter of our individual lives approaches we slow down, trust our hard-learned wisdom, and find the faith in and acceptance of our place in the universe. Our lives progress through these stages as naturally as the world progresses through the seasons.

The Great Talismanic Color Wheel of Influence shows us that we are aligned with the natural world. It shows us that our cycles as people are aligned with the cycles of nature. Like the natural world, we have a time of birth, a time of awakening, a high summer of vigor, an autumn in our lives that gives us the strength and courage to persevere. And we have a winter in which we find our peace and place in the universe as the cycle of life prepares to renew itself again. But, upon reflection, how could this not be so? We are products of this Earth. We are children of the earth. It would be incomprehensible if we were not aligned with the rest of the natural cycle. We change as we age just as the world changes as the year ages. The earth renews itself through periods of birth and death; and, as a part of it, so do we. Our nature is nature. We are the earth. Through the color rays, our talismans can connect us to the earth and its Life Force, combining its natural energy with our minds and spirits. As we examine the true, natural effects of color in our lives, we start where life renews itself annually—at the vernal equinox, the time when spring begins and nature is alive as lush vegetation emerges from the recently frozen ground of winter.

Turquoise Ray of Influence

Turquoise is the color of the world at the vernal equinox as the violets and blues of winter are melted away into the greens of spring. It is the color of the natural birthstones of those born in the beginning of spring, the period of new birth (March 20–April 19). It is the color of the world at a moment of discovery. It is a blending of the cold, winter-blue ray of trust with the approaching warm green ray of growth. It is the color of the earth as the new growth and life emerges. It is a fresh color, a welcome color, and a color that moves us to serenity, knowing that the cycle of life is beginning again. Turquoise is the color of the balance point between the cycles of life. As the old gives way to the new, as winter gives way to spring, and as death gives way to new life, turquoise balances the dark, the cold, and the old, with the light, the warm, and the new.

Turquoise is the color ray of discovery and the color ray of balance. Its vibrations help us find ourselves and return to equilibrium in our lives and feelings. Excesses can be good. Hot passion, cool reason—both have their place. But when we need to re-center and find our true selves, turquoise is the color ray of power that is best suited for such endeavors. When your life is out of balance, whether from too much passion or not enough, or too much activity or not enough, or whatever the imbalance, turquoise rays can get you back to center again.

Turquoise-colored talismans have a wide variety of uses. They temper excesses, restore calm after a storm, soothe us, relieve stress, neutralize extremes, and provide a counter to tendencies to fly off in a single direction. They help us overcome conflict and deal with rage in others or ourselves. They moderate aggressiveness and help us deal with cruelty. They are antidotes to excessive passion, drawing this power from their blue component. Imagine a beach of white sand leading to a tranquil lagoon reflecting a perfect blue sky mixed with the reflections of lush green vegetation—that is turquoise. The turquoise-colored talismans help us relax, rewind, and build our tolerance. When you seek to reestablish your equilibrium and get your emotions under control, use a turquoise-colored talisman.

In lighter shades, turquoise energy is transformed to the power of inner harmony and peace through spiritual realization and understanding. To know your place in the worlds of man and nature, use light blue/green turquoise rays to find the right balance. The concept of inner harmony is vitally important in the quest for well-being. We are constantly pulled in many directions. We have obligations to nation, family, community, and friends. We have our own needs to grow, develop, achieve, and prosper. Modern life is a constant balancing act. We often get out of sorts and stressed as we try to be too much and do too much. It is hard to find the tranquility in our minds that we seem to need to keep our balance. The use of a turquoise talisman can be a tremendous help in efforts to restore our inner harmony as we cope with the pulls and pressures from around us. To become more connected to the brotherhood of man, and to gain true understanding of others and ourselves, use light turquoise talismans.

In darker, richer tones, turquoise brings us a ray of considerable power. It is the color of flexibility. Many of our shortcomings are based on intolerance. We get used to the way we think people should behave, the way the world should work. We grow more intolerant of new things as we age. Dark turquoise rays are potent anti-intolerance rays that will give us the adaptability in our outlook to learn, enjoy, and participate in the newness that is constantly being brought to life. It is a ray that can keep us young in attitude. Dark turquoise rays give us openness to new ideas, foster new perspectives, and help us adapt to new environments.

Besides the mineral turquoise, there are several other minerals and crystals that contain this color ray. Rosasite, selenite, apatite, chrysocolla, topaz, and larimar (pectolite) all are found to contain this potent color ray.

Green Ray of Influence

As spring continues to warm the earth's crust, a frenzy of growth converts barren landscapes into lush glades, and the leaves of plants and trees emerge in a thousand shades of green. Like their counterparts in the plant kingdom, the green gems and minerals are the "growth talismans." They are powerful conduits of the earth's Life Force of birth, development, and creation, and of the power of nature's constant renewal. The green minerals are the natural birthstones of those fortunate enough to be born in the heart of spring (April 20–May 20).

Green is the most restful color, the easiest color for humans to perceive. It is easy on the eye, and easy on the soul. To the human mind, green is the color of spring, new beginnings, and safety in the journey ahead. Green is the most human of colors.[6]

Talismans of pure green are potent aids in nurturing, whether of fledgling family relationships or new business ventures. They are the the symbols of new life in all its manifestations. Use them to encourage growth and development. With a project well started, a gleaming green tourmaline or emerald will ensure that your focus remains constant and your path stays one of successful growth and development. Journeys once started need

---

6 The Franklin Institute, "Light and Color," http://www.fi.edu/color/ (accessed May 26, 2007).

constant vigilance to ensure successful conclusions. Green talismans are perfect for keeping a venture on course, a project on schedule, and a life on track.

Green is the color of fertility and renewal, and the use of green talismans has a long history in aiding efforts to bring new life into a family, a community, or an organization. It is also the color ray of productivity, progress, prosperity, material success, and advancement. Green talismans are potent for efforts directed at career advancement.

The darker green minerals and gems such as chrome tourmaline and aventurine have the strong element of growth muted with the deeper tones of the power, perspective, and mystery of black. These are the talismans of physical growth, and they are excellent aids in our efforts to become stronger, to become more flexible, or just to get into better shape.

Green talismans are also the Safety talismans that are useful in focusing our efforts to make sure we stay safe while we travel or adventure. They are the talismans of profit and good financial results. They are the talismans of security in old age. They will help us in efforts to secure our future and retire comfortably.

In lighter tints, the green talismans are excellent for promoting spiritual growth and renewed commitment to a higher purpose. The lighter green talismans are used in similar pursuits to those of the turquoise ones. However, whereas the lighter turquoise is focused on inner harmony, the lighter green is more focused on spiritual growth and development. Spiritual growth can have many manifestations. Certainly, the light green talismans can help us focus our efforts to improve our devotion to high ideals and strengthen our religious faith.

Olive Ray of Influence

When the vibrant green rays of growth combine with the yellow of pure sunshine, the powerful color ray of olive is produced. The combination awakens us to the possibilities that are rapidly developing. As life on Earth, still in high bloom, sees the promise of the approaching hot summer sun and a time of less vigorous, yet strong growth, we can use the olive talismans to focus our efforts that began well but now need strength to mature. Peridot is the best-known jewel that manifests its power through this color ray. It is one of the true birthstones of those born in the magical month of awakening, as the greens of spring are giving way to the bright yellows of the approaching summer (May 21–June 20).

Olive talismans help focus and enhance our early efforts to seek wisdom, lighting our path to understanding. Olive is the color ray of receptiveness to new meanings and ideas. It is a talisman of the beginning of the search for knowledge and enlightenment. It is the color of the acolyte, the apprentice, and the assistant.

In its deeper tones, the olive talisman is the "Study Stone." It reflects the birth of truth and harmony. It aids us in beginning long searches and quests for vision, insight, understanding, and wisdom. It is the color ray of talismans that aid in perseverance to a long quest, particularly when the end result desired is a higher state of understanding or awareness. Dark olive talismans are excellent for achieving goals that need deep constancy and long-term purpose—not wild, exuberant growth, but the slow, steady development and deep caring of a life's calling. Dark olive talismans are used to promote extended efforts that can span years and decades. They become lifelong companions that magnify and focus our plans for developing our capabilities as we progress in our chosen endeavors.

The lighter shades of olive have a very special purpose in the talismanic arts: perseverance in quests for enlightenment, deep wisdom, and understanding of the natural universe. Astronomers, geologists, paleontologists, and others who spend years in study seeking understanding of the natural world can gain great benefit from the use of light olive talismans. They aid in efforts that require deep concentration and painstaking accuracy. They aid us in efforts to strengthen our resistance, determination, and endurance for mental challenges, particularly those of long duration.

Yellow Ray of Influence

Yellow is the color of the coming of the sun and the warmth it brings. It is the color of the bright days of early summer, and as the sun high in the sky lights up the landscape, its yellow color ray brings us the power of enlightenment, lighting up the landscape of our search for knowledge. It is the color of the summer solstice ushering in the bright time of long days, warm temperatures, and sustained vigor. Yellow is the natural birthstone of those born in the beginning of summer (June 21–July 21). It is the color of midday, midyear, and the beginnings of midlife. Yellow is a color of journeys beginning well, full of promise and sunny optimism.

Yellow talismans give us the power to solidify new interests and new relationships. They help us to see things in new ways and to become enlightened. They add clarity to our lives. They help us wake things up and add zest, optimism, and meaning to lives, relationships, and ideas.

Yellow is a special color for talismans. Yellow Seekers, like yellow sapphires, citrines, and heliodors (yellow beryl), are particularly useful for aiding us in new adventures, new efforts, and new quests. Life is a series of new beginnings. Just as each day is a new beginning in the eternal cycle of the earth's rotation, each equinox and solstice is a beginning of a new season, so in many ways we also have a series of new beginnings in our lives. We all have a series of new jobs, new families, new relationships, and new locations. We start new projects and we begin new efforts. Yellow talismans are specifically for such efforts. They have the special ray of influence to help us focus our energies on beginning new things well.

There is sometimes confusion between the uses of green and yellow talismans when the focus is on beginning and growth. Green is the color of physical growth and renewal. It is used for efforts that are aimed at growth, particularly of physical things. Yellow talismans are used for new efforts, new beginnings, and new projects when the objective is not necessarily the growth of something physical. For efforts that are related to growing a successful garden, a green talisman would be best. For efforts that are aimed at becoming a better cook, yellow is a good choice.

In lighter shades, yellow talismans, such as citrine, are useful for keeping awareness of important things, when day-to-day life can lead to forgetfulness. They are used extensively for ensuring that new relationships get off to a good start by aiding in the establishment of good communication. They give us the power of heightened awareness that lets us focus on the needs of the person or group we are joining. They let us use our energy to be aware of our surroundings and the subtle nuances coming to us from others. Use light yellow talismans for efforts that involve enhancing communications, particularly within families. The power of the light yellow ray can significantly improve communication between parents and children. When used in conjunction with a light turquoise talisman to enhance understanding, the light yellow talisman can provide a potent aid to family interrelationships.

Light yellow talismans are also excellent aids when you desire to improve your organizational skills. They can focus your efforts and allow you to bring order into your life. All of us suffer from an overload of responsibility, duties, and tasks. Our lives are fast and furious at times. Getting things in their proper place, prioritizing activities, and setting an executable plan can be a great boon to our productivity, if not sanity!

Dark yellow talismans bring us the power and energy of clarity that come from true awareness and concentrated yellow energy. Dark, deep yellow mutes the youthfulness of awakening with the maturity of a long wakefulness and a growing maturity. The dark yellow ray of influence is very useful for enjoying a maturing relationship. Use it to spice up a relationship or friendship that might be being neglected. Dark yellow talismans are also excellent aids when decisiveness, precision, or persuasiveness is needed. They are the "Salesman's Stones" that bring success in efforts to sell ourselves, products, or services to others.

One very important use of dark yellow talismans concerns being successful in verbalizing your needs to yourself and to others. Many people are just not aware of exactly what it is that they truly need. Being unable to communicate needs leads to frustration and unhappiness. A talisman that contains a good dark yellow ray of influence can be a great aid in learning to successfully convey your desires. That is always the first step in actually achieving what you seek.

Gold Ray of Influence

The vibrant mix of the enlightenment of pure yellow and the joyfulness of orange produces the king of colors: gold. It is the natural birthstone color of those born in the magical month of midsummer (July 22–August 21). This is a time in the year when we rejoice in the energy of the sun and the growth it creates, which nourishes the body and the soul. The rays of a golden talisman fulfill us and give us the enthusiasm and excitement that make life a wonderful adventure.

Reflecting the exuberance of pure golden light, these talismans, like topaz, aid us in feeling a zest for what life offers. Gold is traditionally the color of kings, riches, and the sun. It is all this and more. Gold is as close to a magical color as exists. It seems to touch a deep part of our minds, conjuring up images of mystical places, treasure, and adventure. We instinctively seek this color. It makes us feel rich, secure, and successful. It is the color of many symbols of power and wealth.

Gold is the color of adventure, success, and power. Gold is the color of the earth fully alive in midsummer. It is the ray of rarity, bespeaking richness and natural value. It enriches the spirit, warms us like yellow, and cheers us like orange. Gold is the high color, the crown of life. It is all life, sweet, warm—growing and reaching its peak. It is brilliant, sometimes blinding, but always tinged with awe and inspiration. Gold is exuberance.

In darker shades, the golden talismans have a deeper and more pronounced sense of devotion and commitment, providing us with a mature enthusiasm and the ability to share a lifelong commitment of care and love. Darker colors of gold also give us a sense of purpose fulfilled. They provide us with the power to lead projects, organizations, and efforts to success. Most important, darker shades of gold are the ultimate power talismans. They exude authority, control, leadership, success, and influence. Dark gold is the talisman when fame is the objective.

Pale gold talismans, like spun flax, offer us the power of toned-down exuberance—they are the talismans of happiness, cheerfulness, and contentment. Talismans that possess the light gold color ray provide us with the pleasure life can offer in simple things. Pale gold talismans like golden beryl, citrine, and the mineral gold are the best all-around talismans when just improving overall happiness and contentment is the goal. We all want to be happy. Using light gold talismans in conjunction with others for more specific purposes can help us to appreciate the value of the changes in our lives.

Happiness is a very elusive quality. The key to achieving it is to appreciate the goodness in daily life. Sure, there are high points in every life, but most days are pretty routine. If we take the time to see the blessings in those days—smiles on children, good weather, comfort in our homes, the conveniences of daily life like hot water at the turn of a knob—we will find happiness much more easily. We are awash in a sea of luxuries that even the kings of the last century couldn't even conceive. Use pale gold talismans in your efforts to see the goodness, the benefits, and the value of your life. They will lead you to happiness.

Orange Ray of Influence

Orange is a most amazing color. It is one of nature's most powerful colors. It is a color that nature uses on a vast canvas. It is the color of the true birthstones of those born at the end of summer (August 22–September 22). The passion of the red ray has an almost multiplicative effect in the orange ray as it combines with the happy elements of gold. This bright, highly noticeable color ray makes a very direct and forceful talisman with little subtlety even in its lighter shades. The forcefulness of the orange ray—its high energy of deep-felt joy and lasting attachments and friendship—give it particular usefulness in making talismans.

Orange is the color of the natural transition from the high hot summer, to the cooler days of autumn. This is a time of passage from the bright yellows and golds to the more somber colors of the waning year. It is a color of the first hints of turning leaves, and the darkening of the earth as the sun moves farther south, shortening the days and light rays.

Some of the most beautiful gems and crystals are orange. The padparadscha, an orange sapphire is one of nature's treasures, and a powerful talisman. Orange is the color of joy and friendship. Joy is a pure emotion, an elusive one, but a heartfelt one. Often as people grow older, they lose the capacity for experiencing pure joy. It can be a simple delight or a deep, lasting feeling. If something seems to be missing but you can't really describe it, perhaps a bit of orange mixed in your daily life is needed. Orange is a happy, outgoing, and sharing color. It brings things and people together. It integrates the parts of our communal lives. It is the "home stone," the "village stone," and the "community stone." The strength of the red rays joined with the powerful fire of the gold rays give the orange talisman powers to combine, integrate, and unite. Orange is the color of physical pleasures, including those of intimacy and sex.

In lighter shades, orange is the color ray of the talisman of friendship. Use talismans of muted orange to find new friends, keep in touch with lifetime friends, and find ways to keep friendships alive. Light orange is the color ray of companionship, loyalty, charm, encouragement, praise, sharing, and affection. It is a very powerful ray, and talismans that possess it are particularly valuable.

Darker shades of orange deepen the sense of belonging and home. If you are lucky enough to find a powerful deep orange stone, use it as a "home stone" by placing it centrally in your house to ensure the hospitality of home and hearth. To keep a family happy together, a team working well, or a congregation united, a dark orange talisman is perfect.

Some of the uses of orange talismans include focusing our energy to overcome distrust, timidity, or shyness. These antisocial behaviors make friendships suffer. Use an orange talisman when the need is to focus energy on developing outgoing, caring, and friendly behaviors.

The major orange talismans include carnelian, orange calcite, orange jade, orange rhodochrosite, fire agate, orange garnet, and orange quartz.

Scarlet Ray of Influence

Scarlet combines the energy of the pure red ray and the exuberance and joy of the orange in a precious gift of nature. Scarlet is the color of strength and vitality, both physical and spiritual. Scarlet talismans are the natural birthstones of those born in the first month of autumn (September 23–October 21).

Scarlet talismans are used when protection from physical harm is needed. Travelers, watchmen, and all who have occasion to fear personal harm from attack or misfortune are well advised to use a scarlet talisman to focus their efforts at self-protection. It usually should be used with a dark green talisman for safety from accidents. Use scarlet-colored talismans in efforts to overcome fear and improve self-reliance. They have great power. They are the talismans of victory, success, and skill. When your challenge is physical, and you need to focus and multiply your physical strength and stamina, use a talisman with the scarlet ray of influence.

Athletes, soldiers, workers, and all for whom physical strength is vital can benefit from the rays of a scarlet talisman. Workout efforts can be enhanced and an overall increase in vitality will be observed with careful use of scarlet talismans. Weightlifters, body build-ers, and track and field competitors can gain significantly from these talismans.

Deep scarlet talismans are the key to the physical pleasures of maturity—in love, in life, and in relationships. Muted with the shades of black, brown, blue, or violet, deep scarlet talismans give us the natural sources of energy to enjoy life's pleasures that extend past the joyfulness of youth. Enjoying life in maturity requires vitality. Vitality has both a mental and physical quality. The darker shades of scarlet are more muted in their uses. Rather than focus on dynamic, explosive physical prowess, the darker shades are more useful for the maintenance of vitality over long periods. Want to feel invincible? Use a scarlet talisman for a while and see how fearless and self-assured you have become.

Lighter shades of scarlet—the lightly tinted red-oranges—are excellent for use in tal-ismans of dedication in young relationships. They combine the pink energy of romantic love with the light orange energy of contentment with family and friends. Light scarlet talismans are unique aids to the newly in love, the new family, or the new relationship. They make excellent "home stones" for the first home of a newly married couple.

Light scarlet talismans have an additional power: increasing willpower and dedication to a difficult mental effort. There are a great many temptations we wish to resist at one time or another. For many, excess weight is a constant battle. We seem to never be able to keep it off. If you are in need of focus and an ability to say no and really mean it, use a light scarlet talisman in your efforts. Among their many uses, the scarlet talismans are the Dieter's Stone. Dispellers and Barriers that possess the light scarlet ray of influence are particular effective. Rhodonite, sunstone, and topaz all can be found possessing this ray of influence. Seek them out.

Red Ray of Influence

Red is the color of passion, energy, and life. It motivates. It is a very strong color—the color of fire and blood. It is emotionally intense and affects humans by raising their blood pressure and speeding up their metabolism. It is a call to action, a battle cry, and a sign of warning. It excites us, raises our enthusiasm, and gives us energy. Red is the natural birth-stone of those born in mid-autumn (October 22–November 20). Red talismans are used when the situation needs passion: active, involved, energetic action. Red empowers, uplifts, and engulfs. It cures apathy. It gets things done. Red is action and drive. If you are suffer-ing from a lack of power, listlessness, or a low emotional state, you need more red. Like the scarlet ray, the red ray brings us a self-confidence built on fearlessness. When the need is for action without hesitation or self-doubt, use a talisman with a fiery ray of bright red.

In lighter shades of red (usually with some light orange mixed in), like pink, the strong passion and power are toned down to subtler, feminine aspects. This is the color ray of determination, commitment, and caring. Simply, pink is love. Also, pink is a soothing color, useful to calm feelings of anger or resentment. Pink is a comfort color that can aid efforts to meditate. Pink shades of tourmaline, jade, corundum, garnet, spinel, and calcite are used to aid us in improving our caring and loving abilities.

Pink is the color of new love, new romance, and new relationships. It is particularly powerful in Seeker and Attractor talismans. For finding a girlfriend or boyfriend, or even a mate, the Seekers such as pink sapphire, rose quartz, cinnabar, and morganite are excellent.

In darker shades, red is tinted with brown or black. Here the power of the color ray is not muted but mixed with darker and more earthy, powerful overtones of brown or the power and mystery of black. Dark red stones are talismans of very hard, durable energy and quiet passion. Strong, deep feelings call for a strong, deep-red talisman. Dark red is a masculine color.

Dark red rays of influence have a wide variety of talismanic uses. The dark red stones are particularly useful for increasing devotion, and seeing the seriousness of life. They are also the Harvest Stones, bringing the power of the season to our efforts to reap the rewards of our productive ventures. They have a power similar to the light scarlet stones in their ability to amplify our tenacity and dedication, particularly in physical efforts.

Ruby, topaz, spinel, carnelian, cuprite, garnet, red jade, moonstone, red jasper, calcite, tourmaline, and sardonyx are some of the red talismans with a wide variety of uses.

Amethyst Ray of Influence

Amethyst, derived from the old Greek word *methy*, meaning wine, is the red-violet ray that connects both time and color. It leads from the old year to the new and connects the red end of the visible spectrum to the violet at the other end of our perception. This potent, powerful color brings things together, wraps them around, and solidifies them. It connects beginnings to ends, joins life to new life, and makes the great circle of life complete once again. It captures the dying rays of the sun, and sends the message that winter is arriving. It is the color of the beginning of the end. Sometimes it is a sad color, but new life follows death, and the wheel of life must continually turn, bringing new life to the planet. There is a time of closure, a time of repose, and a time of passage into new beginnings. Amethyst is the color of that time.

In this way, amethyst is the color of creativity. As the world begins to cycle through a time of renewal once again, creating the means for the rapid growth of the new spring, we too prepare for new creations by allowing a quiet time of reflection and insight.

This color ray, amethyst, the color of the gemstone of the same name, is the color of natural birthstones of those born as the old year wanes and the new is about to arrive at the winter solstice (November 21–December 20). The color ray amethyst combines the fiery passion of the red ray tempered with the intuition of the violet ray. In doing so, it helps us see with both our emotions and our logic. Can there be any more potent combination than imagination and passion? This combination makes amethyst the color ray of vision, insight, and self-knowledge. Great deeds are possible when amethyst rays are employed. These amethyst talismans are used when we want to truly see what exists in the real or spiritual world and not live in a world of misunderstanding. Use amethyst talismans in efforts to correct misconceptions, or protect from tricks or efforts of others to mislead or deceive us. Use amethyst to see behind the masks that other people wear.

Amethyst rays are particularly helpful in artistic endeavors in which new, original results need to be created using the tools and methods of previous times. Amethyst-colored talismans include the Artist's Stone, the Composer's Stone, the Inventor's Stone, the Poet's Stone, and the Painter's Stone. They bring the natural power of creativity to us. They help us visualize, create, and invent. They stimulate our creativity.

Garnets make some of the best amethyst talismans. Garnets are hard, tough, and possess the crystalline properties that hold the power of balance and vision.

Because they reflect the color rays that connect the old and the new, in darker shades amethyst talismans give us the deep vision needed to see the future. When you need to know what lies ahead, when the need is great, use deep amethyst ray talismans to find your way into a difficult future. They give us powerful insight and enhance our perception of the potential effects of our decisions.

In lighter shades, the amethyst ray of vision helps us see into our souls and ourselves. The admonishment "know thyself" is profound advice. A light amethyst crystal can be a tremendous help. It helps us see ourselves as we actually are, and it helps us understand how others see us. When you need to understand why someone reacts to you like they do, use a light amethyst-colored crystal or gemstone talisman to aid in the perception and understanding you seek. Light amethyst is the ray of self-esteem and self-knowledge. It is particularly useful when found in Enhancer talismans such as spinel and halite.

Violet Ray of Influence

At the onset of the darkness of winter, the oranges and reds of autumn give way to the deeper winter tones of violet and blue. The skies are darker with less sunshine; the earth takes on the darker hue of winter's majesty. Violet is the color of natural birthstones of those born at the time when the year is new, just after the winter solstice (December 21– January 19). Like the sleepy, misty time of year that produces its rays, violet is the color ray of intuition, dreams, nobility, and luxury. As the color ray of influence that begins the cycle of life once again, violet is one of the most powerful rays in nature. It inspires awe, and invites a feeling of mystery and magic, reminiscent of the mystery and magic of life's rejuvenation and renewal. Violet color rays are powerful aids in interpreting our dreams, inspiring us to great deeds and accomplishments, and putting the magic back in our lives and relationships. Violet is the color of music; it stirs us, transforms us, and connects us in seemingly mysterious ways to our dreams, our past, and ourselves.

Dark violet talismans have special powers. They are the "dream talismans." They are the windows to the soul and the world beyond our ordinary understanding. They are best for aiding us in interpreting our dreams, and are the entries to places in our minds we don't know exist. They are the legendary third eye that gives us the "sight of insight." Used well, a deep violet talisman can help us see the new visions of reality that we seek. A faceted, translucent, vibrant dark violet crystal is magic on a higher plane. Dark violet is the true color ray of good luck. Luck is a dream manifested. Dark violet is the color ray that connects dreams and reality. There are Seeker and Enhancer crystals such as amethyst, taaffeite, and halite that contain this powerful ray.

Talismans that are lavender, the lighter shade of violet, contain the rays that aid us in the wisdom of self that violet provides, but they are more focused on our feelings and understanding our hidden yearnings. These are the talismans of the free, unfettered intellect and the unfettered heart. Use these beautiful talismans to fulfill your dreams that involve heartfelt desires for love and affection. Use them to gain the knowledge you need to live with grace and style.

Indigo Ray of Influence

As the winter deepens further and the earth tips far from the sun, the color of the winter sky becomes almost inky—a mix of blue and violet. This is a soft color ray that is made for introspection, and it can result in profound wisdom when used well. As such, indigo is the color of virtue and maturity. It is the color of the true birthstone of those born in midwinter (January 20–February 18). The indigo talismans are rare and valuable. They combine the intuition of the violet ray with the trust of the pure blue ray. They can help us find our way to a higher plane of consciousness. The indigo talismans are beautiful and powerful stones of the reflexive awareness and comprehension of complex relationships. Talismanic scholars strive to find the most perfect of these rarities. Even the opaque crystals of sodalite and iolite can be highly effective. They serve as "mind medicine" for those in need of gentle understanding in difficult interpersonal relationships. Indigo is also the color of judgment and long life.

Darkened with brown, black, or blue, the deeper shades of indigo bring us closer to the deep wisdom of the dark violet rays but with the broader connection and communication openness of blue. Use dark indigo talismans when you need to open doors or break down barriers and see the truth that only your soul can fathom. Everyone can use more of this color ray in his or her life. Seek it out.

Dark indigo is the color of honesty. It is powerful in Dispeller talismans such as tanzanite when we need to see through efforts of deception. If we are seeking honest understanding of our place in the universe, Seekers such as covellite are best.

Dark indigo rays are also the best rays for religious and spiritual journeys. When our goals involve developing mastery of spiritual understandings and practices, Enhancers such as lazurite and fluorite that contain this ray of influence are perfect.

When indigo is lightened and diffused in crystals such as those of sodalite or some fluorite, then indigo becomes the ray of connection, having similar power to that of amethyst. The difference in uses is a matter of degree and intent. While amethyst connects the old to the new, the light indigo connects us to the natural world and helps us understand that connection. To maintain a natural connection to life, to be naturally aware of your place, and to keep your soul and mind connected, use a pale indigo talisman.

Lighter shades of indigo are also useful for efforts to increase our humility, develop a sense of dignity, and expand our understanding of the value of virtue in our dealings with others. Finally, talismans containing the light indigo ray of influence are the best ones for efforts at improving our appreciation of others and a sense of thankfulness for life's bounty.

Blue Ray of Influence

Blue is the color of ice reflecting the slowly lightening winter sky as the deep violets depart and the sun climbs higher every day. As the winter slowly gives way to the budding spring, and life quickens, ready to burst forth, blue marks the beginning of life and emotion. Blue is the color of the true birthstones of those born as the world awaits the vernal equinox and spring (February 19–March 19). This is a time when new life is about to burst forth, a time of faith and trust.

Blue talismans are the talismans of trust. When we seek to become more sincere, act more responsibly, or become more trustworthy or faithful, these talismans give us the focus we require. Trust is a complex need. We seek to trust others, and we seek to be trustworthy. Most of our interactions with others depend on mutual trust. Blue talismans are excellent aids in ensuring that we are acting out our lives as worthy of the trust of our friends, acquaintances, and community.

In lighter shades, blue talismans are tempered with subtlety. The color of shallow pools of water reflecting the sky, light blue talismans help us reflect, ponder, question, and relax in our acceptance of the life we have. Use light blue talismans when you need to develop patience, reconcile differences, or seek forgiveness. The light blue rays are excellent for recovery efforts from addictions or destructive behavior patterns. They aid in curbing tempers and helping us become mellower and milder. Their rays are potent, and they can help us to change our lives to become more dependable and cheerful. They are helpful in dealing with grief, letting go of the past, and curing guilt.

The darker shades of blue are for enhancing respect and compassion in ourselves. Dark blue talismans teach us humanity, discretion, and honor. They help us act more charitably, and focus our efforts on service to others. They teach us grace, sensitivity to the needs of others, and tenderness in our dealings.

Other Rays of Influence

White, black, and brown are not colors, per se. White is a combination of all colors, black is really the absence of any color, and brown is a mixed-color ray that is actually a combination of red, green, and blue, or red, green, and orange. Silver is actually a mixture of black and white. However, each of these is a powerful and deeply meaningful ray of influence found in the natural world of minerals.

White Ray of Influence

In today's modern world, white is the color of cleanliness, purity, unity, and innocence. But these are fairly modern meanings and by no means universal.[7] The timeless, natural powers of white rays are those of the moon. White is the color we see when the moon reflects the sun's light to us. White is the color of natural cycles. It is the color of beginning and endings. White is the color of the feminine gender, manifested as the Goddess in many cultures, and, as such, the color of the world of birth, and regeneration. It is a cool color of the night, the sleeping world, and it offers us the best guide to the hidden world beyond understanding, just as the moon is our only illumination in the dark world of night. White is the color of the full moon reflected on a snow-covered field. It is cold, but a sleeping cold reflecting great heat. White is the color of contradictions and opposites. It is the color of freedom and the color of hope.

The white talismans include moonstones, quartz, calcite, selenite, and white forms of lepidolite, topaz, and beryl. Use them to experience and appreciate the cyclic nature of the universe. The white talismans are of the spiritual world that is sensed but not seen. White talismans are guides when we don't know where we are going. They are the guides to understanding and knowledge that we don't even know exists.

Black Ray of Influence

Black is not a color, but rather the lack of color. In nature, black is the color of night when the moon is not in the sky to illuminate the landscape. Dark night is a time of unease in which the familiar world is obscured. Humans naturally fear the unknown and the unseen. Black is naturally associated with such fears. Because we do not know or understand death, black is often associated with death and ending. However, black is actually a very positive color. Dark blacks are very protective and offer us a retreat, the safety of being hidden from our enemies. Black talismans such as hematite, agate, black tourmaline, onyx, and sardonyx are power talismans that, like some red and scarlet minerals, relieve our fears of physical harm. Black is a protective color that actually gives us a sense of power. It makes us feel secure, daring, and physically powerful. Dark-colored crystals deepen our connection to the physical, natural world. They help relieve us of fears specifically associated with our physical existence here on Earth. Black talismans are very synergistic with light green talismans to provide us with safety and confidence.

---

7 Victoria Finlay, *Color: A Natural History of the Palette* (New York: Random House, 2002), 108.

Black talismans are used when we need protection and mental fortitude. They are the talismans to use when we need to feel safe and secure. Black is an excellent color for a Barrier talisman. As we learned in the Second Secret of Talismans, the Barrier talismans have incredible abilities to help us focus and amplify our efforts to keep undesirable elements out of our lives. The crystal energy of a Barrier talisman such as babingtonite, when combined with the black color ray of influence, offers an excellent protective talisman.

Brown Ray of Influence

While there are many colors that can be derived from mixing the natural rays in various degrees, brown is a special mixture because it is the color of many elements of the natural earth. Brown is a very comfortable color to humans. It is the color of home, hearth, and nature. It makes us feel good. Brown is the color of the surface of the earth. It is the color of grounding and connection. It is the relaxation color, the color of being once again "on the ground" and at rest. It is a retreat color, a restful color. It is the most common color on Earth. Most animals and plants are brown in some parts.

Brown talismans are excellent aids in a wide variety of efforts. When we want to regain our composure, relax in our life, reconnect with the natural world, or just find the time to be ourselves a while, brown talismans, like the turquoise ones, are excellent aids. Modern life seems to disconnect us from the earth; we get caught up in the hustle and bustle. We forget to be human, and we ignore our true nature.

Brown is also the color to use when it is necessary to get down from an excited state, or from being "up in the air," undecided, or flighty. When you need to settle down, regroup, and revitalize, use a brown talisman.

There are many brown minerals and crystals. Amber, brown jade, jasper, selenite, tourmaline, cross stones, fire agates, hawk's eyes, and magnetite are just a few of the common ones.

Silver Ray of Influence

Much like pure white, silver is the color of the moon, the feminine, the night, introspection, the cyclic nature of life, coolness, stillness, magic, and ambiguity. Silver is a mirror, a reflection, and a path to the inner consciousness. Silver is a priestess to gold's high priest. It is gray, but a reflective gray. It is lonely, altruistic, and aloof. It is a mystery. As Seekers, silver objects find patterns and the inner meanings of events. Use silver talismans for quiet meditation, finding your real purpose in life, and calm reflection on life's meanings.

Mixed-Color Talismans

Many crystals and mineral specimens are found that are not composed of a single mineral or a single color. For example, bi-colored tourmaline has both red and green in the same crystal. Blue azurite and green malachite are often found together in a single crystal. These types of talismans offer special uses as the strengths of the various color rays are combined. The information in this chapter will allow us to use these special talismans by understanding the individual color rays they possess.

Summary

The human mind resonates to the vibrations of the natural colors. We find meaning because our very existence is tied to this planet. Over eons of survival we have come to associate with the natural world, of which we are a part. We understand this planet, and we instinctively understand the meanings of its colors. The cycle of life is associated with the cycle of color. We understand the natural world. We can use this knowledge to enhance our efforts to understand ourselves. The green rays of spring, as life begins, help us with new undertakings, the gold rays of high summer give us courage, the reds of autumn give us strength, and the cool violets and indigo rays of the waning year offer us inner vision and wisdom. The Third Secret of Talismans is a powerful one indeed, allowing us to use the color rays of influence to fashion talismans that will connect us to the natural world and the Life Force of the planet Earth.

The colors have the same meanings and influence with all talismans. It doesn't matter if you are using a Seeker, a Barrier, or a Dispeller; the colors have only positive meanings. For example, as was mentioned earlier in this chapter, if you were seeking to increase your strength, you might choose a scarlet talisman. Equally, if you were seeking to rid yourself of weakness, you would use a scarlet Dispeller. Why? The color ray of influence is a positive one. Always. Scarlet always sends the influence of strength to the human mind. For another example, if someone were trying to lose weight, the individual might be tempted to look for a color that depicted the undesirable element of his or her life. The Great Talismanic Color Wheel of Influence does not have negative colors. Nature doesn't either. Nature talks to us in a positive, nurturing tone. There actually are many Dispellers that could be used successfully in losing weight. If you were losing weight to gain strength and become more physically fit, scarlet would be a good color to consider. If you were seeking to find a lover, then perhaps red would be a good choice. If your self-worth was suffering because of the failure to maintain your weight, then a light turquoise crystal should be considered.

Color Ray Table

Use / Meaning	Color Ray
Abandonment, dealing with	Dark Orange
Absolution	Light Blue
Abundance	Dark Green
Acceptance	Light Blue
Achievement	Dark Red
Action	Red
Adaptation	Dark Turquoise
Addiction therapy support	Scarlet
Advancement	Green
Adventure	Gold
Affection	Light Orange
Aggression, dealing with	Light Turquoise
Alertness	Light Yellow
Alienation, dealing with	Light Orange
Ambition	Gold
Anger, neutralizing	Light Turquoise
Answers to mysteries	Dark Violet
Anxiety, overcoming	Turquoise
Apathy, curing	Red
Appreciation	Light Indigo
Apprehension, calming	Turquoise
Artistic inspiration	Amethyst
Assertiveness	Dark Scarlet
Authority	Dark Gold
Awakening	Olive
Awareness	Light Yellow
Balance	Turquoise
Beauty	Dark Scarlet
Belief	Blue
Belonging	Dark Orange
Benevolence	Dark Orange
Betrayal, dealing with	Blue
Better life	Light Gold
Bountiful	Dark Red
Bravery	Scarlet

Color Ray Table (continued)

Use / Meaning	Color Ray
Brotherhood	Light Turquoise
Calmness	Turquoise
Capable	Dark Olive
Carefulness	Dark Green
Celebration	Orange
Centering	Brown
Change	Olive
Chaos, fighting	Brown
Charity	Dark Blue
Charm	Light Orange
Cheerfulness	Light Gold
Clarity	Dark Yellow
Cleanliness	Blue
Clear sight	Dark Amethyst
Cohesiveness	White
Comfort	Brown
Commitment	Pink
Commitment to higher purpose	Light Green
Communication	Light Yellow
Community	Dark Orange
Companionship	Light Orange
Compassion	Dark Blue
Completeness	Black
Conceit, overcoming	Light Amethyst
Concentration	Light Olive
Confidence	Light Gold
Conflict, overcoming	Light Turquoise
Connection	Amethyst
Conquering fear	Scarlet
Conquest	Scarlet
Consciousness	Light Yellow
Conservative	Blue
Consideration	Dark Blue
Constructive thought	Dark Yellow
Contemplation	Light Amethyst
Contentment	Light Gold

Color Ray Table (continued)

Use / Meaning	Color Ray
Control	Dark Gold
Conviction	Red
Coolness	Turquoise
Courage	Red
Creation	Green
Creativity	Amethyst
Cruelty, fighting	Light Turquoise
Curses, warding off	Dark Scarlet
Deception, avoiding	Amethyst
Decisiveness	Dark Yellow
Dedication	Light Scarlet
Dedication to higher ideals	Light Green
Dependency, fighting	Scarlet
Depression, dealing with	Orange
Despondency, dealing with	Olive
Destiny	Dark Violet
Determination	Light Olive
Development	Dark Olive
Devotion to others	Dark Red
Dignity	Light Indigo
Diligence	Light Olive
Discernment	Dark Amethyst
Discipline	Light Olive
Discovery	Turquoise
Discretion	Dark Blue
Disrespect, curing	Dark Blue
Dreams	Dark Violet
Drive	Red
Earth	Brown
Ecstasy	Light Gold
Elegance	Lavender
Emotional control	Turquoise
Empathy	Dark Turquoise
Enchantment	Dark Violet
Encouragement	Light Orange
Endurance	Light Olive

Continued on next page

Color Ray Table (continued)

Use / Meaning	Color Ray
Energy	Red
Engagement	Light Gold
Enhanced listening skills	Olive
Enjoyment	Orange
Enlightenment	Yellow
Enthusiasm	Gold
Equilibrium	Turquoise
Evil, protection from	Black
Excitement	Gold
Experience	Indigo
Exuberance	Gold
Facing reality	Light Blue
Failure, easing	Light Olive
Faith	Blue
Faithfulness, dealing with	Blue
Fame	Dark Gold
Family	Dark Orange
Family life	Dark Orange
Farm	Dark Red
Fastidiousness	Light Indigo
Fear, overcoming	Scarlet
Fearlessness	Red
Fertility	Green
Flexibility	Dark Turquoise
Following your heart	Violet
Foolish acts, avoiding	Indigo
Forgetfulness, curing	Light Yellow
Forgiveness	Light Blue
Fortitude	Red
Fortune	Dark Green
Free expression	Dark Yellow
Freedom	White
Friendship	Light Orange
Fright, overcoming	Scarlet
Fulfilling potential	Light Scarlet
Fulfillment	Orange

Color Ray Table (continued)

Use / Meaning	Color Ray
Future	Silver
Generosity	Light Orange
Gentle growth	Light Green
Gentleness	Dark Blue
Glory	Red
Gold	Gold
Good decision making	Dark Amethyst
Good financial results	Dark Green
Good fortune	Dark Green
Good luck	Dark Violet
Good reputation	Dark Orange
Goodness	Light Indigo
Grace	Dark Blue
Grades	Dark Olive
Greater openness	Dark Turquoise
Grief, dealing with	Orange
Grounding	Brown
Growth	Green
Guilt, dealing with	Light Blue
Happiness	Light Gold
Harm, protection from physical	Dark Green
Harmony	Light Turquoise
Harshness, dealing with	Yellow
Harvest	Dark Red
Healing	Green
Health	Dark Green
Heartache, curing	Pink
Hidden knowledge	Amethyst
Home	Dark Orange
Homesickness, curing	Dark Orange
Honesty	Dark Indigo
Honor	Dark Blue
Hope	White
Hospitality	Dark Orange
Humanity	Dark Blue
Humility	Light Indigo

Continued on next page

Color Ray Table (continued)

Use / Meaning	Color Ray
Idealism	Light Green
Ignorance, curing	Dark Olive
Ill wishes, banishing	Dark Scarlet
Illumination	White
Illusion, dispelling	Amethyst
Imagination	Lavender
Immortality	Light Blue
Independence	Olive
Indifference, dealing with	Dark Red
Influence	Dark Gold
Ingeniousness	Lavender
Inhibitions, removing	White
Initiative	Gold
Inner peace	Light Turquoise
Inner strength	Red
Inner truth	Silver
Innocence	White
Insecurity, overcoming	Blue
Insight	Dark Amethyst
Inspiration	Violet
Integrate	Brown
Intelligence	Dark Olive
Introspection	Light Amethyst
Intuition	Violet
Inventiveness	Amethyst
Invincibility	Dark Scarlet
Irritability, reducing	Dark Turquoise
Jealousy, overcoming	Light Green
Joy	Orange
Judgment	Indigo
Justice	Indigo
Kindness	Light Orange
Laziness, curing	Dark Scarlet
Leadership	Dark Gold
Learning	Dark Olive
Lethargy, banishing	Red

Color Ray Table (continued)

Use / Meaning	Color Ray
Liars, revealing	Dark Indigo
Liveliness	Gold
Long life	Indigo
Love	Pink
Love; dealing with loss	Pink
Lover	Pink
Loyalty	Light Orange
Luxury	Lavender
Magic	Dark Violet
Marriage	Dark Orange
Material comfort	Dark Green
Material things	Dark Green
Material wealth	Dark Gold
Mature love	Dark Red
Maturity	Indigo
Meaning	Olive
Meditation	Silver
Mellowness	Light Blue
Merit	Light Green
Merriment	Orange
Mildness	Light Blue
Misfortune, avoiding	Scarlet
Misperceptions, overcoming	Dark Yellow
Misrepresentation, avoiding	Dark Indigo
Modesty	Light Indigo
Money	Dark Green
Morality	Dark Indigo
Mothering	Dark Red
Motivation	Light Olive
Music	Violet
Mystery	Black
Mystical	Dark Violet
Negative thoughts, overcoming	Turquoise
Neglect, dealing with	Light Scarlet
New beginnings	Yellow
New love	Pink

Continued on next page

Color Ray Table (continued)

Use / Meaning	Color Ray
New perspectives	Dark Turquoise
Nightmares, soothing	Dark Violet
Nobility	Violet
Nurturing	Green
Obedience	Blue
Openness	Turquoise
Optimism	Yellow
Order	Blue
Organization	Light Yellow
Originality	Amethyst
Passion	Dark Red
Past, letting go of	Light Blue
Patience	Light Blue
Peace	Light Turquoise
Peace of mind	Light Turquoise
Perception	Dark Amethyst
Perseverance	Light Olive
Persuasiveness	Dark Yellow
Pessimism, overcoming	Light Gold
Philandering, preventing	Light Scarlet
Physical energy	Dark Scarlet
Physical growth	Dark Green
Physical prowess	Scarlet
Pleasure	Orange
Poetry	Amethyst
Popularity	Light Orange
Possessions	Dark Green
Potency	Green
Power	Dark Gold
Practicality	Dark Turquoise
Praise	Light Orange
Precision	Dark Yellow
Prestige	Indigo
Problem solving	Dark Olive
Productivity	Green
Profit	Dark Green

Color Ray Table (continued)

Use / Meaning	Color Ray
Progress	Green
Prosperity	Dark Green
Protection	Scarlet
Purity	White
Purpose	Silver
Quiet	Silver
Rage, dealing with	Light Turquoise
Rarity	Gold
Realism	Yellow
Receptiveness	Olive
Reconciliation	Light Blue
Recovery	Light Blue
Recovering memories	Turquoise
Recreation	Orange
Reflection	Silver
Regeneration	Olive
Rehabilitation	Green
Relaxation	Turquoise
Reliability	Light Scarlet
Religious mastery	Dark Indigo
Renewal	Green
Repentance	Light Blue
Repression, dealing with	Scarlet
Resistance	Light Olive
Respect	Dark Blue
Responsibility	Blue
Rest	Turquoise
Revitalization	Dark Scarlet
Rewards	Dark Red
Riches	Dark Green
Romance	Pink
Sadness, dealing with	Light Gold
Safe place	Dark Green
Safety	Dark Green
Satisfaction	Light Gold
Security	Black

Continued on next page

Color Ray Table *(continued)*

Use / Meaning	Color Ray
Seeing the future	Dark Amethyst
Self-awareness	Turquoise
Self-deceit, revealing	Dark Yellow
Self-doubt, curing	Black
Self-enlightenment	Light Amethyst
Self-esteem	Light Amethyst
Self-knowledge	Light Amethyst
Self-pity, curing	Dark Scarlet
Self-reliance	Scarlet
Self-worth	Red
Selfishness, overcoming	Light Orange
Selflessness	Light Orange
Selling successfully	Dark Yellow
Sense of belonging	Dark Orange
Sense of worth	Olive
Sensitivity	Dark Blue
Sensuality	Pink
Separation, dealing with	Dark Orange
Serenity	Turquoise
Seriousness	Dark Red
Service	Dark Blue
Sex	Orange
Sharing	Light Orange
Shelter	Dark Green
Shyness, overcoming	Light Orange
Sickness, avoiding	Green
Sincerity	Blue
Skill	Scarlet
Solidarity	Light Orange
Solitude	Light Turquoise
Soothing	Turquoise
Sorrow, overcoming	Orange
Soul	Brown
Soul mate	Dark Red
Spiritual development	Light Green
Spiritual guidance	Dark Indigo

Color Ray Table (continued)

Use / Meaning	Color Ray
Spiritual mastery	Dark Indigo
Spiritual wealth	Dark Indigo
Spouse	Light Scarlet
Stability	Turquoise
Stimulating imagery	Amethyst
Strength	Scarlet
Strength of character	Light Green
Stress, dealing with	Turquoise
Subtlety	Amethyst
Success	Dark Gold
Success in exploring the unknown	Red
Success in school	Dark Olive
Support	Dark Orange
Survival	Dark Green
Talent	Dark Red
Temperance	Turquoise
Temptation, resisting	Light Scarlet
Tenacity	Dark Red
Tenderness	Dark Blue
Thankfulness	Light Indigo
Thoughtfulness	Dark Blue
Thoughtlessness, dealing with	Light Yellow
Tolerance	Turquoise
Tranquility	Light Turquoise
Transformation	Black
Travel	Gold
Tricksters, avoiding	Dark Indigo
Trust	Blue
Truth	Dark Indigo
Understanding	Light Turquoise
Unity	White
Verbalizing needs	Dark Yellow
Victory	Scarlet
Vigilance	Light Scarlet
Vigor	Dark Green
Virtue	Light Indigo

Continued on next page

Color Ray Table (continued)

Use / Meaning	Color Ray
Vision	Amethyst
Visualization	Amethyst
Vitality	Dark Scarlet
Warmth	Yellow
Wealth	Dark Green
Weight, losing undesired	Turquoise
Willpower	Light Scarlet
Wisdom	Indigo
Worry, easing	Gold
Youth	Green

The
Fourth Secret
of Talismans

Even deeper within the crystal matrix is hidden the fundamental, elemental earth power of the stone—its raw chemical power base. The very atoms and molecules of carbon, silicon, oxygen, and other elements give minerals their fundamental earth power and form the building blocks of the crystal energy matrices.

The Second Secret of Talismans revealed the power of the crystal energy structure of talismans. Now, modern chemical science has unlocked the Fourth Secret of Talismans. Being able to chemically analyze every mineral has revealed that minerals also have a fundamental earth power that lies beneath the crystal energy structure. This earth power is based on the specific combination of the elements that make up the mineral and its crystal energy matrix.

All minerals are made up of an element or combination of elements. Knowing the fundamental chemical makeup of every mineral has allowed science to understand and now to categorize the mineral kingdom. Knowing that categorization has allowed us to finally understand how the basic earth power of a talisman is formed and how it holds the power of the sun, the moon, and the earth.

Ensuring that the crystal energy matrix and the color ray of power are matched to the user's need or desire is sufficient in many cases to ensure that the right raw material is selected for talismanic use. We learned in the Second Secret of Talismans that there are six natural crystal energy structures and that they are aligned with our human needs. The Seekers, Enhancers, Guardians, Barriers, Dispellers, and Attractors each have unique abilities to aid and enhance human abilities. Using the correct crystal energy structure will facilitate alignment between the human need and the Life Force contained within the crystal. In the Third Secret of Talismans, we learned that the color influence rays of the natural minerals, crystals, and gemstones affect our deepest mind based on the natural cycles of life. The color rays transmit the crystal energy from the talismans to our minds. An alignment of the crystal energy structure and the color ray allows a talisman to focus and amplify our energy and power to achieve our goals. For many needs, an alignment of the crystal energy and the color ray of influence is sufficient to produce a very powerful and useful talisman. This is particularly true when the talisman is made from a transparent or translucent material into which the sunlight can penetrate and be reflected and amplified by the crystal energy matrix. When opaque stones are used, the earth power is often ascendant. Turquoise, tiger's eye, and such opaque minerals are rich in earth power, and their color ray's influence is more directly tied to the earth power of the stone.

Modern science has now organized the mineral kingdom into eight classes based on chemistry. While any good mineralogy or geology book will explain the chemical basis of these mineral classes, we are much more interested in how these different power structures can help us focus and amplify our efforts to better our lives. We already know from the Second Secret that a particular mineral, crystal, or gemstone has a general characteristic use based on its crystal structure. The Fourth Secret further refines that general characteristic use and gives us deeper knowledge and greater understanding. As we explore the eight classes of minerals, we will finally understand the basic earth power of talismans and gain a deeper appreciation of their usefulness in our lives. We will also learn that while the transparent and translucent crystals of the mineral kingdom often take the shape of their internal crystal structure, many minerals, particularly the ones that are opaque, do not. This secret tells us that while opaque minerals have the crystal energy powers, they often derive most of their power from their basic chemical nature.

Class I—The Purifiers

The Purifiers are the natural elements of nature. Everything on this planet is made up of elements. They are the building blocks of matter. Because they combine with other elements to form compounds, most elements are not found in a pure state in nature. Gold, silver, carbon, sulfur, and copper are about the only elements found in a pure state naturally that are useful for talismans. These pure elemental minerals make excellent talismans when help is needed in accomplishing unambiguously righteous goals. Normally this class of minerals is used when absolutely pure motives are involved, and a higher purpose is intended that transcends mere personal needs.

The uses of the natural element class of talismans include promoting honesty, building faith, working for peace, giving joy to others, supporting charity, becoming humble, achieving spiritual growth, building virtues such as patience and courage, and protecting innocence. The pure motives align with the pure elemental power of the Purifiers.

Purifiers do not form transparent gemstones as a rule. The notable exception is carbon, which as we know forms into diamond under the right conditions. Gold, silver, copper, and sulfur are found in a variety of forms from small crystals to distorted thin plates. Copper often forms in thin sheets worked around other rocks in nature. These sheets can be quite attractive and can be used as powerful talismans because their beauty reflects the purity of their power. Gold and silver are often found as small nuggets that are particularly suited to use as Purifier talismans.

Gold, silver, and diamond have extensive uses in the jewelry trade as ornaments and are often used as symbols of affection and devotion. As talismans, in their natural elemental form, they have a similar but somewhat different use and power. They help us achieve high ideals such as devotion, honor, and faithfulness. Even a small nugget of gold, a small diamond crystal, a piece of natural silver wire, or a small segment of natural sulfur can serve as a powerful aid in our quests to remain faithful to a partner or ideal. They can help us dedicate ourselves to a worthy goal in aid of others, or sacrifice our time and possessions in support of the needs of others.

Class I—Purifier Talismans

Purifier talismans, the natural elements, have the earth power to aid us in efforts in which our desires are altruistic and pure. Only a few elements found in their pure state in nature are suitable for talismanic use.

Common Name	MINERAL
ANTIMONY	
Ballas	CARBON (Sphere Diamond)
Black Diamond	CARBON (Diamond)
Black Lead	CARBON (Graphite)
COPPER (Cu)	
Copper Blooms	COPPER
Diamond	CARBON
GOLD (Au)	
GRAPHITE (Carbon)	
IRON	
PLATINUM	
SILVER (Ag)	
SULFUR (S)	

Class II—The Mirrors

The second class of minerals is the sulfides. These minerals are formed from sulfur, or more accurately from hydrogen sulfide. They are usually volcanic in origin. They are normally opaque and have a metallic sheen or luster to them. This mirrorlike surface is an outward manifestation of the power of these talismans to reflect what is normally hidden. These crystals are excellent aids in knowing oneself, as they help reveal to us things that we consciously didn't realize. They reflect us as we are, not as we normally see ourselves. They help strip away pretensions, reveal truths, and give us the ability to see things as they really are. They help us to avoid being deceived by appearances. They make good touchstones of veracity. There are really few in circulation. They are relatively unknown except for pyrite, galena, sphalerite, chalcopyrite, and cinnabar.

Mirrors are particularly useful as self-help talismans. Often the first step in self-improvement is to understand how we got to where we are. We need to learn about ourselves before we can make meaningful change. The Mirror talismans are perfectly suited to help in these efforts to know ourselves better.

The Mirror talismans are often used in conjunction with Class IV Transformers discussed on page 104. Efforts to change ourselves are usually more successful when we really know ourselves and can see the behavior or traits we need to change. You can't improve something until you clearly see what is undesirable. The Mirror talismans allow us to see ourselves truly. Used with Transformers, they help us see the real changes we are making and allow us to maximize the power of the Transformer. There are several notable, powerful Mirror-Transformer talisman combinations.

Pyrite, with its earth power as a Mirror and its gold color ray of power and leadership, can help us accurately assess and understand our progress in developing our leadership abilities. It is often used with the Transformer citrine, which has the same gold color ray of influence. This combination is often very successful in efforts to identify leadership problems and grow new leadership abilities. Many efforts involve trying to influence others to help us achieve our goals. Leadership is an important ability. Pyrite and citrine are excellent aids in quests to gain mastery of this important trait.

Cinnabar, a Mirror, is sometimes found with a deep scarlet ray of physical strength. It is often paired with a green Transformer such as green sapphire or moss agate in efforts to improve physical health through exercise. The cinnabar aids us in critically viewing our progress, allowing the sapphire or agate to help us grow stronger.

Class II—Mirror Talismans

Mirror talismans, the sulfides, have the earth power to aid us by helping us see ourselves as we truly are, and see that which is unclear.

Common Name	MINERAL
Acanthite	ARGENTITE
ARGENTITE	
ARSENOPYRITE	
BERTHIERITE	
Binnite	TENNANTITE
Blackjack	SPHALERITE
BLENDE	SPHALERITE
BORNITE	
BOULANGERITE	
BOURNONITE	
Bravoite	PYRITE
Breithauptite	NICKELINE
Cervantite	STIBNITE
CHALCOPYRITE	
Chloanthite	SKUTTERUDITE
CINNABAR	
COBALTITE	
Cog Wheel Ore	BOURNONITE
Copper Nickel	NICKELINE
COVELLITE	
Dark Ruby Silver	PYRARGYRITE
ENARGITE	
Fool's Gold	PYRITE
GALENA	
GERSDORFFITE	
HAUERITE	
Iron Pyrite	PYRITE
JAMESONITE	
JORDANITE	
Light Ruby Silver	PROUSTITE
MARCASITE	
Niccolite	NICKELINE
NICKELINE	

Class II—Mirror Talismans (continued)

Common Name	MINERAL
ORPIMENT	
Peacock Copper	BORNITE
Peacock Ore	BORNITE
POLYBASITE	
PROUSTITE	
PYRARGYRITE	
PYRITE	
Pyrite Dollars	PYRITE
Pyrite Suns	PYRITE
PYRRHOTITE	
REALGAR	
SKUTTERUDITE	
SPHALERITE	
STEPHANITE	
STIBNITE	
TENNANTITE	
TETRAHEDRITE	

Class III—The Brighteners

The Brighteners are halides, formed by the action of hydrofluoric or hydrochloric acid. When these chemicals come into contact with metals, they form crystals that are often very brightly colored, among the brightest of the mineral kingdom. These crystals and minerals, such as halite and fluorite, are prized for their ability to bring out the beauty in something. As talismans, the Brighteners are particularly useful for enhancing efforts that focus on the sensual aspects of life in which some aspect has become dull, tarnished, or dingy. A longtime relationship can go stale and become dull with repetition or neglect. A Brightener talisman can help focus efforts to make the old seem new, to add luster where there was the patina of neglect, and to polish up skills, capabilities, and approaches to life and love.

The use of Brighteners should seriously be considered by many seeking a talisman. Many desires are for a brighter future in some way. The Brighteners are very utilitarian talismans. They are the generalist talismans. Their uses are not particularly restricted, as are the uses of many of the other talismans. For example, someone who wants to simply enhance his or her life and have a brighter future could start with a Brightener. Using one that has the Enhancer crystal energy structure like a fluorite would be perfect for a general desire to just have a better life in some unspecified way.

The Brighteners also have a specific use in helping us see the best life has to offer. Too often we are focused on our problems, afflictions, and illnesses. Life truly is a great adventure, and this planet truly is a wonderful place. We need help sometimes in recognizing the good things we have and in truly appreciating them. The Brighteners are good for our disposition. They add color and zest to life and give it meaning. They help things seem special. Even if someone has no specific need, a little zest in his or her life is always appreciated.

Class III—Brightener Talismans

Brightener talismans, as halides, have the earth power to aid us in our efforts to bring out the beauty in some element of our lives. There are thousands of minerals, but only a few are halides that give us the earth power of Brighteners.

Common Name	MINERAL
ATACAMITE	
BOLEITE	
DIABOLEITE	
FLUORITE	
HALITE	
SAL AMMONIAC	
Sylvine	SYLVITE
SYLVITE	
THOMSENOLITE	

Class IV—The Transformers

Transformers are oxides that form as less stable chemical compositions become more stable ones when they come into contact with oxygen. The transformative powers of these stones and crystals are legendary. Rubies and sapphires are well-known examples of Transformer talismans from this class.

Quartz is also of this class, and its use in gem therapy is well documented. Much of its power comes from the internal structure that enhances such transformative efforts. As a note to talismanic scholars, some experts place quartz in the Filter class, which is a group of silicates discussed later in this chapter. However, modern research (based on the Strunz mineral classification) shows quartz has much more transforming properties than filtering properties, and rightfully is a Transformer. The earth is rich in a wide variety of quartz. There are hundreds of varieties of quartz from which excellent Transformer talismans can be made. Agate, chalcedony, and other forms of quartz offer a great variety of capabilities. Virtually all the color rays of influence are available in quartz and other Transformer minerals.

Transformers are an extremely important class of talismans. Efforts to change our situations, our prospects, our health, our relationships, our outlook, and ourselves can all be enhanced by using a Transformer talisman.

Transformation is a key use of talismans. Many human activities are aimed at transforming ourselves into something more desirable, more employable, happier, or more capable. The bookstores are filled with self-help books. Many people are searching for a better life and know that transforming themselves is a necessary first step.

Some examples of the uses of Transformers include aiding in efforts to develop new capabilities like learning to dance, speaking a new language, growing stronger, becoming a better spouse or child, replacing bad habits, and improving our disposition. Transformation is a key element of many of our efforts to better our lot in life. By transforming ourselves we can transform our lives.

Although it is beyond the scope of this book, the famous Transformer, quartz, has extensive uses in physical therapy and healing. These are efforts that seek to transform a disease state into a healthy state. Quartz is a Seeker crystal with the earth power of the Transformer. Its success in the healing arts is due to the combination of its crystal energy matrix and its earth power to transform. Some of the other Transformers, such as cuprite, the beautiful spinels, alexandrite, and cassiterite, are not as well known as quartz but are excellent aids in efforts to make significant changes in our lives through the earth power of Transformation.

Class IV—Transformer Talismans

This list is not all-inclusive; there are thousands of minerals and many thousands of common names for them. If you are in need of a talisman to help you transform some part of your life, these Transformers are the place to start.

Common Name	MINERAL
Abraciated Jasper	Jasper QUARTZ
African Queen Picture Jasper	Jasper QUARTZ
Agate	Chalcedony QUARTZ
Agate Jasper	Jasper QUARTZ
Agatized Coral	Agate Chalcedony QUARTZ
ALEXANDRITE	CHRYSOBERYL
Amberine	Agate Chalcedony QUARTZ
Amethyst	QUARTZ
Amethyst Sage Agate	Agate Chalcedony QUARTZ
Ametrine	QUARTZ
ANATASE	
Arroyo Picture Jasper	Jasper QUARTZ
Australian Jasper	Red/White Chalcedony QUARTZ
Aventurine	QUARTZ
Azeztulite	QUARTZ
Azurlite	Turquoise Chalcedony QUARTZ
Basanite	Jasper Chalcedony QUARTZ
Basinite	Chalcedony QUARTZ
Bayate	Jasper QUARTZ
Beta Quartz	QUARTZ
Bi-color Quartz	QUARTZ
Bi-color Sapphire	CORUNDUM
Biggs Jasper	Jasper QUARTZ
Biggs Picture Jasper	Jasper QUARTZ
Binghamite	Hawk's Eye Chalcedony QUARTZ
Bird of Paradise	Brown Jasper QUARTZ
Black Onyx	Dyed Chalcedony QUARTZ
Black Skin Agate	Agate Chalcedony QUARTZ
Black Spinel	SPINEL
Black Star Sapphire	CORUNDUM
Black Zebra Agate	Agate Chalcedony QUARTZ
Blood Agate	Agate Chalcedony QUARTZ
Blood Jasper	Bloodstone Chalcedony QUARTZ

Continued on next page

Class IV—Transformer Talismans (continued)

Common Name	MINERAL
Bloodstone	Chalcedony QUARTZ
Blue Chalcedony Quartz	Chalcedony QUARTZ
Blue Chrysoprase	Chalcedony QUARTZ
Blue Lace Agate	Chalcedony QUARTZ
Blue Mist Chalcedony Quartz	Chalcedony QUARTZ
Blue Mountain Picture Jasper	Jasper QUARTZ
Blue Sapphire	CORUNDUM
Blue Spinel	SPINEL
Blue Star Sapphire	CORUNDUM
Bog Iron Ore	GOETHITE
BORACITE	usually artificial
BORAX	
Botswana Agate	Chalcedony QUARTZ
Brazil Agate	Agate Chalcedony QUARTZ
Breccia	Agate Chalcedony QUARTZ
Brecciated Jasper	Jasper QUARTZ
BROOKITE	
Bruneau Jasper	Brown/White Chalcedony QUARTZ
Bruno Canyon Jasper	Jasper QUARTZ
Buchanan Thundereggs	Agate Chalcedony QUARTZ
Burrow Creek Jasper	Jasper QUARTZ
Cactus Quartz	QUARTZ
California Moonstone	Chalcedony QUARTZ
Cambay	Carnelian Chalcedony QUARTZ
Cameo (Agate)	Agate Chalcedony QUARTZ
Canadian Ocean Rock	Jasper QUARTZ
Canary Stone	Yellow Chalcedony QUARTZ
Candy Rock	Jasper QUARTZ
Carnelian	Chalcedony QUARTZ
Carnelian Onyx	Sardonyx Chalcedony QUARTZ
Caribbean Blue Chalcedony	Chalcedony QUARTZ
Carrie Plume Agate	Agate Chalcedony QUARTZ
CASSITERITE	
Catalinaite	Jasper QUARTZ
Cathedral Agate	Agate Chalcedony QUARTZ
Cat's Eye	CHRYSOBERYL

Class IV—Transformer Talismans (continued)

Common Name	MINERAL
Cave Creek Jasper	Red Jasper QUARTZ
Caviar Agate	Chert QUARTZ
Ceragate	Yellow Chalcedony QUARTZ
Chalcedony	QUARTZ
Chalcotrichite	CUPRITE
Champagne Citrine	QUARTZ
Chapinite	Jasper QUARTZ
Chicken Track Picture Jasper	Jasper QUARTZ
Chinese Opal	White Chalcedony QUARTZ
Chrome Chalcedony	Green Chalcedony QUARTZ
Chrysojasper	Green Jasper QUARTZ
Chrysoprase	Chalcedony QUARTZ
Cinnabar Matrix	Jasper QUARTZ
Citrine	QUARTZ
Cloud Agate	Agate Chalcedony QUARTZ
COLUMBITE	
CORUNDUM	
Crazy Lace Agate	Agate Chalcedony QUARTZ
Creolite	Red/White Jasper QUARTZ
Cripple Creek Picture Jasper	Jasper QUARTZ
CUPRITE	
Cuyunite	Chalcedony QUARTZ
Cymophane	CHRYSOBERYL (Cat's Eye)
Dallasite	Green/White Jasper QUARTZ
Dalmatian Jasper	White/Black Jasper QUARTZ
Damsonite	Lilac Chalcedony QUARTZ
Demion	Carnelian Chalcedony QUARTZ
Dendritic Agate	Agate QUARTZ
Denio Dendritic Agate	Agate Chalcedony QUARTZ
Depalite	Olive Chert QUARTZ
Deschutes	Jasper QUARTZ
Desolation Canyon Thundereggs	Agate Chalcedony QUARTZ
Donnybrook Thundereggs	Agate Chalcedony QUARTZ
Dougway Thundereggs	Agate Chalcedony QUARTZ
Drusy Quartz	QUARTZ
Dumortierite Quartz	Blue QUARTZ

Continued on next page

Class IV—Transformer Talismans (continued)

Common Name	MINERAL
Dyed Agate	Dyed Agate Chalcedony QUARTZ
Eagle Rock Plume Agate	Agate Chalcedony QUARTZ
Edinite	Prase Chalcedony QUARTZ
Egyptian Jasper	Brown Jasper QUARTZ
Eldoradoite	Blue Chalcedony QUARTZ
Elephant Jasper	Brown/Black Jasper QUARTZ
Ellensburg Blue Agate	Agate Chalcedony QUARTZ
Ezteri	Bloodstone Chalcedony QUARTZ
Fallen Tree Thundereggs	Agate Chalcedony QUARTZ
Ferruginous Quartz	Red QUARTZ
Fire Agate	Agate Chalcedony QUARTZ
Flame Agate	Agate Chalcedony QUARTZ
Flint	White/Black Chert QUARTZ
FRANKLINITE	
Fred Bed Thundereggs	Agate Chalcedony QUARTZ
Frieda Thundereggs	Agate Chalcedony QUARTZ
Friend Ranch Thundereggs	Agate Chalcedony QUARTZ
Frogskin Jasper	Tan/Green Jasper QUARTZ
Frost Agate	Gray Chalcedony QUARTZ
Fryite Picture Jasper	Jasper QUARTZ
GAHNITE	
GIBBSITE	
Glory Blue	Blue Chalcedony QUARTZ
GOETHITE	
Gold Included Quartz	QUARTZ
Golden Sapphire	CORUNDUM
Graveyard Point Agate	Agate Chalcedony QUARTZ
Green Gold Quartz	Irradiated QUARTZ
Green Moss Agate	Agate Chalcedony QUARTZ
Green Onyx	Chrysoprase QUARTZ
Green Sapphire	CORUNDUM
Gray Quartz	QUARTZ
Gray Star Sapphire	CORUNDUM
Hampton Butte Moss Agate	Agate Chalcedony QUARTZ
HAUSMANNITE	
Hawk's Eye	QUARTZ polymorph of Crocidolite

Class IV—Transformer Talismans (continued)

Common Name	MINERAL
Heliotrope	Bloodstone QUARTZ
Hemachate	Red Jasper QUARTZ
HEMATITE	
Holly Blue	Chalcedony QUARTZ
Holly Blue Agate	Agate Chalcedony QUARTZ
Hornstone	Chert QUARTZ
HUBNERITE	
Ice Stone	White Chert QUARTZ
ILMENITE	
Imperial Jasper	Jasper QUARTZ
Indian Star Ruby	CORUNDUM
Iolanthite	Jasper QUARTZ
Iris Agate	Agate Chalcedony QUARTZ
Jasp-Agate	Jasper QUARTZ
Jasper	Jasper QUARTZ
Jasper Breccia	Jasper QUARTZ
Jasperine	Jasper QUARTZ
Jasponyx	Agate Chalcedony QUARTZ
Joshua Tree Agate	Agate Chalcedony QUARTZ
Kidney Ore	HEMATITE
Kinradite	Jasper QUARTZ
Lantana	Agate Chalcedony QUARTZ
Lazurquartz	Blue Chalcedony QUARTZ
Lemon Chrysoprase	Chrysoprase Chalcedony QUARTZ
Lemon Yellow Citrine	QUARTZ
Leolite	Agate Chalcedony QUARTZ
Leopard Jasper	Jasper QUARTZ
Leopardskin Jasper	Jasper QUARTZ
LEPIDACHROSITE	found in QUARTZ
Lydian Stone	BASANITE
Lingam	Jasper QUARTZ
Lucky Strike Thundereggs	Agate Chalcedony QUARTZ
Madagascar Mariposite	Yellow Chalcedony QUARTZ
Madeira Citrine	QUARTZ
MAGNETITE	
Man Yü	Red Carnelian Chalcedony QUARTZ

Continued on next page

Class IV—Transformer Talismans (continued)

Common Name	MINERAL
MANGANITE	
MANGANOTANTALITE	
Marra Mamba	Jasper QUARTZ (Tiger Iron)
Maury Mt. Moss Agate	Agate Chalcedony QUARTZ
McDermitt Thundereggs	Agate Chalcedony QUARTZ
Mecca Stone	Carnelian Chalcedony QUARTZ
Mohave Blue	Violet Chalcedony QUARTZ
Mojave Moonstone	Blue Chalcedony QUARTZ
Montana Moss Agate	Agate Chalcedony QUARTZ
Morlop	Jasper QUARTZ
Morrisonite	Jasper QUARTZ
Mosaic Agate	Agate Chalcedony QUARTZ
Moss Agate	Agate Chalcedony QUARTZ
Moss Jasper	Jasper QUARTZ
Moukaite	Pink Jasper QUARTZ
Mozarkite	Multicolored Chert QUARTZ
Mtorolite	Dark Green Jasper QUARTZ
Munjina Stone	Agate Chalcedony QUARTZ
Myrickite	Red Chalcedony QUARTZ with CINNABAR
Neon Quartz	Irradiated QUARTZ
Novaculite	White Chert QUARTZ
Nunderite	EPIDOTE in QUARTZ
Nunkirchner Jasper	Brown Jasper QUARTZ
Ocean Jasper	Jasper QUARTZ
OLIVINE (usually FORSTERITE)	a mineral group
Onyx	Jasper QUARTZ
Oolitic Chert	Chert QUARTZ
Oolitic Hematite	HEMATITE
Oolitic Jasper	Jasper QUARTZ
Opal Butte Thundereggs	Agate Chalcedony QUARTZ
Ora Verde Quartz	Irradiated QUARTZ
Orange Chalcedony	Chalcedony QUARTZ
Orange Sapphire	CORUNDUM
Orange Tourmaline	TOURMALINE
Orbicular Jasper	Jasper QUARTZ
Oregon Jade	Plasma Chalcedony QUARTZ

Class IV—Transformer Talismans (continued)

Common Name	MINERAL
Oregonite	Jasper Chalcedony QUARTZ
Owyhee Picture Jasper	Jasper QUARTZ
Padparadscha Sapphire	CORUNDUM
Paradise Jasper	Red Jasper QUARTZ
Pastelite	Pink/Green Jasper QUARTZ
Peach Aventurine	QUARTZ
PERICLASE	
PEROVSKITE	
Petersite	QUARTZ
Petrified Wood	Jasper QUARTZ
Picture Jasper	Jasper QUARTZ
Pietersite	Hawk's Eye Chalcedony QUARTZ
Pigeon Blood Agate	Carnelian Chalcedony QUARTZ
Pink Sapphire	CORUNDUM
Pink Spinel	SPINEL
Pisolitic Chert	Chert QUARTZ
Plasma	Chalcedony QUARTZ
PLATTNERITE	
Polianite	PYROLUSITE
Polka-dot Agate	Agate QUARTZ
Polka-dot Jasper	Jasper QUARTZ
Pony Butte Thundereggs	Agate QUARTZ
Poppy	Red/Orange/Yellow Jasper QUARTZ
Poppy Jasper	Jasper QUARTZ
Poppy Stone	Jasper QUARTZ
Prase	Green QUARTZ
Prase Malachite	Green Chalcedony QUARTZ
Prasiolite	QUARTZ
Priday Plume Agate	Agate Chalcedony QUARTZ
Priday Thundereggs	Agate Chalcedony QUARTZ
Psilomelane	ROMANECHITE
PYROLUSITE	
QUARTZ	
Rainforest Jasper	Jasper QUARTZ
Red Jasper	Jasper QUARTZ
Red Spinel	SPINEL

Continued on next page

Class IV—Transformer Talismans (continued)

Common Name	MINERAL
Riband Jasper	Banded Jasper QUARTZ
Richardson's Thundereggs	Agate Chalcedony QUARTZ
ROCK CRYSTAL	QUARTZ
Rocky Butte Picture Jasper	Jasper QUARTZ
Rogueite	Green Jasper QUARTZ
ROMANECHITE	
Rose Cat's Eye Quartz	QUARTZ
Rose de France Amethyst	QUARTZ
Rose Quartz	QUARTZ
Ruby	CORUNDUM
Ruin Agate	Agate Chalcedony QUARTZ
Russian Agate	Agate Chalcedony QUARTZ
Russian Jasper	Red-Flecked Jasper QUARTZ
Rutilated Quartz	QUARTZ
RUTILE	
Saddle Mountain Fire Agate	Agate Chalcedony QUARTZ
Sagenite	QUARTZ
Saint Stephen's Stone	Bloodstone Chalcedony QUARTZ
Sapphire	CORUNDUM
Sapphirine	Blue Chalcedony QUARTZ
Sard	Chalcedony QUARTZ
Sardonyx	Chalcedony QUARTZ
Scenic Jasper	Tan Jasper QUARTZ
Sea Jasper	Jasper QUARTZ
Seftonite	Green Chalcedony QUARTZ
SENARMONTITE	
Sioux Falls Jasper	Jasper QUARTZ
Smoky Quartz	QUARTZ
Specularite	HEMATITE
SPINEL	
Spirit Quartz	QUARTZ
Star Malachite	Green Chalcedony QUARTZ
Star Quartz	QUARTZ
Star Ruby	CORUNDUM
STAUROLITE	
Steins Pillar Thundereggs	Agate Chalcedony QUARTZ

Class IV—Transformer Talismans (continued)

Common Name	MINERAL
STIBICONITE	
Stinking Water Plume Agate	Agate Chalcedony QUARTZ
Stone Yard	Jasper QUARTZ
Succor Creek Thundereggs	Agate Chalcedony QUARTZ
Sunset Agate	Agate Chalcedony QUARTZ
Swiss Lapis	Dyed Blue Chalcedony QUARTZ
TAAFFEITE	
TANTALITE	
Teanaway Agate	Agate Chalcedony QUARTZ
Tiger's Eye	Jasper QUARTZ
Tree Agate	Agate Chalcedony QUARTZ
Turgite	HEMATITE
Turritella Agate	Agate Chalcedony QUARTZ
Utica Jewelstone	White-Banded Chert QUARTZ
Vabanite	Red/Yellow Jasper QUARTZ
VALENTINITE	
Valley View Thundereggs	Agate Chalcedony QUARTZ
Variegated Jasper	Jasper QUARTZ
VILLIAUMITE	
Violet Sapphire	CORUNDUM
Violet Spinel	SPINEL
Violite	Violet Chalcedony QUARTZ
Whistler Springs Thundereggs	Agate Chalcedony QUARTZ
White Fir Springs Thundereggs	Jasper QUARTZ
White Sapphire	CORUNDUM
White Spinel	SPINEL
Whiteskins	Agate Chalcedony QUARTZ
Wild Horse Jasper	Jasper QUARTZ
Wilkite	Multicolored Jasper QUARTZ
Willow Creek Jasper	Jasper QUARTZ

Class V—The Builders

The Builders are carbonates—minerals that are rarely in their final forms, but rather in a transitional state. The class also includes the nitrates and borates that are similar in chemistry and earth power. Azurite, malachite, dolomite, and rhodochrosite are all Builders. These minerals are similar to Transformers in use. The difference is that Builders are more useful when the beginning state is not undesirable. Transformers are more focused on changing an undesirable situation into one that is more desirable. Builders are used when there is nothing particularly wrong with the current situation, but the desire is to build something new that might somehow have value in our future. They help in development efforts, in learning new skills and knowledge, and in building new relationships.

The Builders are excellent in applications in which something new needs to be made from something old. Woodworkers, stoneworkers, artists, painters, and others involved in the creative arts benefit from this type of talisman. The Builder talismans can help artists and craftspersons to focus on the artistic outcome they are trying to achieve.

The uses of azurite and malachite in particular are based on both their crystal energy structure of a Dreamholder, and on their earth power as a Builder. These two attributes give azurite and malachite the power to help us build our dreams into reality. Many uses of talismans focus on efforts to achieve a highly desirable goal. Finding our true love, getting our perfect home, or having a financially secure retirement are all dreams that take a great deal of focus and energy to accomplish. The Builder talismans are perfect aids.

Calcite, rhodochrosite, dolomite, and other Builders that form in the Seeker crystal energy structure have the power to help us when we are seeking to develop new skills and capabilities. Their crystal structure helps us focus our energy on gaining those new skills. Their Builder earth power helps us to put together the new abilities and use them with other skills and knowledge to accomplish our goals.

Class V—Builder Talismans

Builder talismans, the carbonates, have the earth power to aid us in our efforts to build on what we have to improve our lives and ourselves.

Common Name	MINERAL
ANKERITE	
ARAGONITE	
ARTINITE	
AURICHALCITE	
AZURITE	
Azurite-Malachite	mixed minerals
BASTNASITE	
BAYLDONITE	
Bluebird	AZURITE with CUPRITE
Bonamite	SMITHSONITE
Brown Spar	CALCITE
Calamine	SMITHSONITE
CALCITE	
CERUSSITE	
Chessylite	AZURITE
Clay Ironstone	SIDERITE
Cobaltian Calcite	CALCITE
Cobaltian Dolomite	DOLOMITE
COLEMANITE	
Cotton Balls	ULEXITE
DOLOMITE	
GASPEITE	
GAYLUSSITE	
HAMBERGITE	
HENMILITE	
HYDROBORACITE	
HYDROMAGNESITE	
HYDROZINCITE	
Iceland Spar	CALCITE
KERNITE	
MAGNESITE	
MALACHITE	
PHOSGENITE	

Continued on next page

Class V—Builder Talismans (continued)

Common Name	MINERAL
RHODIZITE	
RHODOCHROSITE	
ROSASITE	
SIDERITE	
SINHALITE	
SMITHSONITE	
SPHAEROCOBALTITE	
STICHTITE	
Tarnowitzite	ARAGONITE
Television Stone	ULEXITE
TINCALCONITE	
TRONA	
ULEXITE	
WOLFEITE	

Class VI—The Solidifiers

The Solidifiers are a class of minerals that include the sulfates, which are crystals that result from the action of sulfuric acid. Sulfuric acid is a very dense, very stable liquid. These are the most powerful talismans when the need is to solidify a relationship or a new habit. They are used to add permanence to anything that is temporary. All of the talismans from the Solidifier class share this ability to solidify and add permanence. These talismans are often used after the Transformers or Builders.

The Solidifier talismans are particularly useful in efforts to stabilize a situation. For someone who has finally achieved a desired state, the use of a Solidifier will help him or her maintain that state. They are very useful for people who have dieted effectively and don't want to regain weight. They are useful for people who have established a relationship and now want to make it permanent. If someone has finally gotten the fame, the fortune, or the relationship of his or her dreams, then a Solidifier should be used to ensure that the fame is not fleeting, that the fortune isn't dissipated, or that the relationship doesn't sour.

Selenite, crocoite, barite, celestite, anglesite, scheelite, wulfenite, and gypsum are some of the common Solidifiers.

Solidifiers with the red, scarlet, and orange rays of influence such as crocoite, scheelite, and wulfenite are very useful in efforts to hold on to the joy, strength, and passion in our lives. The golden barite is excellent to help us hold on to our financial wealth or to hold on to our enthusiasm for a project. The pure white gypsum, or a crystalline mass of anhydrite, can be an excellent talisman to help us focus on keeping our freedom safe, and our hopes alive in times of difficulty.

Class VI—Solidifier Talismans

Solidifier talismans, the sulfates, have the earth power to aid us by helping add permanence to our accomplishments.

Common Name	MINERAL
Alabaster	GYPSUM
Aluminilite	ALUNITE
ALUNITE	
Angelsite	ANHYDRITE
ANGLESITE	
ANHYDRITE	
ANTLERITE	
BARITE	
Bologna Stone	BARITE
BROCHANTITE	
CALEDONITE	
CELESTINE	
Celestite	CELESTINE
CHALCANTHITE	
CHENEVIXITE	
CONNELLITE	
CROCOITE	
Desert Rose	BARITE
EMMONSITE	
ETTRINGITE	
FERBERITE	
GLAUBERITE	
GYPSUM	
JAROSITE	
LINARITE	
Linerite	LINARITE
LUDLAMITE	
MOTTRAMITE	
POLYHALITE	
POWELLITE	
PSEUDOMALACHITE	

Class VI—Solidifier Talismans (continued)

Common Name	MINERAL
Satin Spar	GYPSUM
SCHEELITE	
Selenite	GYPSUM
SPANGOLITE	
STURMANITE	
THAUMASITE	
WOLFRAMITE	
WULFENITE	

Class VII—The Buffers

Most Buffers, sometimes called Balancers, are phosphates derived from phosphoric acid, which forms compounds that buffer, balance, and neutralize both acids and alkalis. Other talismans from this class have similar chemistry. The talismanic uses include promoting stability, balance, and centering. The Buffers are often referred to as Balancers because turquoise is the most commonly used Buffer and its color of the same name is the color ray of balance. The Buffers are excellent at restoring the natural balance in situations that have become unstable. They can help us restore equilibrium in our lives and world.

Equilibrium is a vital part of life. As humans we all need a center, a place of repose, a place of balance. We have passion; we need rest. We have growth; we need renewal. We have community; we need space. When we have too much of something, we start to need some of its opposite. We are creatures of the middle. We want to be wise, but want to learn again. We want strength, but need help. We want understanding, but need joy. We seek vision, but want wonder. We want knowledge, but we want to be surprised sometimes.

We also need Buffers in this world to help us cope with the many demands of society. We are constantly buffeted by conflicting demands on our time and efforts. We are pulled, pushed, and prodded to go certain ways, act certain ways, or be a certain type of person. We need an insulator, something we can use to keep our balance by buffering us from the pressures of life. These Buffer talismans are just the ticket. Drawing on their earth power they can help us buffer, balance, and neutralize external forces that threaten our desires in this life.

Buffers are weathering stones that help us get through hard times. They soften a blow and put things right. They are able to protect us from outside influences, temper shocks, and add some emotional padding to our efforts to deal with the bumps and bruises of life.

In addition to turquoise, other common Buffers include adamite, lazulite, and mimetite.

Class VII—Buffer Talismans

Buffer talismans, the phosphates, have the earth power to buffer, balance, and neutralize external forces that threaten our desires in this life. Some of the common ones are included in this listing.

Common Name	MINERAL
ADAMITE	
AGARDITE	
AMBLYGONITE	
ANNABERGITE	
APATITE	
ARROJADITE	
ARTHURITE	
ATELESTITE	
BERYLLONITE	
BRAZILIANITE	
Campylite	MIMETITE
CARMINITE	
CARNOTITE	
Cat's Eye Apatite	APATITE
CERULÉITE	
CHALCOPHYLLITE	
CHILDRENITE	
Chinese Turquoise	TURQUOISE
Chlorapatite	APATITE
CHRYSOBERYL	
CLINOCLASE	
Cobalt Bloom	ERYTHRITE
CONICHALCITE	
CORNETITE	
CREEDITE	
Cuproadamite	ADAMITE
DESCLOIZITE	
DUFRENITE	
DUFTITE	
EOSPHORITE	
ERYTHRITE	
FLUORAPATITE	
GORMANITE	
GUANACOITE	

Continued on next page

Class VII—Buffer Talismans (continued)

Common Name	MINERAL
HANKSITE	
Heterosite	PURPURITE
HOPEITE	
HUREAULITE	
Hydroxylapatite	APATITE
Knaufite	VOLBORTHITE
LAZULITE	
LEGRANDITE	
LIBETHENITE	
MIMETITE	
MONAZITE	
MONTEBRASITE	
Nickel Bloom	ANNABERGITE
PARADAMITE	
PARAVAUXITE	
PHOSPHOPHYLLITE	
PLUMBOGUMMITE	
PURPURITE	
PYROMORPHITE	
ROSELITE	
SCHOLZITE	
SCORODITE	
SCORZALITE	
STRENGITE	
STRUNZITE	
THENARDITE	
TSUMEBITE	
TURQUOISE	
VANADINITE	
VARISCITE	
VAUXITE	
VESZELYITE	
VOLBORTHITE	
WARDITE	
WAVELLITE	
WENDWILSONITE	
WHITEITE	
WOLFEITE	

Class VIII-1—The Strengtheners (Resisters)

The first of the silicate class is the Strengtheners or, as they are sometimes called, the Resisters (scientific names are island silicates, nesosilicates, or orthosilicates). They are formed when tetrahedrons of silicate form islands between the metal ions of the compound. This class of minerals forms very compact materials that are strong, resistant, and unyielding. They provide us with the energy to resist temptations and resist distractions from our goals.

Garnets are the best know of the Strengtheners, and they are the best talismans to aid us in efforts to stay on our courses and not be swayed by external sources from achieving our goals and ultimately our rightful destiny. It is interesting that so many garnets are in shades of scarlet and red. The red section of the Great Talismanic Color Wheel of Influence is concerned with both physical and intellectual strength. Garnets such as pyropes, almandine, and mixtures of these minerals have both the chemical earth power of strength and the reddish color rays of strength. The garnets are the most potent talismans of strength, vigor, and resistance because of this convergence of the color ray and chemical earth power. The green garnets such as demantoid, grossular, and tsavorite combine the earth power of the Strengtheners with the color rays of growth, awakening, and perseverance, giving us excellent talismans for growing strength and power in both our physical and spiritual lives.

Strengthener talismans are often used in conjunction with others when new, positive changes are desired, yet negative influences still prevail. Giving up a bad habit (smoking, overeating, arguing with loved ones, drinking to excess, etc.) is tough. The behavior has an attraction that somehow provides pleasure. Resisting that pleasure takes special strength. A garnet or other Strengthener talisman can aid us in pushing back against the allure of the destructive behavior. Another talisman then is usually needed to focus and amplify our efforts to substitute more positive, desirable actions. Usually good success is found by combining the use of a Strengthener with a Class V Builder talisman such as malachite, azurite, or rhodochrosite.

Class VIII-1—Strengthener Talismans

Strengthener talismans, the island silicates, have the earth power to aid us by strengthening our efforts.

Common Name	MINERAL
African Jade	GROSSULAR
ALLANITE	
ALMANDINE (Garnet)	
Almandite (Garnet)	ALMANDINE
ANDALUSITE	
ANDRADITE	
BAKERITE	
Basalt Bomb	FORSTERITE
Blue Topaz	TOPAZ
BOLTWOODITE	
BULTFONTEINITE	
CACHEMIRINE Garnet	
Carbuncle	ALMANDINE (Garnet)
Cat's Eye Kornerupine	KORNERUPINE
Chiastolite	ANDALUSITE
Chrysolite	FAYALITE
Cinnamon Stone	GROSSULAR
CLINOHUMITE	
Cyanite	KYANITE
DATOLITE	
Demantoid Garnet	ANDRADITE
DUMORTIERITE	
Evening Emerald (Peridot)	FORSTERITE
FAYALITE	
Fibrolite	SILLIMANITE
FORSTERITE	
GADOLINITE	
Garnet	a mineral group
Grandite Garnet	ALMANDINE (mostly)
Green Topaz	TOPAZ
Imperial Garnet	SPESSARTINE
KINOITE	
KORNERUPINE	

Class VIII-1—Strengthener Talismans (continued)

Common Name	MINERAL
KYANITE	
London Blue Topaz	Irradiated TOPAZ
Malaya Garnet	Mixed GARNET
Mandarin Garnet	Mixed GARNET
Melanite	ANDRADITE
Merelani Mint Garnet	ALMANDINE (mostly)
Mozambique Garnet	Mixed GARNET
Peacock Topaz	TOPAZ
Peridot	FORSTERITE
PHENAKITE	
Precious Topaz	TOPAZ
Purple Garnet	ALMANDINE-PYROPE
Pyrope Garnet	PYROPE
Pyrope-Almandine Garnet	ALMANDINE-PYROPE
Queensland Garnet	ALMANDINE-PYROPE
Rhodolite	ALMANDINE-PYROPE
SILLIMANITE	
Silver Topaz	TOPAZ
Sky Blue Topaz	TOPAZ
SPESSARTINE	
Spessartite	SPESSARTINE
Sphene	TITANITE
Swiss Blue Topaz	Irradiated TOPAZ
Tanzanite Topaz	TOPAZ
Teal Topaz	TOPAZ
TEPHROITE	
Thai Garnet	ALMANDINE
TITANITE	
TOPAZ	
Topazolite	ANDRADITE
Tourmalinated Quartz	QUARTZ
Tsavorite	GROSSULAR
Umbalite Garnet	ALMANDINE-PYROPE
UVAROVITE	
White Topaz	TOPAZ
WILLEMITE	

Class VIII-2—The Unifiers

Called group silicates, or sorosilicates in scientific terms, the Unifiers contain silicate molecules bound in pairs or small groups. Unifiers like tanzanite and zoisite are the most common of these minerals with talismanic uses. The basic elemental forces of pairing make these particularly valuable talismans for focusing energy on relationships either between two people or within a family.

If you have a strong relationship you want to ensure continues to succeed in fulfilling your life, a tanzanite is an excellent source of the energy you will need to focus. It will also amplify your efforts to bond with the other person. Many uses for talismans are focused on relationships with a single person or within a family. Efforts to keep unity within a partnership or family group can always use a bit of help. Unifiers are the right talismans to aid us in keeping people together and happy.

Unifiers are also great talismans for community group efforts. If you are the leader of a small group and seek to ensure it works well together, accomplishes its goals, and continues to be effective, a Unifier will be a big help to you. Unifiers are very useful for efforts that require instilling allegiance or loyalty. Political efforts particularly benefit from using a Unifier.

The Unifiers are fairly uncommon and rare, but worth seeking out. Vesuvianite and pumpellyite are not too rare, and should be carefully considered for talismans in which the need is for unity of a small group or family.

Class VIII-2—Unifier Talismans

Unifier talismans, the group silicates, have the earth power to aid us by helping bring together things in our lives that have fallen apart.

Common Name	MINERAL
Anyolite	ZOISITE
BERTRANDITE	
Breislakite	ILVAITE
Californite	VESUVIANITE
Cerian	VESUVIANITE
Chlorastrolite	PUMPELLYITE
DANBURITE	
Green Starstone	Chlorastrolite PUMPELLYITE
Greenstone	Chlorastrolite PUMPELLYITE
HARDYSTONITE	
HEMIMORPHITE	
HUBEITE	
Idocrase	VESUVIANITE
ILVAITE	
JENNITE	
PIEDMONTITE	
PUMPELLYITE	Chlorastrolite PUMPELLYITE
SUOLUNITE	
Tanganyika Artstone	ZOISITE, with Ruby
Tanzanite	ZOISITE
Turtleback	Chlorastrolite PUMPELLYITE
Uigite	Chlorastrolite PUMPELLYITE
VESUVIANITE	
ZOISITE	

Class VIII-3—The Energizers

This class—called the ring silicates or cyclosilicates by scientists has—crystal lattices that contain three to twelve rings of silicate tetrahedrons. There are two basic energy structures that can result. The first is a pillar structure that is a fantastic energy conduit, and the second is a spongelike structure that is a powerful absorber of energy directed at it. The pillar-structure crystals are mostly transparent; the spongelike ones are mostly opaque, as you would expect. The beryls, like aquamarine and emerald, are of the first type; sugilite and chrysocolla are talismans of the second type.

The conduit Energizers are talismans that can help us in many efforts to gain what we seek, enhance our lives, protect that which we value, and defend us from the undesirable elements of life on Earth. For example, the beryls, like emerald and aquamarine, are powerful Seekers, based on their crystal energy matrices. Combining that energy with their earth power as Energizers makes these minerals perfect talismans for focusing and amplifying the Universal Life Force and our energy to accomplish our quests. Everyone gets tired and discouraged from time to time. The conduit Energizers are a good antidote to allow us to keep our energy level up and our efforts focused.

The absorber Energizers, like sugilite and chrysocolla, are mostly opaque and function more like batteries. They can serve to augment our energy during periods we are not at our peak. The green color ray exhibited by chrysocolla, for example, augments and amplifies its earth Energizer power for growth and development.

Class VIII-3—Energizer Talismans

Energizer talismans, the ring silicates, have the earth power to aid us in having the energy we need to accomplish our goals.

Common Name	MINERAL
Achroite	ELBAITE TOURMALINE
Almandine Spar	EUDIALYTE
Aphrizite	TOURMALINE
Aquamarine	BERYL
AXINITE	
BENITOITE	
BERYL	
Bi-color Tourmaline	TOURMALINE
Black Tourmaline	TOURMALINE
BUERGERITE	
Cat's Eye Tourmaline	ELBAITE
Chrome Tourmaline	TOURMALINE
CHRYSOCOLLA	
CORDIERITE	
Dark Blue Beryl	Irradiated BERYL
DIOPTASE	
Dravite	TOURMALINE
ELBAITE TOURMALINE	
Emerald	BERYL
EUDIALYTE	
Golden Beryl	BERYL
Goshenite	BERYL
Green Beryl	BERYL
Green Tourmaline	ELBAITE TOURMALINE
Heliodor	BERYL
Indicolite Tourmaline	ELBAITE TOURMALINE
Indigolite	TOURMALINE
Iolite	CORDIERITE
Morganite	BERYL
Orange Beryl	BERYL
PAPAGOITE	
Peach Beryl	BERYL
Pink Tourmaline	TOURMALINE

Continued on next page

Class VIII-3—Energizer Talismans (continued)

Common Name	MINERAL
Red Beryl	BERYL
Rubellite	ELBAITE TOURMALINE
SCHORL	Black TOURMALINE
SUGILITE	
TOURMALINE	a mineral group
UVITE	TOURMALINE
VERDELITE	TOURMALINE
Water Sapphire (Iolite)	CORDIERITE
Watermelon Tourmaline	TOURMALINE
Yellow Tourmaline	TOURMALINE

Class VIII-4—The Harmonizers

The Harmonizers, called the chain and band silicates or inosilicates in scientific journals, contain silicate tetrahedrons bound together in a long chain. They distribute energy in a balanced, long-term way, promoting harmony. For efforts aimed at smoothing a path through difficulties, or aiding in promoting a harmonious relationship within a larger group, like an extended family, then a Harmonizer is an excellent choice.

Jade has a long tradition of promoting harmony. Certainly some of it power comes from its Guardian crystal energy structure, but much also comes from its earth power as a Harmonizer. The Chinese in particular have recognized this inherent power in jade. They have used it for centuries for many efforts that involve promoting peaceful acceptance of situations and ending friction between warring parties. Jade is often the talisman of peace. Its Guardian crystal structure, its Harmonizer earth power, and its green color ray provide a powerful combination for ensuring long-term mutual understanding and cooperation.

Kunzite and Rhodonite are also valuable talismans from this class. They are both powerful Harmonizers. Kunzite is often a light red color and its uses mostly focus on enhancing personal relationships between the sexes. Rhodonite is usually a dark red or scarlet color. As a Harmonizer, it is used to correct misconceptions or to protect people from tricks or deception. Use rhodonite Harmonizers to see behind the masks that other people wear.

Class VIII-4—Harmonizer Talismans

Harmonizer talismans, the chain and band silicates, have the earth power to aid us by helping add harmony to our lives.

Common Name	MINERAL
Acmite	AEGIRINE
ACTINOLITE	
AEGIRINE	
ANTHOPHYLLITE	
ARFVEDSONITE	
AUGITE	
BABINGTONITE	
Black Star Diopside	DIOPSIDE
Blue Asbestos	Crocidolite RIEBECKITE
Bronzite	ENSTATITE
BUSTAMITE	
Cat's Eye Diopside	DIOPSIDE
Cat's Eye Enstatite	ENSTATITE
Cat's Eye Jade	NEPHRITE
CHAROITE	
Chrome Diopside	DIOPSIDE
Crocidolite	RIEBECKITE
DIOPSIDE	
Eakleite	XONOTLITE
EDENITE	
ENSTATITE	
EPIDIDYMITE	
EPIDOTE	
EUDIDYMITE	
FLUORRICHTERITE	
HEDENBERGITE	
Hiddenite	SPODUMENE
HORNBLENDE	
HOWLITE	
Hypersthene	ENSTATITE
INESITE	
Jade	Nephrite ACTINOLITE, or JADEITE
JADEITE	

Class VIII-4—Harmonizer Talismans (continued)

Common Name	MINERAL
Kidney Stones	JADEITE
Kunzite	SPODUMENE
Larimar	PECTOLITE
Lorimar	PECTOLITE
Nephrite (Jade)	ACTINOLITE
NEPTUNITE	
Nuumite	ANTHOPHYLLITE
OKENITE	
PECTOLITE	
PLANCHÉITE	
RHODONITE	
RICHTERITE	
RIEBECKITE	
Schizolite	PECTOLITE
Serandite	PECTOLITE
SHATTUCKITE	
SPODUMENE	
Tawmawite	EPIDOTE
TREMOLITE	
TUNDRITE	
Violan	Blue DIOPSIDE
Withamite	Red EPIDOTE
WOLLASTONITE	
XONOTLITE	

Class VIII-5—The Bonders

Bonders are called sheet silicates or phylosilicates by scientists. These crystals are formed when silicate tetrahedrons connect in sheets, producing very cohesive minerals. They are very tough to cut. They are outstanding minerals to use as talismans when there is need to create something that is bound tightly. Like glue bonding wooden planks together, Bonder talismans are useful in cementing relationships and agreements. They help us hold things together. Serpentine is the best-known example. Biotite and lepidolite are less known, but they are powerful minerals of this class.

Bonder talismans are particularly well suited to efforts that involve getting a consensus, working out difficulties caused by differing points of view, and negotiating. The Bonders' power is to get people working together. They help us form relationships that get better with age. Bonders help make contracts work out in the long term by ensuring that they are based on clear understandings, and that each party is a beneficiary of the contract. They help keep families, communities, and organizations together. They have power that is similar to that of the Unifiers, but they are more focused on sealing nonfamily relationships than the Unifiers.

Class VIII-5—Bonder Talismans

Bonder talismans, the sheet silicates, have the earth power to aid us in our efforts to hold things together or gain a consensus. There are thousands of minerals; some of the common ones that have the earth power of a Bonder are included in this listing.

Common Name	MINERAL
Agalmatolite	PYROPHYLLITE
AJOITE	
ANTIGORITE	
APOPHYLLITE	
ASTROPHYLLITE	
Atlantisite	Serpentine with STICHTITE
BIOTITE	
Biotite Lens	BIOTITE
Bowenite	ANTIGORITE (Serpentine)
CARLETONITE	
CAVANSITE	
CLINOCHLORE	
ELPIDITE	
EUCLASE	
Fuchsite	MUSCOVITE
Garnierite	NÉPOUITE
GYROLITE	
Infinite	ANTIGORITE
Kämmererite	CLINOCHLORE
KAOLINITE	
Lavenderine	LEPIDOLITE
Lemon Jade	Serpentine
LEPIDOLITE	
MUSCOVITE	
NÉPOUITE	
PENTAGONITE	
PETALITE	
PHLOGOPITE	
POLYLITHIONITE	
PREHNITE	

Continued on next page

Class VIII-5—Bonder Talismans (continued)

Common Name	MINERAL
PYROPHYLLITE	
Ricolite	Serpentine and TALC
SANBORNITE	
Seraphinite	CLINOCHLORE
Serpentine	a mineral group
Soapstone	TALC
TALC	

Class VIII-6—The Filters

This class, the framework silicates (or tectosilicates), is formed by three-dimensional grids of tetrahedrons of silicates that very much look and act like a filter. They absorb certain things and allow others to pass. They filter energy, allowing positive charges to flow and blocking negative ones when properly used and aligned. The feldspars are common Filters, and they have a wide variety of uses in the talismanic world.

Filters are similar to Buffers, but have a more specific use. The Buffers are general talismans used when the need is to achieve balance in life by buffering pressures. The Filters, on the other hand, are used to keep negative energy away from us. When we want help to see the best in others, to give others the benefit of the doubt, to see the good side of something, we need a Filter. It is too easy in life to see the glass half empty, the child as a poor student, or the spouse as a slob. Filters help us see the glass half full, the child as a loving, well-meaning young lady, and the spouse as an excellent provider, devoted to his family. The Filters are not "rose-colored glasses," but rather, they aid in helping us to constantly see the positive in people or situations and not be overwhelmed by the negative. The Filters also work to keep harmful electromagnetic forces from sapping our energy and health. The modern world is awash in cell phone, computer network, TV, radio, and other created-energy transmissions. Use the Filters to protect against the adverse effects of these hazards.

The Filters are a fairly widespread and abundant group of minerals. Nature seems to find it necessary to make them readily available. This is fortuitous. Their positive energy is important to all of us. We all need help seeing the beauty in life, the good in humanity, and the glory that is the natural Earth. Many efforts to gain what we lack depend on a constant positive outlook and an ability to see the goodness in life. The Filter talismans, particularly the ones with the crystal energy of Seekers and Enhancers, are excellent talismans for a wide variety of efforts.

Lapis lazuli, sodalite, and stilbite in particular are Enhancers with the earth power of Filters. These crystals are excellent for improving everyone's life by giving them more of a positive outlook and enabling them to appreciate the bounty of this Earth. When found in a light blue color, lapis lazuli is a superb talisman for finding peace and calmness through acceptance and enjoyment of the earth's bounty.

Class VIII-6—Filter Talismans

Filter talismans, the framework silicates, have the earth power to help us filter out the unpleasant parts of our lives.

Common Name	MINERAL
Adularia	Moonstone ORTHOCLASE/ALBITE
AFGHANITE	
ALBITE	
Amazonite	MICROCLINE
ANALCIME	
Analcite	ANALCIME
ANDESINE	
Azulicite	SANIDINE
Blue Moonstone	ORTHOCLASE
BYTOWNITE	
CHABAZITE	
Chrysotile	Serpentine
Cleavelandite	ALBITE
Cryptoperthite	Moonstone ORTHOCLASE/ALBITE
Desmine	STILBITE
EPISTILBITE	
GMELINITE	
GOOSECREEKITE	
Green Moonstone	ORTHOCLASE
Gray Moonstone	ORTHOCLASE
Hackmanite	SODALITE
HEULANDITE	
LABRADORITE	
Lapis Lazuli	LAZURITE (mostly), PYRITE, CALCITE
LAZURITE	
LEIFITE	
LEUCITE	
MESOLITE	
MICROCLINE	
Moonstone	ORTHOCLASE/ALBITE
NATROLITE	
OLIGOCLASE	
ORTHOCLASE	

Class VIII-6—Filter Talismans (continued)

Common Name	MINERAL
PALYGORSKITE	
Peach Moonstone	ORTHOCLASE/ALBITE
Peristerite	ALBITE
Perthite	MICROCLINE
PHILLIPSITE	
Rainbow Moonstone	LABRADORITE
SANIDINE	
SCAPOLITE	
SCOLECITE	
SODALITE	
Spectrolite	LABRADORITE
STELLERITE	
STILBITE	
Sunstone	OLIGOCLASE Feldspar
THOMSONITE	
WERNERITE	SCAPOLITE

Summary

In the First Secret of Talismans we learned that only natural things have the power to help us as talismans. In the Second Secret it was discovered that the internal crystal energy matrices contain the energy we need to help us in our efforts. The Third Secret revealed the color rays of influence. Now in the Fourth Secret we have learned that the third attribute of any mineral, its chemical composition, gives it a specific power. The table below summarizes these specific uses of talismans based on their earth power.

Earth Power Table

Earth Energy	Class	Scientific Type	Earth Power Best Used For
Purifiers	I	Natural Elements	Pure motives and high purposes
Mirrors	II	Sulfides	Seeing hidden attributes
Brighteners	III	Halides	General improvement in the future
Transformers	IV	Oxides	Changing a poor environment for the better
Builders	V	Carbonates	Adding new capabilities and possibilities to our lives
Solidifiers	VI	Sulfates	Adding permanence to things and relationships
Buffers	VII	Phosphates	Helping with balancing lives and demands
Resisters	VIII-1	Island Silicates	Keeping negative energy away
Unifiers	VIII-2	Group Silicates	Bringing two people together
Energizers	VIII-3	Ring Silicates	Channeling or absorbing energy
Harmonizers	VIII-4	Chain and Band Silicates	Promoting harmony, understanding, and tolerance
Bonders	VIII-5	Sheet Silicates	Joining things together
Filters	VIII-6	Framework Silicates	Promoting an optimistic view

With the first four Secrets of Talismans now revealed and understood, we know that talismans draw their energy and power from the earth, sun, and moon. And we know they carry that energy in their crystal energy structure. We have learned that the color rays are power influences on the human mind. Now from the Fourth Secret we know that talismans also draw power from their very chemical makeup.

The use of this knowledge from the first four Secrets allows us finally to understand how certain minerals, crystals, and gems can be used in our human efforts to achieve our goals and protect us from harm. Using just these first four Secrets allows an unprecedented ability to refine a particular need to virtually the exact raw material required for our purpose. We must understand first what basic need we desire to pursue. Then we must understand the power of colors. Finally we need to consider the power in the talisman's chemical composition. Putting these three attributes together will allow us to select the perfect talisman for any purpose.

Having the perfect raw material for a talisman is an excellent beginning. The first four Secrets have successfully led us to ensuring that we use the right mineral for the purpose we envision. But there is more to using talismans than just picking the right mineral. We now need to understand how we should prepare this material for use. Fortunately, the Fifth Secret of Talismans will reveal the methods we need to ensure we use the raw material correctly.

The
Fifth Secret
of Talismans

Talismans must be made in a way that is consistent
with the intrinsic power and energy of the mineral
and matched to its potential uses in focusing and
magnifying human power.

The proper preparation of a talisman is one of the great secrets to the successful use of these seemingly wondrous artifacts. We already know from the First Secret of Talismans that the raw materials from which they are fashioned must be natural materials. From the discovery of the Second, Third, and Fourth Secrets we learned to understand the specific powers of each mineral, crystal, and gemstone based on its crystal energy structure, its color ray of influence, and its earth power. Once we know what raw material we need for a specific talisman, the next step is to actually find the right material and fashion it to our needs. The Fifth Secret of Talismans reveals to us how to ensure we have maximized the power of the mineral, crystal, or gemstone talisman by selecting and fashioning it effectively.

Finding the Right Material

Finding natural minerals is not difficult. The earth is made of them! However, many gemstones, minerals, and crystals are being manufactured, imitated, altered, faked, and adulterated. The jewelry industry constantly tries to produce new, different, and less expensive alternatives to natural products. Identifying these unnatural products can be difficult. Usually minerals in their unaltered state are much easier to identify as natural because there is less opportunity for alteration in their preparation. Using faceted gemstones as a beginning point in making a talisman can be problematic.

Being able to absolutely certify a particular gemstone as a natural stone often takes the skills and expertise of a gemologist. A gemologist will perform scientific tests to identify a gemstone and to determine if it is a natural mineral crystal or not. There are many tests used by gemologists. These tests include studying a gem's specific gravity, refractive index, and other physical characteristics and properties. Often high magnification of the interior of a gemstone offers valuable hints. For example, some synthetic stones have veils of the tiny particles of the flux used in their manufacture, and some contain gas bubbles that are visible when the stone is examined under high magnification. Such stones are not natural minerals, and have no power to focus and amplify our power and combine it with the Life Force of the planet Earth.

Emeralds, rubies, diamonds, garnets, and many other gemstones are now grown in laboratories. Natural rubies and emeralds are repaired, filled with glass, and oiled. Opals are faked by gluing slices of an opal to a backing material. Black onyx is often just dyed chalcedony. There are numerous other tricks and treatments for many gems. Beware: do not use such material in making a talisman. If you are using faceted gemstones as the raw material for making talismans, either obtain your materials from a reputable source or enlist the services of a gemologist.

The world today offers tremendous opportunities to obtain excellent natural minerals and crystals for making talismans. Many miners advertise their mines and their minerals on the Internet. Several, such as as the Arkansas quartz crystal miners, offer the opportunity for you to dig your own crystals. The Web is also home to many very reputable mineral dealers who are skilled in their trade and able to procure almost any mineral you desire. Dealing with established merchants will virtually ensure that you are getting authentic material. Don't be fooled by low prices or unknown, unproven dealers. If a particular crystal, mineral, or gemstone seems to be "too good to be true," it probably is not a pure, natural specimen. Use only proven sources.

Fashioning Minerals and Crystals into Talismans

Once suitable natural material is obtained (assuming it is not yet fashioned), the next step is to decide if it is to remain in its natural state or if it is to be fashioned in some way. Fashioning does not, in itself, adversely affect a material's use as a talisman. Often, it actually enhances it. It is important to realize that the talisman has to focus human energy. In doing so, it must relate effectively to the human mind. Fashioning often brings out the mineral's or crystal's natural attributes in a more visible way, adding to its usefulness in focusing and amplifying our personal power. For example, if you intend to make a Seeker talisman, using a mineral such as quartz is necessary because it forms in the Seeker crystal system and helps us focus the Life Force of the planet Earth into pointing our way forward to a desired goal. That energy can be further enhanced by matching the external shape of the talisman to its use. In the case of a Seeker, our human brains would relate more to a Seeker talisman shaped like a pointer or arrow than to something like a ball. The external pointer or arrow shape would reinforce our mind's understanding of the power of the crystal. An effort to align the internal energy structures with the external appearance will enhance the overall effectiveness. Seekers, as mentioned, should have some exterior shape that reinforces to the mind the talismans' ability to focus and amplify our power to find what we are looking for. Enhancers should be similar. Barrier and Guardian talismans can be much more effective if their shape is like a wall, a barrier, or a shield. Dispeller talismans work particularly well when they appear with a myriad of sharp points, which reinforce their ability to dissipate the elements of our lives we no longer desire. Attractor talismans seem to work in a variety of shapes. In exploring this Secret of Talismans we will discover the best approaches for each type of talisman.

Generally talismans come in two types. The first type, Specimen talismans, are used when there is a need or desire for a talisman to be used by a group, when one is being designed for a specific location such as a room, or when the material needed for a certain purpose is unsuitable for the various methods of fashioning, usually due to its softness. The second type of talisman is the more familiar Personal talisman. They are usually fashioned in some manner that makes them easy to carry and handle without damage. As this Secret reveals, the fashioning also allows the material to be worked in such a way that its external shape aids in its effectiveness. To understand this Secret of Talismans, we will examine both types.

Specimen Talismans

The first type of talismans, Specimen talismans, are usually not fashioned (the exception being large spheres), but after being mined, they are cleaned but otherwise mostly left as they were found in or on the earth. Crystal and mineral specimens are mined throughout the world, and avidly collected by crystal and mineral collectors. This trade allows us access to the raw materials we need. The same dealers that supply the collectors with collectable mineral specimens can also serve as the source of the talisman maker's raw materials. Specimen talismans can be any size, but normally vary from just about an inch in all dimensions to about eight inches or more in one or more dimensions. For talismans to be used in a large space or for a group need, the large sizes work well. For individual use, excellent results are obtained from specimens just an inch or so in size.

There are major advantages to Specimen talismans. These talismans are often available just as they formed in nature, retaining all of their natural attributes such as color, shape, symmetry, and size. Their crystal faces are naturally occurring. Sometimes they are composed of more than one mineral, and have more than one color ray of influence. For special needs that might require a mix of talismans, sometimes a mixed-mineral specimen

Specimen talisman

can be found that combines the needed attributes. Mixed-mineral Specimen talismans can have combinations of chemical earth powers, crystal energy structures, and color rays. These combinations can be potent indeed. Because of the incredible number of potential combinations of minerals, the variety of Specimen talismans is unlimited.

Specimen talismans are also the easiest to make, in that there is little or no fashioning to be done once a mineral specimen has been obtained. The major benefit of Specimen talismans is that they allow the use of many more minerals than Personal talismans do. Many minerals are really too soft to fashion effectively into Personal talismans. Imagine trying to grind a large salt crystal. It would just crumble. The soft minerals are usually always used as Specimen talismans. The Mohs hardness scale is a good guide. On that scale, any mineral with a hardness of less than 5 should probably always be left as a Specimen talisman.

Personal Talismans

Personal talismans are the other type of talisman. These are usually fashioned in some manner because they are meant to be carried or worn. For many uses, talismans must be available during the normal day. Cutting and polishing a gem or mineral specimen can make it much more portable and useful. Personal talismans are usually made from the harder minerals that can respond well to the cutting, grinding, and polishing involved in fashioning. Most material with a Mohs hardness of 5 or more can be fashioned in some manner. Personal talismans are usually faceted, made into cabochons, carved, or tumbled. The fashioning technique depends both on the material and the intended use of the resulting talisman. Each of these fashioning techniques has a special application in making talismans.

Faceting

The first method of fashioning a Personal talisman is by faceting. A facet is a flat face on a stone. Faceting is a process of grinding patterns of flat surfaces on a crystal or stone to give it a shape. Faceting is not difficult, but it involves the use of a faceting machine. This machine has a spinning plate with the surface of the plate impregnated with hard material like sapphire or diamond. The mineral or crystal is held against the plate and the hard sapphire or diamond effectively grinds a flat surface. By rotating the crystal or mineral specimen in precise ways, the crystal or mineral is fashioned one flat surface after another until the desired shape is achieved. There are many different cuts that can be used in faceting crystals to be used as talismans. However, many are just variations on several well-known shapes. The usual shapes are wands, triangles, rectangles, circles, and ovals.

Seeker and Enhancer talismans are usually faceted into wands, trillions (triangles), or round brilliant cuts. These shapes offer a sharp point that can further focus the crystal energy of the material. Fortunately, many of the minerals that form in the Seeker crystal structure are hard enough for faceting. Some are even found naturally in these shapes, making faceting easy. For example, quartz crystals often naturally form in the shape of wands, and thus can be either used as Specimen talismans or faceted and polished easily into the wand shape for a Personal talisman.

Other minerals that form in the Seeker crystal structure are not hard enough for faceting. In particular, the Seeker crystalline structure minerals that have the earth power of Builders and Filters are mostly too soft. Calcite, a Seeker with the earth power of the Builder class, for example, has a Mohs hardness of 3. Gmelinite, a Seeker with the earth power of the Filter class, is only a 4 on the hardness scale. Such minerals are better used as Specimens.

When making Seekers and Enhancers, some designs do not work too well for Personal talismans. Oval cuts, with their elongated culets, don't provide the needed focus. Other designs that lack a focus or clear pointing direction do not give the best results. A faceted sphere would make a poor Seeker or Enhancer. It would not stimulate the brain in such a

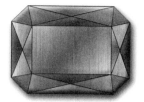

Faceted talisman

way as to aid in focusing our personal power to find a path to what we desire. The external shape would serve to run us around in a circle rather than provide the visual stimulation of pointing out the way to our goal. While Enhancers don't need to have quite the focus of the Seekers, they still need orientation and some direction.

Although there are few suitable minerals, faceting Guardian and Barrier talismans is straightforward. These talismans help us focus our energy and augment it with the Life Force of the planet Earth to guard what we possess and value, and to protect us from unwanted elements of life. They are used for guarding and blocking actions, not pointing. If faceted, they should be made into solid, chunky cuts like cushions, square cuts, or large ovals that appear to be shields. The result should be a design that is consistent with their regular inner structure and one that appears to be solid and substantial. Personal Guardian and Barrier talismans are usually carried on one's person. As such, the hardest, most durable materials should be used to ensure long use.

Minerals that are to be used as Dispellers are usually best left in their natural form. Often these minerals can be found in clusters of numerous tightly intergrown crystals with a myriad of sharp crystal points. Such a specimen offers the visual representation of a radiator, and it helps us focus our thoughts and energy to dispel or radiate out the undesirable elements of our lives. However, if a Personal Dispeller is needed, and a faceted gem is desired, the best cut is a round brilliant cut. This cut normally has fifty-eight facets, and the multiple flashes of light energy radiating from it as it is rotated in sunlight can directly stimulate the human brain.

Attractors are usually not made by faceting. There are no common minerals that form transparent crystals with the Attractor crystal energy structure. Attractors are usually Specimen talismans, or they are occasionally made by cutting the material into cabochons.

Cabochons

The second method of fashioning material is to make cabochons. Making cabochons is easier to do than faceting, and it does not require the expensive equipment that faceting does. Cabochons are the most common Personal talismans. Beginning talisman makers are encouraged to learn a bit of lapidary art and develop some skill in making cabochons. Mastery of the talismanic arts requires a deep knowledge of the characteristics of minerals. The act of physically forming natural minerals into suitable cabochon Personal talismans will provide the aspiring talisman maker with the deep understanding needed for long-term success.

A cabochon does not have numerous flat faces ground on a crystal. Rather, it is usually a convex shape, often flat on one side, although any fashioning that does not involve faceting, carving, or tumbling is considered to be making a cabochon. Cabochons are often cut into oval shapes, but irregular shapes are also common. A cabochon is made by slicing a piece of a mineral with a rock saw, then cutting out the desired outline, again with a rock saw. Then the resulting rough piece is ground by holding it against a rotating grinding wheel until it is formed into its final shape. It is then polished on a polishing wheel. The process is similar to faceting, but where faceting is done by grinding numerous tiny facets and requires great accuracy in each cut, making a cabochon involves just shaping the top of the material. The bottom is usually just polished flat.

While opaque material is used more frequently, cabochons made from translucent and transparent material are important. Rubies, sapphires, emeralds, and other gems are often cut en cabochon to bring out special qualities of the crystal. For example, some sapphires can show a reflected star when cut into a cabochon. Chatoyant crystals, such as some chrysoberyls, form an "eye" due to fibrous inclusions. These eyes would not be visible if the stone were faceted. Transparent or translucent material that is not of the quality to warrant the time and expense of faceting is still of great value to the talisman maker. The color and chemical composition may be exactly what is needed for a particular talisman. Cutting the material en cabochon produces an excellent talisman without undue expense or effort.

Many Seeker and Enhancer talismans are made by forming the mineral into cabochons, particularly when the material is opaque. However, these are usually made by cutting free-form shapes like triangles rather than the traditional oval shape of a cabochon. Seeker and Enhancer talismans need to suggest direction. Pointed shapes that remind us of an arrow work best. In addition, minerals that form strong eyes when cut into cabochons can be

Cabochon

very suggestive of assistance in seeing the future. In this way they can be valuable Seekers. They can help us see possibilities where perhaps on our own we might miss them.

Barriers and Guardians are often made by cutting minerals into cabochons. When cut into the traditional oval, or into square shapes, they give the strong suggestion of a shield. Cabochon Dispeller talismans can be made, but require shapes that are more like stars rather than ovals. Attractor talismans seem to work in any shape of cabochon as long as they are cut to maximize the attractive powers of their surface sheen.

As we learned in the Fourth Secret of Talismans, opaque minerals gain more of their power to focus and enhance human energy from their chemical composition than from their crystal energy structure. For opaque material, cutting en cabochon is the standard practice. An exception is made for manufacturing wands, but beyond this shape, little is gained by faceting an opaque material because the light cannot enter the stone and be reflected, which is the purpose of the faceting process.

Forming cabochons allows the talisman maker to take the structure and appearance of the mineral into consideration in the design of the final talisman. Here is where art meets science in talisman making. The art is in the understanding of the suitability of a particular mineral specimen for a specific talismanic use. A good talisman maker has a deep appreciation for the intrinsic attributes of the particular raw material. The science is in ensuring that only natural materials are used. When the science found in the first four Secrets of Talismans is combined effectively with the art of the Fifth Secret, the result can be quite stunning and highly effective talismans with great power to focus our efforts and align our power with the Life Force of our planet and universe.

Carving

Carving is an ancient and respected method of preparing talismans. Spheres, blocks, eggs, cubes, and figurines of all description are possible. Most hand-carved talismans are made from the softer materials that are easy to work and shape. Like faceting and making cabochons, carving is accomplished by grinding away elements from a mineral sample, but rather than always holding the material against a large spinning plate or wheel, hand carving is done by using a small, often hand-held, spinning grinding wheel or drill. Materials with hardness of 6 or less on the Mohs scale can be carved with inexpensive hand tools. For harder materials, most talisman makers procure commercially carved material, which is widely available in the marketplace.

Spheres are a very interesting form for talismans. "Scrying" (divination using a polished surface, such as a crystal ball) is an ancient practice. One rarely sees a statue of a magician without the magician holding a crystal ball. Humankind seems to instinctively see magic in a crystal ball. As a shape for a talisman, the sphere is used with both transparent and opaque materials. It can be a small sphere, and used as a Personal talisman, or a larger sphere can be carved making an effective Specimen talisman. Spheres normally are not used for Seeker or Enhancer talismans unless the material is transparent, and the intent is to use it for scrying by looking deep within it for guidance and direction. Some talisman makers report success with using spheres as Barriers and as Guardians. The idea seems to be that the shape reminds the user of ammunition, like cannon balls. Spheres have very limited use as Dispeller talismans. With a smooth surface, spheres don't seem to work as well as other shapes, which offer many sharp points of radiation. Attractor talismans in the shape of spheres work well. Spheres are also used with all six crystal structures, particularly the Seeker and Enhancer ones, when the primary purpose of the talisman is to harness its earth power. Spheres make excellent Harmonizers, Mirrors, Energizers, Solidifiers, and Bonders.

Cubes and blocks also make great talismans, particularly Barriers and Guardians. Their external shape matches the internal crystal structure and gives the appearance of strength and power. This appearance enhances their ability to align their protective Life Force with the power of the human mind. They also work well with opaque materials that are being used primarily for their earth power. They are particularly useful for Energizers, Solidifiers, and Bonders.

Eggs and figurines are rarely used in making talismans. They often have a fragile appearance, and really don't work well in efforts to focus and magnify human power. Special shapes

Carved talisman

Tumbled talismans

like crosses can be used, but the effects of their symbolism are hard to predict and control. The symbolism might overshadow the inherent capabilities of the mineral and make it less effective for a particular user. On the other hand, if the symbolism is clearly understood, special shapes can enhance the power of a talisman. A cross carved from a mineral with the Guardian crystal structure is a good example. Such a talisman could be used effectively for spiritual protection by a believer in one of the Christian faiths. A nephrite jade cross would be an excellent talisman for such a person.

Tumbling

Tumbling is an inexpensive way to prepare a talisman. The equipment is not difficult to operate, and the results with many minerals are very good. The shape of the resulting crystal or stone is difficult to plan accurately, but the tumbling process cleans up the crystal or mineral and shows the color clearly.

Tumbling is not a good solution if a sharp, pointed crystal is desired. Tumbling rounds off a crystal, and results in a smooth shape. It is a good method, though, for making Personal talismans from hard, opaque materials. Seekers and Enhancers are not usually tumbled—their external shape is important. Barriers, Enhancers, and Guardians can be made from tumbled stones. Dispellers should not be tumbled. Attractors can be made effectively by tumbling.

General Fashioning Guidelines

The following table is a general guide to fashioning talismans. It is a starting point. There are thousands of minerals. Each mineral and each specimen of a mineral is unique. For example, if you are in need of a talisman to help you seek to transform your life in some way, you might chose a Seeker crystal that has the earth power of a Transformer. The table tells you that there are minerals with those powers that can be faceted or made into cabochons.

Fashioning Table

	Seekers	Enhancers	Guardians	Barriers	Dispellers	Attractors
Purifiers	Specimen	Specimen			Specimen	
Mirrors	Specimen	Specimen	Specimen	Specimen	Specimen	Specimen
Brighteners		Specimen	Specimen		Specimen	Specimen
Transformers	Facet/Cab	Facet/Cab	Facet/Cab		Facet/Cab	Facet/Cab
Builders	Cabochon		Cabochon	Cabochon	Cabochon	Cabochon
Solidifiers			Specimen	Specimen	Specimen	Specimen
Buffers	Cabochon		Cabochon	Cabochon	Cabochon	Cabochon
Strengtheners	Facet	Facet	Facet	Facet	Facet	Facet
Unifiers	Facet		Facet	Facet	Facet	Facet
Energizers	Facet				Facet	
Harmonizers	Cabochon		Cabochon	Cabochon		Cabochon
Bonders			Specimen	Specimen		Specimen
Filters		Cabochon	Cabochon	Cabochon	Cabochon	

Looking across the table, examining the various crystal energy structures, we see there are compromises to be made. Ideally all Seekers, Enhancers, and Dispellers would be either left as Specimen talismans or faceted to provide the sharp points needed. However, some of the minerals that form in these crystal structures are not suitable for faceting. These crystals should either be left in their natural state and used as Specimen talismans or made into as appropriate a shape as possible if formed into cabochons.

Looking down the columns of the table from the earth power perspective, we see that the Purifiers, being natural elements, are rare enough that they are usually not fashioned when found. They are usually always used as Specimen talismans. So too are the Mirrors and the Brighteners. Among the Brighteners, the fluorites are often found in large, naturally formed crystals that need little work. The Transformers, on the other hand, are usually faceted or cut into cabochons. They include a number of very hard minerals that form very durable and transparent gemstones. These are best faceted to bring out their color rays, particularly for Seekers, Enhancers, and Dispellers. The Builder talismans are usually cut into cabochons and work best that way. They contain minerals that form very interesting patterns within the stones that are best observed by carefully designing a cabochon cut. Shield or block shapes work best. Solidifiers are usually left as Specimen talismans due to their fragile nature. The major Buffer talisman is turquoise. It can be very effectively cut into cabochons, and this is the usual method. Strengtheners, Unifiers, and Energizers are mostly prepared by faceting. Like the Transformers, they often form colorful transparent gem material that is best used by allowing the light to enter the stone to produce powerful color rays. Harmonizers are almost all cut into cabochons for use. Bonders are used primarily as Specimen talismans due to their softness. Filter talismans are almost all cut into cabochons if not used as Specimen talismans. The blank areas in the table are where few or no known talismans exist. Most of the minerals that are normally made into cabochons are also commonly tumbled or carved. Both tumbling and carving work well for talismans when the primary intention is to use the mineral's earth power.

Clearly, the nature of the mineral dictates its method of fashioning. Most minerals that are fashioned can also be used as Specimen talismans. The decision to fashion a mineral crystal or leave it natural is one that must be based on the physical properties of the crystal and its intended use.

Setting and Mounting Talismans

There is much debate within the talisman and amulet community on the advisability of mounting talismans into rings, necklaces, and other jewelry items. It is worth devoting some time to understand this issue.

Talismans are tools, not jewelry. As will be seen in the Seventh Secret, they are used daily to focus and amplify our energy. Our minds will respond to them if we perceive them as tools and not as pretty jewelry. No one thinks jewelry is for any purpose beyond adornment. Fancy settings will only detract from the usefulness and value of a talisman.

Certainly, Specimen talismans are not set into jewelry of any kind. Personal talismans should only be set into the most simple of necklaces to allow them to be accessible. The necklace must be worn so that the talisman is not visible to others. If it were visible, the necklace would be a piece of jewelry, not a talisman. The settings should be made of natural elements, like gold, silver, or copper. Talismans should not be set into rings or bracelets. Again these are jewelry, and the stones in jewelry are ornaments, not talismans.

The most important element in setting or mounting a talisman is to consider how the setting will affect your ability to use the talisman for its intended purpose. Remember, a talisman or amulet is used to focus and amplify your personal power and ability. Many users find that a pendant is the best way to keep the talisman available and to have it ready to use. In making talismans for others, keeping the setting as simple as possible is recommended. Use only natural materials infused with the Life Force, and ensure that the purpose of the setting is not to make the stone into jewelry.

Summary

The Fifth Secret of Talismans reveals the necessity of proper preparation when fashioning talismans. Whether Specimen or Personal talisman, assuring the shape's consistency with the mineral's properties and the talisman's intended use is fundamental to success. Use the charts in this chapter as a beginning. They are a guide. Refine the design of every talisman to align its appearance as closely as possible to its crystal energy and its earth power. Consider the congruency of the external shape with the internal structure, composition, and power of the crystal. Strive for unity of design and purpose. With practice, and deepening understanding, you will be able to fashion talismans and amulets that will aid you and others to focus the Universal Life Force and amplify your natural abilities for whatever the need or desire.

Applying the first five Secrets will produce powerful talismans and amulets with truly amazing powers. In fact, these five Secrets reveal everything needed to make talismans. All that remains to reveal is the secret of using them effectively. However, before exploring the proper use of talismans in the Seventh Secret, the Sixth Secret will reveal a remarkable method for making our talismans and amulets even more effective and powerful.

THE
SIXTH SECRET
OF TALISMANS

**Talismans gain tremendous power when connected
physically and spiritually to places and times of highly
focused Life Force energy.**

Minerals are part of the earth. Because elements and compounds formed within this planet, they contain the Life Force of the planet Earth, a form of the Universal Life Force. Like we humans, talismans made from natural minerals each have their individual strength and power, but also like us, they are more powerful when they are highly charged with the Universal Life Force.

The Universal Life Force runs through time and space. It is an energy matrix that encompasses the spiritual world and the physical one. It runs through the past, the present, and into the future. Its energy is manifested to us through the sun, the moon, and the earth. Bringing a talisman to a place where the Universal Life Force is particularly strong, at a time when it is strongest, will make that talisman an even more powerful conduit of the Life Force of the planet Earth, and it will better focus our personal power. It will draw increased effectiveness from this source, just as a rechargeable battery is recharged when connected to the power grid. This Secret tells us that if we can somehow find a place and a time to connect our talismans even more strongly to the Life Force, we can enhance their talismanic power. We need to identify such a place and determine when to take our talismans there to connect them to the highly focused Universal Life Force.

We know we need a place where the Life Force is strong. From the First Secret of Talismans, we know the Life Force stems from the energy of the sun, the moon, and the earth, so we need a place where their energy is concentrated. We know the Life Force runs through time, so we know we need a place where we are connected to the past, the present, and the future. We know the Universal Life Force encompasses and powers both the spirit world and the physical world, so we need a place that connects these worlds.

Stonehenge

Fortunately, at least one such place does seem to exist. It is located west of London, England, on the Salisbury Plain. It is known as Stonehenge. We do not know why it was built over periods of thousands of years by peoples of several cultures, but we do know it is a natural celestial observatory that marks the solstices and equinoxes, and can be used to measure and predict other celestial events such as moon cycles and eclipses.[1] Thus it is a place that connects the earth, the sun, and the moon—a nexus of power and energy. While there are certainly similar, more secret places in lands with ancient cultures such as Egypt, Iran, China, and India, the history of Europe and England is documented sufficiently to allow us to know the power of Stonehenge.

Stonehenge is an ancient place that, because it is made of giant, very hard stones, will exist well into the future. It connects the Life Force in time. Its origin is lost in myth and legend. Even today, all of its mysteries are not solved. We still have no clear understanding of why three different cultures over a period of several thousand years spent so much time and energy on its construction. Some of its secrets remain for the future to reveal.

But is this the right place? It does seem so, but the Sixth Secret tells us that the place also needs to be one that connects the physical world and the spiritual one. Does Stonehenge do that?

Yes, Stonehenge does connect the physical world and the spiritual one. First of all, there is a strong link to the physical world there. Stonehenge is a very physical place, with its large circles of massive stones that dwarf observers. It is physically awe inspiring. Even with many of the original stones missing from the site, today, as a World Heritage Site, it attracts close to a million visitors a year.

But Stonehenge is much more than just some large stones arranged in a circle serving to identify celestial events. It is also a very spiritual place. Located at a major connection point of fourteen ley lines[2] that join many of the most sacred places in England, it has served for over five thousand years as a gathering place for incalculable numbers of religious, cultural, and spiritual rituals by people from many different cultures and religions.[3]

---

1 Gerald S. Hawkins and John B. White, *Stonehenge Decoded* (New York: Dell Publishers, 1965), 107.

2 Alfred Watkins, *The Old Straight Track: The Classic Book on Ley Lines*, (London: Abacus 2005), xv. A ley line is an ancient line or track marked by hills, barrows, and bairns that connects spiritual sites in the United Kingdom.

3 Sahar Huneidi, "Sacred Stonehenge: A Spiritual Tour," http://www.psychicsahar.com/artman/publish/article_562.shtml (accessed June 16, 2007).

Without doubt, its spirituality is tied strongly to its location on the nexus of the many ley lines, but there is more to its spirit world connection than just its location. Its connection to the spiritual world is also very strong because of the spiritual power of its inner stone circle of megaliths, all sixty of which were made of tons of Preseli bluestone.

Preseli Bluestone

The power and energy of Preseli bluestone is considered to be virtually magical. It is mined in the Preseli Hills in Pembrookshire, Wales. The Preseli Hills, the center of Welsh mythology, are the origins of the Welsh legends called the *Mabinogion*, which means "Tales of Youth." The legends of *Annwn*, the Underworld, originated here. The Preseli Hills are home to Carn Ingli, where angels reportedly communicate, and to Pentre Ifan, a stone megalith made of Preseli bluestone. Pentre Ifan, also known as the Womb of Cerridwen, is said to be one of the main gateways to the land of the fairies.[4] It's little wonder that the makers of Stonehenge knew that they needed to bring the power and magic of Preseli to Stonehenge.

With our modern instruments, and knowledge of the Secrets of Talismans, we can now begin to understand some of the magic. Our modern instruments reveal that Preseli bluestone is a pyroxene mineral, composed of augite mixed with some plagioclase feldspar. Preseli bluestone is therefore a mix of a Guardian mineral (augite) and a Barrier mineral (plagioclase feldspar). This is a rare, powerful combination of protection. The inner circle of Stonehenge is composed of a material containing minerals with two crystal energy structures, both of which help protect us spiritually and physically. But there is more. The Preseli bluestone contains the chemical earth powers of Harmonizers (augite) and Filters (plagioclase feldspar). Bluestone is opaque, and we have discovered that opaque minerals are normally used for their earth power. Minerals that have the earth power of Harmonizers are built from silicate tetrahedrons bound together in a long chain. They distribute energy in a balanced, long-term way that promotes harmony. The Filter minerals are built of silicate tetrahedrons bound in a three-dimensional arrangement that filters out negative energy and allows only positive energy to flow. Stonehenge was built on the major nexus of ley lines that connect the key spiritual centers of England. Putting a powerful circle of bluestone in that location allows for distribution of positive spiritual energy

---

4 Preseli Bluestone Limited, "The Secret of Preseli Bluestones," http://www.stonehengestones.com/ (accessed June 16, 2007).

in a long-term, balanced way and simultaneously blocks negative energy from flowing. This very physical presence of megaliths of bluestone forms a powerful spiritual energy center that connects the past, the present, and the future in both the physical and the spiritual world. The inner circle of Stonehenge is made of tons of this seemingly magical bluestone, which was transported over two hundred miles from Wales. Stonehenge, by its location at the nexus of ley lines, and by its use of Preseli bluestone, connects the physical and the spiritual worlds. It is surely the place we need where the Universal Life Force is highly focused.

So we know where we need to be. Stonehenge is a place that strongly connects the sun, the moon, and the earth. It is a place where the past, the present, and the future seem to meld together, and it is certainly a place where the spiritual world and material world join together. Just stepping into the outer ring of sarsen stones at Stonehenge will convince even the strongest skeptic that here the Life Force is strong indeed. What else could have prompted people from three different cultures to spend thousands of years building the stone circles? The people of those times, like people today, need only be in the place to know it is a major nexus of the Universal Life Force. Moving into the inner circle of Preseli bluestones intensifies the feelings and experience.[5] Here the connection to the sun, the moon, and the earth is strongest as the very stones are aligned with the heavens. Here the past blends into the future, as the cycles of the sun, the moon, and the earth's seasons are melded together. And being here, we seem to leave the physical world behind and melt into one of magic, spirituality, and dreams.

Time of Powering Talismans

Knowing where we need to be to connect our talismans to the focused Life Force, the next part of the Secret to unravel is to determine when we need to be there. Fortunately, the answer is found in the nature of the place itself. Stonehenge is an astronomical observatory that is designed to mark the solstices and equinoxes. Obviously these are the times we seek. There are two equinoxes: the vernal equinox and the autumnal equinox. These days mark the beginning of spring and fall. There are two solstices: the summer solstice and the winter solstice, marking the beginning of those seasons. We know then that there

---

5 Access to Stonehenge is now controlled by the English Heritage Foundation. Stone circle access can be arranged by contacting the foundation. They are on the Web at http://www.english-heritage.org.uk. At the time of writing, free access into the stone circle was available on the solstices and equinoxes.

are four times a year we need to be at Stonehenge. We are not alone in that knowledge. Modern-day Druids and people of many religions converge on Stonehenge at these times. These people, like their ancient ancestors, understand the importance of these dates, and the connection to the spiritual world Stonehenge provides at these times particularly. Taking our prospective talismans to Stonehenge on the day of a solstice or equinox and placing them in the Inner Ring of bluestones will charge them with the focused Universal Life Force that connects the past and the future, the physical and spiritual worlds, in a place on Earth that is a nexus of spiritual connections, and one that is devoted to the power of the sun and the moon, whose travels are marked by the alignments of the stones.

Understanding this Secret, however, is a bit disconcerting. Certainly we can make powerful talismans using the first five Secrets of Talismans. But if we want to enhance their power by connecting them to the focused Universal Life Force, we need to continually go to England every three months and take our prospective talismans to Stonehenge. Surely there is a more convenient and less expensive way. Is there a practical way to charge our talismans with focused Universal Life Force? Is there a way to somehow transport at least some of the power of Stonehenge?

The Circle of Bluestone

We know much of the power of Stonehenge is derived from its location on the ley lines that connect the spiritual locations in England. Obviously, we cannot transport that aspect of its power. But we can transport the power of the circle of bluestone. We certainly can't carry giant megaliths of bluestone around, but we can carry a small circle or ring of bluestone.[6] Such a ring could be a great surrogate for the circle of bluestones at Stonehenge. If such a ring had been physically at Stonehenge, its connection to that place would be strong. So, a ring of bluestone that has been physically connected to the circle of bluestone at Stonehenge could be an excellent extension of the spiritual power of Stonehenge for connecting talismans to concentrated Universal Life Force. Bluestone is a powerful energy conduit. While it certainly would be most desirable to actually take the talismans to Stonehenge, practically speaking, bringing some of the power of Stonehenge to the talismans will markedly increase their effectiveness.

---

6 Such rings of bluestone are now commercially available. They are called "Merlin Rings" and are available from Preseli Bluestone, Ltd., at http://www.stonehengestones.com.

The Five Transport Talismans

One problem that arises with this approach is only relatively small rings of bluestone are available. Larger talismans, particularly Specimen talismans, could not be placed within a small ring at an equinox or a solstice. They would be too large. We need some way of using the ring with larger talismans. One solution is to use some small talismans that can be passed through the ring to transport the Life Force to our other talismans that are too large. If we were to do so, we would want to ensure that those smaller talismans were the best possible conduits of the focused Life Force at that time.

Here the knowledge contained in the Fourth Secret of Talismans can be of great help. The Great Talismanic Color Wheel of Influence tells us which color rays of influence are associated with the solstices and equinoxes. If we look up the colors associated with the key times we have to be at Stonehenge, we learn that the vernal equinox occurs as the colors transition to turquoise, the summer solstice occurs as the colors change to yellow, the autumnal equinox as they change to scarlet, and the winter solstice as they change to violet. Small Transport talismans that contain these color rays of influence could be passed through the bluestone ring at the appropriate time, then connected physically with our talismans. But we are missing something. These four Transport talismans just give us the necessary color rays of influence of daytime. Stonehenge is a place of both the sun and the moon, and Stonehenge is a lunar observatory, built to predict eclipses and other lunar events. We need an additional, fifth small talisman to represent the moon and its power over human activities. The connection of the pentacle to the moon goddess Morrigan in Celtic lore tends to support this supposition. Since the colors of the moon and night are silver, white, and black, it is reasonable to assume we need a fifth Transport talisman that is one or more of these colors.

So we need five stones: one representing each season of the earth-and-sun relationship, and a fifth one to represent the power of the moon. While any talismans with the right color ray of influence would be perfectly suitable, perhaps using minerals that have been employed for talismans since the distant past would give us an enhanced connection. Many gems and jewels were unknown in very ancient times, but several have been mined and used since earliest recorded history.

Turquoise, once called *mafkat* by the ancient Egyptians, has been mined on the Sinai Peninsula for over three thousand years.[7] The mineral has the color ray of influence we

---

7 Cerrillos Hills Park Coalition, "Turquoise and the Park," The Santa Fe County Cerrillos Hills Historic Park, http://www.cerrilloshills.org/minerals/turquoise.html (accessed June 17, 2007).

need to use at the vernal equinox to transport the focused Life Force into our turquoise, green, and olive talismans. It comes in small sizes and is not expensive. A small piece of blue-green turquoise makes an excellent vernal equinox Transport talisman.

Since the times of ancient Egypt, people have mined transparent yellow quartz, a gem we now know as citrine. A small crystal of citrine can be used to pass through the blue-stone ring on the summer solstice, then used to transport the Life Force to our yellow, gold, and orange talismans.

There are many minerals with the scarlet color ray. Carnelians have been mined in the Alps since at least 900 AD. A good scarlet-colored carnelian crystal is an excellent choice for our third Transport talisman. We can use it on the autumnal equinox to transport the focused Life Force to our scarlet, red, and amethyst talismans by passing it through our bluestone ring, then touching it to our new talismans to transport the focused Life Force to them.

There are several minerals that have been known since antiquity that can provide a violet ray. Several types of garnets such as pyropes and umbalites can be found with the right color ray. Also, the mineral amethyst can be found with violet rays. Some jadeite also contains this ray of influence. The easiest to find are dark amethyst crystals. We can use one on the winter solstice to transport the focused Life Force to our violet, indigo, and blue talismans in the same manner as we use the other Transport talismans. We pass the violet Transport talisman through the bluestone ring, and then use it to touch our new talisman, thereby transporting the focused Life Force to our new talisman.

This leads us to the last stone. The last stone has to reflect the influence of the moon. Unfortunately, the moonstone of today was not known to ancient cultures. Neither was the diamond. But there are two possible minerals that have been mined for thousands of years: onyx and silver. Onyx is actually chalcedony quartz that is black and white. The white is often just a thin line in the black quartz, an excellent representation of the path of the moon through the night sky. Silver is a mineral that has been mined since ancient times, and it clearly reflects the mystery and powerful influence of the moon. A piece of either black onyx or silver can serve us well for our fifth talisman.

Connecting Talismans with the Focused Life Force

As we now know, we need to take our talismans to Stonehenge to enhance their effectiveness by steeping them in the focused Universal Life Force found there, particularly at the solstices and equinoxes. If we cannot be there to pass them through the Inner Ring, then we can use our bluestone ring as a surrogate. Our smaller talismans can be passed through it instead of through the Inner Ring at Stonehenge at the appropriate time. For connecting our larger talismans, we can pass our Transport talismans through the ring at the appropriate time and then bring them into contact with our talismans. With any of these three methods, we can use the Sixth Secret of Talismans to increase the power of our talismans by connecting them physically and spiritually to a place of highly focused Universal Life Force.

There is one limitation of which we need to be aware. While the Universal Life Force is certainly universal and all-pervasive, the Life Force of the planet Earth varies by season. It is a developing, growing force in the spring; a warming, harmonizing force in the summer; a maturing, ripening force in the autumn; and a rebirth force in the winter. The best results are obtained when the talismans associated with a particular season are connected at the appropriate times. The Great Talismanic Color Wheel of Influence illustrates the correct times for either taking talismans to Stonehenge, or charging them using our bluestone ring. The winter-colored talismans of violet, indigo, and blue are best charged on the winter solstice. The turquoise, green, and olive ones are best charged on the vernal equinox. The yellow, gold, and orange are best charged on the summer solstice. And the scarlet, red, and amethyst ones are best charged on the autumnal equinox. This might account for the rarity of powerful talismans. There is only one day each year on which they can best be connected to the focused Universal Life Force.

We now know the first four Transport talismans are used at the solstices and equinoxes to charge talismans associated with the coming season. But we have talismans that are white, silver, brown, and black that are not associated with a particular season. And we have a silver or black onyx Transport talisman. How are such talismans connected with the focused Universal Life Force? And what is the use of the silver or black and white Transport talisman?

Talismans that are black, brown, silver, or white are more associated with the night and the moon than the daytime and the sun. The current school of thought is that they should be charged on the moon/Earth cycle, not on events that define the sun/Earth cycle like equinoxes and solstices. The moon's power is highest when the moon is full, so it is believed that black, brown, silver, and white talismans can be connected to this power on any full moon, but preferably the one nearest the winter solstice. If these talismans cannot be brought to Stonehenge at a full moon, then they can be passed through the bluestone ring on the night of a full moon. If they are too large, then the silver or onyx Transport talisman can be passed through the ring, then physically touched to them. We have more opportunities throughout the year to enhance the power of our brown, black, silver, and white talismans than the colored ones.

Summary

The Sixth Secret of Talismans offers us a way to make our talismans even more effective in amplifying our personal energy with the power and energy of the Life Force of the planet Earth. This Secret gives us the ability to make talismans with much more power and energy than normal. Talismans that are made using the first five Secrets are powerful aids in any effort. Talismans that are enhanced using the Sixth Secret of Talismans are extraordinary aids in our efforts to achieve our desires.

The Seventh Secret of Talismans

Talismans must be selected, activated, and used according to their special powers and in alignment with the desires of a human mind.

Selecting a Talisman

A talisman must provide the right crystal energy, earth power, and color ray of influence for its intended purpose. Selecting a suitable talisman involves understanding and applying the first six Secrets of Talismans, but that is not enough. The Seventh Secret teaches us that the talisman must connect with the human mind to actually work.

The first step in selecting a talisman is to take the time to really understand what you want. A talisman focuses and multiplies a person's own power and energy. There are many powerful talismans, but we know from the first six Secrets that minerals and stones have specific capabilities to help us focus and magnify our power. Selecting a talisman starts with knowing what you want it to help you accomplish. Frankly, if you don't really know what you want, no talisman can work because there is nothing to focus and multiply. If you aren't going anywhere, you don't need a talisman. If you can write down exactly what you want, and be specific about it, you are ready to select a talisman.

Applying the Second Secret of Talismans

Start the talisman selection process by applying the Second Secret of Talismans. If you are seeking something that you currently don't have, then a Seeker talisman is probably the place to begin. If you desire to enhance or enrich something in your life, then an Enhancer crystal is called for. If you desire to focus on guarding something of value to you, say a possession, a relationship, or a special person, a talisman from the Guardian system is a good choice. Should you need to protect yourself from some misfortune like disease or violence, then a talisman should be selected from the Barrier crystal structure. Finally, if you feel you have something now that you wish to be rid of, an affliction of some sort, a Dispeller should be your choice.

Just as there is more than one way to accomplish most things, there are multiple paths to selecting just the right talisman. For example, if you desire to be healthier, you might start with a Seeker, because you are seeking better health. However, an Enhancer might be more appropriate if you are already in good health and just want to be in even better shape. But if, on reflection, you determine you want to focus on achieving better health by avoiding illness, then a Barrier talisman might be a good choice. And, for the sake of completeness, if your desire was to get better health by losing twenty pounds, then a Dispeller might be called for. The more specifically you express your need, the easier it is to chose the best talisman.

Applying the Third Secret of Talismans

The next step in selecting a talisman is to apply the Third Secret of Talismans and refer to the Great Talismanic Color Wheel of Influence to determine the color of the talisman you need. Again, as in selecting the appropriate crystal energy matrix, there are various approaches that need to be considered. Still, using the same example of someone desiring better health, let's examine the Color Wheel and see which color ray is needed.

In looking at the Color Wheel, it is again useful if we have precisely defined what we desire. Perhaps we want to improve our health by getting stronger. A scarlet talisman would be appropriate. Scarlet is the color ray of influence for physical strength. Maybe we want to improve our health by becoming more active. Then a yellow or perhaps an orange one would be useful. As you can discern, there are many paths to most goals. Selecting a talisman can help you narrow down many paths to a single path that you can travel. Already the power of talismans is beginning to help by illuminating the path to your goal. Pick the color most aligned with your need, using the Color Wheel and the tables provided.

Applying the Fourth Secret of Talismans

Once you have identified the crystal energy structure needed and the color ray that best suits your desire, the next step is to harness the basic earth power of talismans. In this step, you must refine your goal even further and decide what kind of change is needed to accomplish your goal. At this point, you will find you may have several choices, a few choices, a single choice, or none at all! There are not talismans of all crystalline structures in all colors in all earth power types. The mineral kingdom is rich, but not that rich. If you find you have several choices, then select the one that seems best. If none exist, you will have to start over and find a new path to your goal.

Continuing our example, perhaps we are seeking to improve our health by growing some real muscles to gain strength. We might consider either a Seeker or an Enhancer. Then we could further refine our selection by choosing either a green crystal to give us the green ray of growth or a scarlet crystal for its effects on physical strength. We could then carefully apply the Fourth Secret and decide that we really want to transform ourselves by building new muscles. This would tell us to select a green Seeker or Enhancer talisman from the Transformer class. Another way to travel this path might be to focus on just the building of strength. A Builder-class talisman would work in this case. It is important to consider various paths and ways to travel those paths. Although as mentioned earlier, not every path is available, the good news is there is a path to help us focus on achieving virtually every goal conceivable.

In our example we have decided to first focus on growing our strength, so we are going to choose a green Seeker or Enhancer crystal from either the Transformer or the Builder class. Let's see if any such talisman exists.

Looking into the listing of Enhancer crystal structures for green Transformers, using the charts in the color insert, we find there are really no common minerals that fit the bill. Cuprite and spinel are Enhancer crystals that form in the Transformer class, but spinel is the only green one. In the Seeker crystal class there are a few from which to choose. Chrysoprase is a light green crystalline form of quartz. Green sapphires are also Seeker crystals in the Transformer class. In the Builder class, green calcite is available in the Seeker crystal structure. Refining the selection, a review of the power of the green color ray reveals that light green is the color of spiritual growth and darker shades are for physical purposes. Since chrysoprase is found only in light shades of green, the best choice for our purpose seems to be a green sapphire. These crystals come in darker shades that are perfect for our purpose. Since they are found both in opaque and in transparent crystals, they can be used as Personal talismans. Since we often go to health clubs and gyms to build new muscles, a faceted green sapphire would be an excellent choice for our example.

We might later decide that we are concerned with maintaining the new physical strength we possess. That might at first lead us to looking for a Guardian that possesses the scarlet ray of influence. We would particularly desire a dark scarlet ray because it is the specific ray of physical strength. We find that realgar is available. However, in checking its properties we learn it is an unstable mineral, and therefore not well suited for our purpose. We might then look into an Enhancer. Here we find that nature has provided us with several species of garnets that provide the scarlet ray of influence. One of the grossular garnets will work nicely. They are from the Buffer class of minerals and give us the earth power of promoting stability and balance. They are hard and durable. They will be perfect.

Applying the First and Fifth Secrets of Talismans

The process of selecting a talisman to this point has just directed us to a particular mineral species and color. The next step is to select a particular crystal or stone for our exact purpose. Applying the First Secret of Talismans, we know we need to ensure that we are selecting a natural crystal or mineral, not a fake or synthetic one. Applying the Fifth Secret we seek to acquire either a Specimen talisman, or a Personal talisman of the appropriate shape. In our example we are looking for a talisman to aid us in focusing and magnifying our efforts to grow stronger by building new muscles. A Seeker or Enhancer should be formed to provide direction and focus. A round or spherical design would not be helpful. A triangular cut with a sharp focus would be best. A heart shape or wand would work as well.

Applying the Sixth Secret of Talismans

The final step is to apply the Sixth Secret of Talismans to our selected talisman. Enhancing its powers by connecting it to the focused Life Force of the planet Earth will significantly magnify its powers. Since we have a talisman that contains the green ray of influence, we can either take it to Stonehenge on the vernal equinox or use our bluestone ring and turquoise Transport talisman on the vernal equinox to connect it to the focused Life Force. Our talisman will certainly work well without this step; it just won't have maximum power.

At this point we will have used natural green sapphire that has been faceted and connected to the focused Life Force of the planet Earth to make a powerful Seeker/Transformer talisman almost ready to focus and amplify our abilities to become physically stronger.

Through this process, talismans for every purpose can be selected. It takes some time and effort, and a bit of flexibility to find the right path and the right talisman, but it works.

Activation of a Talisman

Now that we know how to select a talisman, we need to understand how to activate it and how to use it.

Activating a talisman is actually one of the easiest aspects of making, selecting, and using talismans, but it is a vital step. Activation releases the energy flow from the talisman to the human mind, and focuses it on the exact desire to be accomplished. This process aligns the natural crystal energy, the earth power, and the color ray of the talisman to the exact human desire. Should this step not be done, or done improperly, the power of the talisman will still be there; it just won't be working for any purpose. It will be like a battery in a flashlight that is turned off—available but unused.

Since we have harnessed the energy of the earth forces in selecting the talisman's crystal energy and earth power, and we have harnessed the energy of the sun in the color ray of influence, all that is left to complete the talisman is to harness the power of the moon. The cool light of the moon is needed to give completeness to the talisman, and to allow us to focus on exactly what we seek. The process is simple. Take the talisman in your hand in the light of the moon. While looking directly at the talisman illuminated by the light of the moon, state your goal exactly and clearly, and feel the energy lines form between you and the talisman. This can take from a few seconds to a few minutes, depending on the strength of your desire and the exactness of the match to the talisman's intrinsic power. Exact matches take but a few seconds. Selecting a talisman imprecisely can make this take several minutes. If you do not feel the energy align, you need to either clarify the goal or select a different talisman. Once you have done this step with any particular talisman, it need not be repeated. You will find the talisman will always be ready to amplify and focus your efforts whenever you use it.

Using a Talisman—The Principle of Causal Duality

The final step in making, selecting, and using talismans is to actually use the talisman to focus, multiply, and enhance your own power. Remember, a talisman is not a lucky stone. It doesn't do anything on its own; it is a conduit. A talisman works through the process of Causal Duality.

Causal Duality is the final key to unlocking the last Secret of Talismans. Once you understand what this principle involves and you know how to apply it, you will have mastered all the Secrets of Talismans. You will be able to use the crystal energy matrices and the fundamental earth power of talismans. You will know how to get the most from the color rays of influence. You will be able to make talismans work.

The principle of Causal Duality is simple to understand, but it can be both easy and hard to use. The principle states that equal benefit comes from action toward a goal and inaction away from it. The causes of our success are to be found both in efforts to move forward and in the absence of actions that can cause us to move backward. Many people do not achieve their goals because they do not understand this principle and they do not apply it. Consider the case of people trying to become happier. Many times they work only on efforts to do things that will make them feel better. They forget the efforts of avoiding complaining or becoming angry at little things that may be sapping their good humor. Or consider the person who desires a better relationship with a spouse. He or she may focus on doing new, more thoughtful things for his or her mate, but neglect the correction of actions that cause friction. Causal Duality tells us effort must have both positive and negative elements and must stay in balance. The journey to a goal consists of daily efforts to both move toward the goal and to avoid moving away from it.

Using a talisman harnesses the power of Causal Duality. To use a talisman, each day take the talisman in your hand. Clear you mind, and carefully state your desire. This is exactly the process used in activating it, except moonlight is not needed. Now the second important part is to apply the power of Causal Duality. At this point, while still holding the talisman, state one thing that you will do that day that will move you closer to your goal. And equally importantly, state one thing you will refrain from doing that would have moved you away from that goal. Although this thought is simple, the idea is profound and key to the successful use of any talisman. Remember, a talisman focuses and amplifies your personal powers and abilities. You have to use it. It is a tool, not a magic wand. If you use it, it will work for you. If you don't use it, it can't help. So each day, take the talisman in your hand. Clear your mind. Carefully state your desire. Then state one thing you will do that day to further your goal. Finally, state one thing you will avoid doing that will keep you from attaining your goal. Then, if you have a Specimen talisman, put it where you will see it during the day, if possible. If you have a Personal talisman, put it in a safe place on your person, where you can see it, and feel its energy and power during the day.

Now consider: if in a single year, you did 365 actions that would move you closer to your goal, and you refrained from taking 365 actions that might thwart your efforts, it is extraordinarily likely that at the end of a single year you will be far down the path to any goal. Some will not take so long; some will take much longer. It doesn't matter. The process is exactly the same. The talisman will focus your energy and it will multiply it with its internal crystal matrix and its fundamental power of the Life Force on this planet.

Selecting and Using a Talisman—An Example

STEP ONE: To begin any use of a talisman or amulet, you must decide what you desire to accomplish.

Example: "I want to be more attractive by losing some excess weight."

STEP TWO: Turn to the Second Secret chapter and read the descriptions of each of the six crystal types, or refer to the charts to determine what crystal energy structure you need.

*Example: "I think I need an Enhancer. Enhancers have the crystal energy to help me improve my life. Or maybe I need a Dispeller. Actually, that would be better. Dispellers are used specifically to get rid of things I have but don't want. That excess weight is exactly what I have and don't want. OK, a **Dispeller** it is."*

STEP THREE: Turn to the Third Secret chapter and read the descriptions of the color rays of influence. Refer to the Color Wheel or the tables to find the color of talisman or amulet you need.

*Example: "Well I see that gold is the color of happiness, and I will be happy when the weight is off. However, I see that turquoise is the color ray of balance. Maybe I need to focus on just getting my body back in balance, free of the excess weight. OK, the table agrees; it says turquoise is for losing weight and restoring balance. I need a talisman that has the **turquoise** ray. Now, I wonder if there are any Dispellers that come in turquoise?"*

STEP FOUR: Review the Fourth Secret chapter and also refer to the color insert tables. Determine if any minerals exist that fit your quest.

*Example: "Turning to the color tables, I found the **Dispeller and Restorer** tables that have the turquoise rows. I see I can use aragonite, a talisman with the **Builder** earth power; or topaz, a talisman with the **Strengthener** earth power; or shattuckite, a **Harmonizer**; or cavansite, a **Bonder**. I have some good choices."*

STEP FIVE: If choices are available, go to step six. If nothing is available, repeat the first four steps and look for a different approach.

STEP SIX: Review the descriptions found in the Fourth Secret to narrow down your choice to the best one.

Example: "OK, according to the book, Builders are generally for making something new from something that already exists. Well, I am trying to build a new body, so maybe the ara-

*gonite will be good. Strengtheners, according to the chapter, are sometimes called Resisters because they are good for resisting temptations and strengthening willpower. Wow, that would be exactly what I need. But, let's check the other two. The Harmonizers are used for smoothing a path through difficulties. Well, dieting will be difficult. I could use some help making it easier. The Harmonizer might be a good choice too. There was also a Bonder available. Bonders I see are for getting people to agree and getting people working together. Not too good for my purpose. Well, I think the topaz is my best bet if I can find a turquoise-colored one. If not, I don't know what shattuckite is, but it will also work. So I need either a turquoise-colored **topaz** or **shattuckite**. Got it."*

STEP SEVEN: Find the necessary material for your talisman. Make sure it is natural. Refer to The Fifth Secret to determine if you need a Personal talisman or if a Specimen one will work. If you need a Personal talisman, again refer to the Fifth Secret chapter to determine what shape you need.

Example: "I searched the Internet, and I found that shattuckite is only found in groups of very small crystals, so it is only available as a Specimen talisman. I think I need something to carry around to remind me not to eat too much. The topaz is a gemstone that is fairly common. I found that topaz comes in quite a few colors, and I found several sources listed on various websites. The Fifth Secret chapter points out that the best shapes for a Barrier talisman include cubes and blocks and solid chunky cuts that appear substantial. I'll look for some square-cut turquoise-colored topaz. That will be perfect."

STEP EIGHT: Using the knowledge of the Sixth Secret of Talismans, next connect the talisman to the focused Universal Life Force by either taking it to Stonehenge, or using your bluestone ring and Transport talisman at the appropriate time.

Example: "OK, I know that turquoise, green, and olive talismans are connected to the focused Life Force at the vernal equinox. Well, it is quite a while until the vernal equinox, and I want to use my talisman now. I know that my new turquoise-colored topaz will be a much more potent talisman after I connect it to the focused Life Force at the vernal equinox, but for now, I will at least begin using its considerable power and energy. Since I don't have a trip planned to England any time soon, I will plan to use my bluestone ring and turquoise Transport talisman on the vernal equinox and supercharge my talisman."

STEP NINE: Follow the guidance in the Seventh Secret to activate and use the talisman.

Example: "OK, I have taken the talisman out into the moonlight, held it in my hand, and stated my goal of losing thirty pounds by Christmas. I start each day by holding the talisman and deciding one thing I am going to do to help me lose weight, and one thing I am going to refrain from doing that would make me gain weight. I carry the stone with me and look at it often during the day. I feel its power helping. I am succeeding each day."

Summary

The Seventh Secret of Talismans reveals how to use a talisman effectively. The Secret is to select a talisman using the first six Secrets. Then it must be activated to harness the power of the moon. After activation, the Secret tells us we must use the principle of Causal Duality to allow our talisman to amplify and focus our personal power by combining it with the Life Force of the planet Earth. As we have explored the Seven Secrets of Talismans, we have learned that talismans are indeed wondrous objects that can focus our energy to accomplish the seemingly impossible. They can magnify our abilities through combining them with the Universal Life Force and the Life Force of the planet Earth. They can help us gain what we seek, improve upon what we possess, guard our health and life, protect us from adversity, and help us rid ourselves of afflictions. Until now, their secrets had been undiscovered and their powers had been hidden. But their secrets have been revealed. We now understand what was previously thought to be magic. We know how to make talismans that actually work! We have learned the Seven Secrets of Talismans.

APPENDIX ONE

The Seven Secrets of Talismans

I

The power of a talisman comes from the natural energy of the sun, the moon, and the planet Earth.

II

Nature has hidden crystal energy structures in virtually all minerals. Each mineral has a specific crystal energy structure that controls its power. These crystal energy structures are completely aligned with basic human needs.

III

The color influence rays of talismans align the power of the crystals to the power of our minds.

IV

Even deeper within the crystal matrix is hidden the fundamental, elemental earth power of the stone—its raw chemical power base. The very atoms and molecules of carbon, silicon, oxygen, and other elements give minerals their fundamental earth power and form the building blocks of the crystal energy matrices.

V

Talismans must be made in a way that is consistent with the intrinsic power and energy of the mineral and matched to its potential uses in focusing and magnifying human power.

VI

Talismans gain tremendous power when connected physically and spiritually to places and times of highly focused Life Force energy.

VII

Talismans must be selected, activated, and used according to their special powers and in alignment with the desires of a human mind.

APPENDIX TWO

Listing of Common Talismans

The mineral kingdom consists of about six thousand recognized species of minerals. In addition, the jewelry and mineral marketplace has given these minerals a variety of common and trade names. For example, cerian is actually the mineral vesuvianite. Copper nickel is the trade name of nickeline. There are hundreds of varieties of quartz. Most of these are names of unique colorations found only in a certain location. Examples include crazy lace agate, fallen tree thundereggs, and Ellensburg blue agate. With the constant pressures in the marketplace to innovate, there is constant change in the names of many minerals and rocks as individuals try to market their wares as new and different.

The listing presented here provides a reference to some of the more common minerals and trade names. The valid mineral species are in BLOCK CAPITALS. The trade or common names are in small letters and cross-referenced to their proper species. For example, the entry for desert rose (a trade name) shows it is actually the mineral BARITE.

In the event that a mineral or crystal is not listed, an Internet search will find it quickly. At the time of the writing of this book, www.mindat.org was the most complete listing. By identifying the mineral's species, its crystal structure and mineral classification can be determined. These can then be used to find its talismanic properties by referring to the tables at the end of the Second Secret chapter and the color insert in this book. For example, touchonite is not listed. By searching for it on the Internet, the listing at www.mindat.org says it is another name for carnelian. The entry for carnelian states that carnelian is quartz. The listing for quartz shows that it forms in the hexagonal crystal system and is a Class IV oxide. The listings in the Second Secret chapter tell us that the hexagonal crystals are Seekers. The tables in the color insert tell us that Class IV oxides are Transformers. So a touchonite is a Seeker/Transformer talisman. In this manner, any mineral's or crystal's talismanic properties can be determined.

Common Name or MINERAL	MINERAL	Crystal Matrix	Earth Power
Abraciated Jasper	Jasper QUARTZ	Seeker/Simplifier	Transformer
Acanthite	ARGENTITE	Enhancer	Mirror
Achroite	ELBAITE TOURMALINE	Seeker/Simplifier	Energizer
Acmite	AEGIRINE	Guardian/Dreamholder	Harmonizer
ACTINOLITE		Guardian/Dreamholder	Harmonizer
ADAMITE		Dispeller/Restorer	Buffer
Adularia	Moonstone ORTHOCLASE/ ALBITE	Guardian/Dreamholder/ Barrier	Filter
AEGIRINE		Guardian/Dreamholder	Harmonizer
AFGHANITE		Seeker/Simplifier	Filter
African Jade	GROSSULAR	Enhancer	Strengthener
African Queen Picture Jasper	Jasper QUARTZ	Seeker/Simplifier	Transformer
Agalmatolite	PYROPHYLLITE	Guardian/Dreamholder	Bonder
AGARDITE		Seeker/Simplifier	Buffer
Agate	Chalcedony QUARTZ	Seeker/Simplifier	Transformer
Agate Jasper	Jasper QUARTZ	Seeker/Simplifier	Transformer
Agatized Coral	Agate Chalcedony QUARTZ	Seeker/Simplifier	Transformer
AJOITE		Barrier	Bonder
Alabaster	GYPSUM	Guardian/Dreamholder	Solidifier
ALBITE		Barrier	Filter
ALEXANDRITE	CHRYSOBERYL	Dispeller/Restorer	Transformer
ALLANITE		Guardian/Dreamholder	Strengthener
ALMANDINE (Garnet)		Enhancer	Strengthener
Almandine Spar	EUDIALYTE	Seeker/Simplifier	Energizer
Almandite (Garnet)	ALMANDINE	Enhancer	Strengthener
Aluminilite	ALUNITE	Seeker/Simplifier	Solidifier
ALUNITE		Seeker/Simplifier	Solidifier
Amazonite	MICROCLINE	Barrier	Filter
Amber	not a crystal	none	none
Amberine	Agate Chalcedony QUARTZ	Seeker/Simplifier	Transformer
AMBLYGONITE		Barrier	Buffer
Amethyst	QUARTZ	Seeker/Simplifier	Transformer

Common Name or MINERAL	MINERAL	Crystal Matrix	Earth Power
Amethyst Sage Agate	Agate Chalcedony QUARTZ	Seeker/Simplifier	Transformer
Ametrine	QUARTZ	Seeker/Simplifier	Transformer
Ammolite	amorphous	mixed	mixed
Ammonite	fossil	mixed	mixed
ANALCIME		Barrier	Filter
Analcite	ANALCIME	Barrier	Filter
ANATASE		Attractor	Transformer
ANDALUSITE		Dispeller/Restorer	Strengthener
ANDESINE		Barrier	Filter
Andesite	a rock	mixed	mixed
ANDRADITE		Enhancer	Strengthener
Angelsite	ANHYDRITE	Dispeller/Restorer	Solidifier
ANGLESITE		Dispeller/Restorer	Solidifier
ANHYDRITE		Dispeller/Restorer	Solidifier
ANKERITE		Seeker/Simplifier	Builder
ANNABERGITE		Guardian/Dreamholder	Buffer
Anorthosite	a rock	mixed	mixed
ANTHOPHYLLITE		Dispeller/Restorer	Harmonizer
ANTIGORITE	Serpentine	Guardian/Dreamholder	Bonder
ANTIMONY		Seeker/Simplifier	Purifier
ANTLERITE		Dispeller/Restorer	Solidifier
Anyolite	ZOISITE	Dispeller/Restorer	Unifier
Apache Gold	glass (not a crystal)	glass	glass
Apache Tear	glass (not a crystal)	glass	glass
APATITE		Seeker/Simplifier	Buffer
Aphrizite	TOURMALINE	Seeker/Simplifier	Energizer
APOPHYLLITE		Attractor	Bonder
Aquamarine	BERYL	Seeker/Simplifier	Energizer
ARAGONITE		Dispeller/Restorer	Builder
ARFVEDSONITE		Guardian/Dreamholder	Harmonizer
ARGENTITE		Enhancer	Mirror
ARROJADITE		Guardian/Dreamholder	Buffer
Arroyo Picture Jasper	Jasper QUARTZ	Seeker/Simplifier	Transformer
ARSENOPYRITE		Guardian/Dreamholder	Mirror
ARTHURITE		Guardian/Dreamholder	Buffer
ARTINITE		Guardian/Dreamholder	Builder

Continued on next page

Common Name or MINERAL	MINERAL	Crystal Matrix	Earth Power
ASTROPHYLLITE		Barrier	Bonder
ATACAMITE		Dispeller/Restorer	Brightener
ATELESTITE		Guardian/Dreamholder	Buffer
Atlantisite	Serpentine with STICHTITE	Guardian/Dreamholder	Bonder
AUGITE		Guardian/Dreamholder	Harmonizer
AURICHALCITE		Dispeller/Restorer	Builder
Australian Jasper	Red/White Chalcedony QUARTZ	Seeker/Simplifier	Transformer
Aventurine	QUARTZ	Seeker/Simplifier	Transformer
AXINITE		Barrier	Energizer
Azeztulite	QUARTZ	Seeker/Simplifier	Transformer
Azulicite	SANIDINE	Guardian/Dreamholder	Filter
AZURITE		Guardian/Dreamholder	Builder
Azurite-Malachite	mixed minerals	Guardian/Dreamholder	Builder
Azurlite	Turquoise Chalcedony QUARTZ	Seeker/Simplifier	Transformer
BABINGTONITE		Barrier	Harmonizer
BAKERITE		Guardian/Dreamholder	Strengthener
Ballas	CARBON (Sphere Diamond)	Enhancer	Purifier
Band (or Banded) Jasper	Jasper QUARTZ	Seeker/Simplifier	Transformer
BARITE		Dispeller/Restorer	Solidifier
Basalt	a rock	mixed	mixed
Basalt Bomb	FORSTERITE	Dispeller/Restorer	Strengthener
Basanite	Jasper Chalcedony QUARTZ	Seeker/Simplifier	Transformer
Basinite	Chalcedony QUARTZ	Seeker/Simplifier	Transformer
BASTNASITE		Seeker/Simplifier	Builder
Bayate	Jasper QUARTZ	Seeker/Simplifier	Transformer
BAYLDONITE		Guardian/Dreamholder	Builder
BENITOITE		Seeker/Simplifier	Energizer
BERTHIERITE		Dispeller/Restorer	Mirror
BERTRANDITE		Dispeller/Restorer	Unifier
BERYL		Seeker/Simplifier	Energizer
BERYLLONITE		Guardian/Dreamholder	Buffer
Beta Quartz	QUARTZ	Seeker/Simplifier	Transformer
Bi-color Quartz	QUARTZ	Seeker/Simplifier	Transformer
Bi-color Sapphire	CORUNDUM	Seeker/Simplifier	Transformer
Bi-color Tourmaline	TOURMALINE	Seeker/Simplifier	Energizer

Common Name or MINERAL	MINERAL	Crystal Matrix	Earth Power
Biggs Jasper	Jasper QUARTZ	Seeker/Simplifier	Transformer
Biggs Picture Jasper	Jasper QUARTZ	Seeker/Simplifier	Transformer
Binghamite	Hawk's Eye Chalcedony QUARTZ	Seeker/Simplifier	Transformer
Binnite	TENNANTITE	Enhancer	Mirror
BIOTITE		Guardian/Dreamholder	Bonder
Biotite Lens	BIOTITE	Guardian/Dreamholder	Bonder
Bird of Paradise	Brown Jasper QUARTZ	Seeker/Simplifier	Transformer
Bismuth	synthetic only	mixed	mixed
Bismuth Crystals	synthetic only	mixed	mixed
Black Diamond	CARBON (Diamond)	Enhancer	Purifier
Black Lead	CARBON (Graphite)	Seeker/Simplifier	Purifier
Black Onyx	Dyed Chalcedony QUARTZ	Seeker/Simplifier	Transformer
Black Skin Agate	Agate Chalcedony QUARTZ	Seeker/Simplifier	Transformer
Black Spinel	SPINEL	Enhancer	Transformer
Black Star Diopside	DIOPSIDE	Guardian/Dreamholder	Harmonizer
Black Star Sapphire	CORUNDUM	Seeker/Simplifier	Transformer
Black Tourmaline	TOURMALINE	Seeker/Simplifier	Energizer
Black Zebra Agate	Agate Chalcedony QUARTZ	Seeker/Simplifier	Transformer
Blackjack	SPHALERITE	Enhancer	Mirror
BLENDE	SPHALERITE	Enhancer	Mirror
Blood Agate	Agate Chalcedony QUARTZ	Seeker/Simplifier	Transformer
Blood Jasper	Bloodstone Chalcedony QUARTZ	Seeker/Simplifier	Transformer
Bloodstone	Chalcedony QUARTZ	Seeker/Simplifier	Transformer
Blue Asbestos	Crocidolite RIEBECKITE	Guardian/Dreamholder	Harmonizer
Blue Chalcedony Quartz	Chalcedony QUARTZ	Seeker/Simplifier	Transformer
Blue Chrysoprase	Chalcedony QUARTZ	Seeker/Simplifier	Transformer
Blue Lace Agate	Chalcedony QUARTZ	Seeker/Simplifier	Transformer
Blue Mist Chalcedony Quartz	Chalcedony QUARTZ	Seeker/Simplifier	Transformer
Blue Moonstone	ORTHOCLASE	Guardian/Dreamholder	Filter
Blue Mountain Picture Jasper	Jasper QUARTZ	Seeker/Simplifier	Transformer
Blue Sapphire	CORUNDUM	Seeker/Simplifier	Transformer
Blue Spinel	SPINEL	Enhancer	Transformer
Blue Star Sapphire	CORUNDUM	Seeker/Simplifier	Transformer
Blue Topaz	TOPAZ	Dispeller/Restorer	Strengthener
Bluebird	AZURITE with CUPRITE	Guardian/Dreamholder	Builder

Continued on next page

Common Name or MINERAL	MINERAL	Crystal Matrix	Earth Power
Bog Iron Ore	GOETHITE	Dispeller/Restorer	Transformer
Boji Stone	mixed minerals (a rock)	mixed	mixed
BOLEITE		Attractor	Brightener
Bologna Stone	BARITE	Dispeller/Restorer	Solidifier
BOLTWOODITE		Guardian/Dreamholder	Strengthener
Bonamite	SMITHSONITE	Seeker/Simplifier	Builder
BORACITE	usually artificial	Dispeller/Restorer	Transformer
BORAX		Guardian/Dreamholder	Transformer
BORNITE		Enhancer	Mirror
Botswana Agate	Chalcedony QUARTZ	Seeker/Simplifier	Transformer
BOULANGERITE		Enhancer	Mirror
BOURNONITE		Dispeller/Restorer	Mirror
Bowenite	ANTIGORITE (Serpentine)	Guardian/Dreamholder	Bonder
Bravoite	PYRITE	Enhancer	Mirror
Brazil Agate	Agate Chalcedony QUARTZ	Seeker/Simplifier	Transformer
BRAZILIANITE		Guardian/Dreamholder	Buffer
Breccia	Agate Chalcedony QUARTZ	Seeker/Simplifier	Transformer
Brecciated Jasper	Jasper QUARTZ	Seeker/Simplifier	Transformer
Breislakite	ILVAITE	Dispeller/Restorer	Unifier
Breithauptite	NICKELINE	Seeker/Simplifier	Mirror
BROCHANTITE		Guardian/Dreamholder	Solidifier
Bronzite	ENSTATITE	Dispeller/Restorer	Harmonizer
BROOKITE		Dispeller/Restorer	Transformer
Brown Spar	CALCITE	Seeker/Simplifier	Builder
Bruneau Jasper	Brown/White Chalcedony QUARTZ	Seeker/Simplifier	Transformer
Bruno Canyon Jasper	Jasper QUARTZ	Seeker/Simplifier	Transformer
Buchanan Thundereggs	Agate Chalcedony QUARTZ	Seeker/Simplifier	Transformer
BUERGERITE	TOURMALINE	Seeker/Simplifier	Energizer
BULTFONTEINITE		Barrier	Strengthener
Burrow Creek Jasper	Jasper QUARTZ	Seeker/Simplifier	Transformer
BUSTAMITE		Barrier	Harmonizer
Butterstone	a rock	mixed	mixed
BYTOWNITE		Barrier	Filter
CACHEMIRINE Garnet		Enhancer	Strengthener
Cactus Quartz	QUARTZ	Seeker/Simplifier	Transformer
Calamine	SMITHSONITE	Seeker/Simplifier	Builder

Common Name or MINERAL	MINERAL	Crystal Matrix	Earth Power
CALCITE		Seeker/Simplifier	Builder
CALEDONITE		Dispeller/Restorer	Solidifier
California Moonstone	Chalcedony QUARTZ	Seeker/Simplifier	Transformer
Californite	VESUVIANITE	Attractor	Unifier
Cambay	Carnelian Chalcedony QUARTZ	Seeker/Simplifier	Transformer
Cameo (Agate)	Agate Chalcedony QUARTZ	Seeker/Simplifier	Transformer
Campylite	MIMETITE	Seeker/Simplifier	Buffer
Canadian Ocean Rock	Jasper QUARTZ	Seeker/Simplifier	Transformer
Canary Stone	Yellow Chalcedony QUARTZ	Seeker/Simplifier	Transformer
Candy Rock	Jasper QUARTZ	Seeker/Simplifier	Transformer
Carbonatite	a rock	mixed	mixed
Carbuncle	ALMANDINE Garnet	Enhancer	Strengthener
Caribbean Blue Chalcedony	Chalcedony QUARTZ	Seeker/Simplifier	Transformer
CARLETONITE		Attractor	Bonder
CARMINITE		Dispeller/Restorer	Buffer
Carnelian	Chalcedony QUARTZ	Seeker/Simplifier	Transformer
Carnelian Onyx	Sardonyx Chalcedony QUARTZ	Seeker/Simplifier	Transformer
CARNOTITE		Guardian/Dreamholder	Buffer
Carrie Plume Agate	Agate Chalcedony QUARTZ	Seeker/Simplifier	Transformer
CASSITERITE (Tin Oxide)		Attractor	Transformer
Catalinaite	Jasper QUARTZ	Seeker/Simplifier	Transformer
Cathedral Agate	Agate Chalcedony QUARTZ	Seeker/Simplifier	Transformer
Cat's Eye	CHRYSOBERYL	Dispeller/Restorer	Transformer
Cat's Eye Apatite	APATITE	Seeker/Simplifier	Buffer
Cat's Eye Diopside	DIOPSIDE	Guardian/Dreamholder	Harmonizer
Cat's Eye Enstatite	ENSTATITE	Dispeller/Restorer	Harmonizer
Cat's Eye Jade	NEPHRITE	Guardian	Harmonizer
Cat's Eye Kornerupine	KORNERUPINE	Dispeller/Restorer	Strengthener
Cat's Eye Opal	amorphous	mixed	mixed
Cat's Eye Tourmaline	ELBAITE	Seeker/Simplifier	Energizer
CAVANSITE		Dispeller/Restorer	Bonder
Cave Creek Jasper	Red Jasper QUARTZ	Seeker/Simplifier	Transformer
Caviar Agate	Chert QUARTZ	Seeker/Simplifier	Transformer
CELESTINE		Dispeller/Restorer	Solidifier
Celestite	CELESTINE	Dispeller/Restorer	Solidifier

Continued on next page

Common Name or MINERAL	MINERAL	Crystal Matrix	Earth Power
Ceragate	Yellow Chalcedony QUARTZ	Seeker/Simplifier	Transformer
Cerian	VESUVIANITE	Attractor	Unifier
CERULÉITE		Barrier	Buffer
CERUSSITE		Dispeller/Restorer	Builder
Cervantite	STIBNITE	Dispeller/Restorer	Mirror
CHABAZITE		Seeker/Simplifier	Filter
CHALCANTHITE		Barrier	Solidifier
Chalcedony	QUARTZ	Seeker/Simplifier	Transformer
CHALCOPHYLLITE		Seeker/Simplifier	Buffer
CHALCOPYRITE		Attractor	Mirror
Chalcotrichite	CUPRITE	Enhancer	Transformer
Chalk	Limestone (a rock)	mixed	mixed
Champagne Citrine	QUARTZ	Seeker/Simplifier	Transformer
Chapinite	Jasper QUARTZ	Seeker/Simplifier	Transformer
CHAROITE		Guardian/Dreamholder	Harmonizer
CHENEVIXITE		Guardian/Dreamholder	Solidifier
Chessylite	AZURITE	Guardian/Dreamholder	Builder
Chiastolite	ANDALUSITE	Dispeller/Restorer	Strengthener
Chicken Track Picture Jasper	Jasper QUARTZ	Seeker/Simplifier	Transformer
CHILDRENITE		Dispeller/Restorer	Buffer
Chinese Opal	White Chalcedony QUARTZ	Seeker/Simplifier	Transformer
Chinese Turquoise	TURQUOISE	Barrier	Buffer
Chloanthite	SKUTTERUDITE	Enhancer	Mirror
Chlorapatite	APATITE	Seeker/Simplifier	Buffer
Chlorastrolite	PUMPELLYITE	Guardian/Dreamholder	Unifier
Chloromelanite	Nebula Stone (a rock)	a rock	a rock
Chrome Chalcedony	Green Chalcedony QUARTZ	Seeker/Simplifier	Transformer
Chrome Diopside	DIOPSIDE	Guardian/Dreamholder	Harmonizer
Chrome Tourmaline	TOURMALINE	Seeker/Simplifier	Energizer
CHRYSOBERYL		Guardian/Dreamholder	Buffer
CHRYSOCOLLA		Dispeller/Restorer	Energizer
Chrysojasper	Green Jasper QUARTZ	Seeker/Simplifier	Transformer
Chrysolite	FAYALITE	Dispeller/Restorer	Strengthener
Chrysoprase	Chalcedony QUARTZ	Seeker/Simplifier	Transformer
Chrysotile	Serpentine	Guardian/Dreamholder	Filter
CINNABAR		Seeker/Simplifier	Mirror
Cinnabar Matrix	Red Jasper QUARTZ	Seeker/Simplifier	Transformer

Common Name or MINERAL	MINERAL	Crystal Matrix	Earth Power
Cinnamon Stone	GROSSULAR	Enhancer	Strengthener
Citrine	QUARTZ	Seeker/Simplifier	Transformer
Clarkeite	Gummite (a rock)	mixed	mixed
Clay	a rock	mixed	mixed
Clay Ironstone	SIDERITE	Seeker/Simplifier	Builder
Cleavelandite	ALBITE	Barrier	Filter
CLINOCHLORE		Guardian/Dreamholder	Bonder
CLINOCLASE		Guardian/Dreamholder	Buffer
CLINOHUMITE		Guardian/Dreamholder	Strengthener
Cloud Agate	Agate Chalcedony QUARTZ	Seeker/Simplifier	Transformer
COBALT (Co)	synthetic only	mixed	mixed
Cobalt Bloom	ERYTHRITE	Guardian/Dreamholder	Buffer
Cobaltian Calcite	CALCITE	Seeker/Simplifier	Builder
Cobaltian Dolomite	DOLOMITE	Seeker/Simplifier	Builder
COBALTITE		Dispeller/Restorer	Mirror
Cog Wheel Ore	BOURNONITE	Dispeller/Restorer	Mirror
COLEMANITE		Guardian/Dreamholder	Builder
COLUMBITE		Dispeller/Restorer	Transformer
CONICHALCITE		Dispeller/Restorer	Buffer
CONNELLITE		Seeker/Simplifier	Solidifier
COPPER (Cu)		Enhancer	Purifier
Copper Blooms	COPPER	Enhancer	Purifier
Copper Nickel	NICKELINE	Seeker/Simplifier	Mirror
CORDIERITE		Dispeller/Restorer	Energizer
CORNETITE		Dispeller/Restorer	Buffer
CORUNDUM		Seeker/Simplifier	Transformer
Cotton Balls	ULEXITE	Barrier	Builder
COVELLITE		Seeker/Simplifier	Mirror
Crazy Lace Agate	Agate Chalcedony QUARTZ	Seeker/Simplifier	Transformer
CREEDITE		Guardian/Dreamholder	Buffer
Creolite	Red/White Jasper QUARTZ	Seeker/Simplifier	Transformer
Cripple Creek Picture Jasper	Jasper QUARTZ	Seeker/Simplifier	Transformer
Crocidolite	RIEBECKITE	Guardian/Dreamholder	Harmonizer
CROCOITE		Guardian/Dreamholder	Solidifier
Cryptoperthite	Moonstone ORTHOCLASE/ ALBITE	Guardian/Dreamholder/ Barrier	Filter
CUPRITE		Enhancer	Transformer

Continued on next page

Common Name or MINERAL	MINERAL	Crystal Matrix	Earth Power
Cuproadamite	ADAMITE	Dispeller/Restorer	Buffer
Cuyunite	Chalcedony QUARTZ	Seeker/Simplifier	Transformer
Cyanite	KYANITE	Barrier	Strengthener
Cymophane	CHRYSOBERYL (Cat's Eye)	Dispeller/Restorer	Transformer
Dallasite	Green/White Jasper QUARTZ	Seeker/Simplifier	Transformer
Dalmatian Jasper	White/Black Jasper QUARTZ	Seeker/Simplifier	Transformer
Damsonite	Lilac Chalcedony QUARTZ	Seeker/Simplifier	Transformer
DANBURITE		Dispeller/Restorer	Unifier
Dark Blue Beryl	Irradiated BERYL	Seeker/Simplifier	Energizer
Dark Ruby Silver	PYRARGYRITE	Seeker/Simplifier	Mirror
DATOLITE		Guardian/Dreamholder	Strengthener
Demion	Carnelian Chalcedony QUARTZ	Seeker/Simplifier	Transformer
Demantoid Garnet	ANDRADITE	Enhancer	Strengthener
Dendritic Agate	Agate QUARTZ	Seeker/Simplifier	Transformer
Denio Dendritic Agate	Agate Chalcedony QUARTZ	Seeker/Simplifier	Transformer
Depalite	Olive Chert QUARTZ	Seeker/Simplifier	Transformer
Deschutes	Jasper QUARTZ	Seeker/Simplifier	Transformer
DESCLOIZITE		Dispeller/Restorer	Buffer
Desert Rose	BARITE	Dispeller/Restorer	Solidifier
Desmine	STILBITE	Enhancer	Filter
Desolation Canyon Thundereggs	Agate Chalcedony QUARTZ	Seeker/Simplifier	Transformer
DIABOLEITE		Attractor	Brightener
Diamond	CARBON	Enhancer	Purifier
DIOPSIDE		Guardian/Dreamholder	Harmonizer
DIOPTASE		Seeker/Simplifier	Energizer
DOLOMITE		Seeker/Simplifier	Builder
Donnybrook Thundereggs	Agate Chalcedony QUARTZ	Seeker/Simplifier	Transformer
Dougway Thundereggs	Agate Chalcedony QUARTZ	Seeker/Simplifier	Transformer
DRAVITE	TOURMALINE	Seeker/Simplifier	Energizer
Drusy Quartz	QUARTZ	Seeker/Simplifier	Transformer
DUFRENITE		Guardian/Dreamholder	Buffer
DUFTITE		Dispeller/Restorer	Buffer
DUMORTIERITE		Dispeller/Restorer	Strengthener
Dumortierite Quartz	Blue QUARTZ	Seeker/Simplifier	Transformer
Dunite	a rock	mixed	mixed

Common Name or MINERAL	MINERAL	Crystal Matrix	Earth Power
Dyed Agate	Dyed Agate Chalcedony QUARTZ	Seeker/Simplifier	Transformer
Eagle Rock Plume Agate	Agate Chalcedony QUARTZ	Seeker/Simplifier	Transformer
Eakleite	XONOTLITE	Guardian/Dreamholder	Harmonizer
EDENITE		Guardian/Dreamholder	Harmonizer
Edinite	Prase Chalcedony QUARTZ	Seeker/Simplifier	Transformer
Egyptian Jasper	Brown Jasper QUARTZ	Seeker/Simplifier	Transformer
ELBAITE TOURMALINE		Seeker/Simplifier	Energizer
Eldoradoite	Blue Chalcedony QUARTZ	Seeker/Simplifier	Transformer
Elephant Jasper	Brown/Black Jasper QUARTZ	Seeker/Simplifier	Transformer
Ellensburg Blue Agate	Agate Chalcedony QUARTZ	Seeker/Simplifier	Transformer
ELPIDITE		Dispeller/Restorer	Bonder
Emerald	BERYL	Seeker/Simplifier	Energizer
EMMONSITE		Barrier	Solidifier
ENARGITE		Dispeller/Restorer	Mirror
ENSTATITE		Dispeller/Restorer	Harmonizer
EOSPHORITE		Dispeller/Restorer	Buffer
EPIDIDYMITE		Dispeller/Restorer	Harmonizer
EPIDOTE		Guardian/Dreamholder	Harmonizer
EPISTILBITE		Guardian/Dreamholder	Filter
ERYTHRITE		Guardian/Dreamholder	Buffer
ETTRINGITE		Seeker/Simplifier	Solidifier
EUCLASE		Guardian/Dreamholder	Bonder
EUDIALYTE		Seeker/Simplifier	Energizer
EUDIDYMITE		Guardian/Dreamholder	Harmonizer
Evening Emerald (Peridot)	FORSTERITE	Dispeller/Restorer	Strengthener
Ezteri	Bloodstone Chalcedony QUARTZ	Seeker/Simplifier	Transformer
Fallen Tree Thundereggs	Agate Chalcedony QUARTZ	Seeker/Simplifier	Transformer
FAYALITE		Dispeller/Restorer	Strengthener
FERBERITE		Guardian/Dreamholder	Solidifier
Ferruginous Quartz	Red QUARTZ	Seeker/Simplifier	Transformer
Fibrolite	SILLIMANITE	Dispeller/Restorer	Strengthener
Fire Agate	Agate Chalcedony QUARTZ	Seeker/Simplifier	Transformer
Fire Opal	amorphous (not a crystal structure)	mixed	mixed
Flame Agate	Agate Chalcedony QUARTZ	Seeker/Simplifier	Transformer

Continued on next page

Common Name or MINERAL	MINERAL	Crystal Matrix	Earth Power
Flint	White/Black Chert QUARTZ	Seeker/Simplifier	Transformer
FLUORAPATITE		Seeker/Simplifier	Buffer
FLUORITE		Enhancer	Brightener
FLUORRICHTERITE		Guardian/Dreamholder	Harmonizer
Fool's Gold	PYRITE	Enhancer	Mirror
FORSTERITE		Dispeller/Restorer	Strengthener
FRANKLINITE		Enhancer	Transformer
Fred Bed Thundereggs	Agate Chalcedony QUARTZ	Seeker/Simplifier	Transformer
Frieda Thundereggs	Agate Chalcedony QUARTZ	Seeker/Simplifier	Transformer
Friend Ranch Thundereggs	Agate Chalcedony QUARTZ	Seeker/Simplifier	Transformer
Frogskin Jasper	Tan/Green Jasper QUARTZ	Seeker/Simplifier	Transformer
Frost Agate	Gray Chalcedony QUARTZ	Seeker/Simplifier	Transformer
Fryite Picture Jasper	Jasper QUARTZ	Seeker/Simplifier	Transformer
Fuchsite	MUSCOVITE	Guardian/Dreamholder	Bonder
Fulgarite	Lechatelierite (glass)	mixed	mixed
GADOLINITE		Guardian/Dreamholder	Strengthener
GAHNITE		Enhancer	Transformer
GALENA		Enhancer	Brightener
Garnet	a mineral group	Enhancer	Strengthener
Garnierite	NÉPOUITE	Dispeller/Restorer	Bonder
GASPEITE		Seeker/Simplifier	Builder
GAYLUSSITE		Guardian/Dreamholder	Builder
GERSDORFFITE		Enhancer	Mirror
GIBBSITE		Guardian/Dreamholder	Transformer
GLAUBERITE		Guardian/Dreamholder	Solidifier
Glory Blue	Blue Chalcedony QUARTZ	Seeker/Simplifier	Transformer
GMELINITE		Seeker/Simplifier	Filter
GOETHITE		Dispeller/Restorer	Transformer
GOLD (Au)		Enhancer	Purifier
Gold Included Quartz	QUARTZ	Seeker/Simplifier	Transformer
Golden Beryl	BERYL	Seeker/Simplifier	Energizer
Golden Sapphire	CORUNDUM	Seeker/Simplifier	Transformer
GOOSECREEKITE		Guardian/Dreamholder	Filter
GORMANITE		Barrier	Buffer
Goshenite	BERYL	Seeker/Simplifier	Energizer
Grandite Garnet	ALMANDINE (mostly)	Enhancer	Strengthener

Common Name or MINERAL	MINERAL	Crystal Matrix	Earth Power
Granite	a rock	mixed	mixed
Granodiorite	a rock	mixed	mixed
GRAPHITE (Carbon)		Enhancer	Purifier
Graveyard Point Plume Agate	Agate Chalcedony QUARTZ	Seeker/Simplifier	Transformer
Green Beryl	BERYL	Seeker/Simplifier	Energizer
Green Gold Quartz	Irradiated QUARTZ	Seeker/Simplifier	Transformer
Green Moonstone	ORTHOCLASE	Guardian/Dreamholder	Filter
Green Moss Agate	Agate Chalcedony QUARTZ	Seeker/Simplifier	Transformer
Green Onyx	Chrysoprase Chalcedony QUARTZ	Seeker/Simplifier	Transformer
Green Sapphire	CORUNDUM	Seeker/Simplifier	Transformer
Green Starstone	Chlorastrolite PUMPELLYITE	Guardian/Dreamholder	Unifier
Green Topaz	TOPAZ	Dispeller/Restorer	Strengthener
Green Tourmaline	ELBAITE TOURMALINE	Seeker/Simplifier	Energizer
Greenstone	Chlorastrolite PUMPELLYITE	Guardian/Dreamholder	Unifier
Gray Moonstone	ORTHOCLASE	Guardian/Dreamholder	Filter
Gray Quartz	QUARTZ	Seeker/Simplifier	Transformer
Gray Star Sapphire	CORUNDUM	Seeker/Simplifier	Transformer
GROSSULAR		Enhancer	Strengthener
Grossular Garnet	GROSSULAR	Enhancer	Strengthener
GUANACOITE		Guardian/Dreamholder	Buffer
GYPSUM		Guardian/Dreamholder	Solidifier
GYROLITE		Barrier	Bonder
Hackmanite	SODALITE	Enhancer	Filter
HALITE		Enhancer	Brightener
HAMBERGITE		Dispeller/Restorer	Builder
Hampton Butte Moss Agate	Agate Chalcedony QUARTZ	Seeker/Simplifier	Transformer
HANKSITE		Seeker/Simplifier	Buffer
HARDYSTONITE		Attractor	Unifier
HAUERITE		Enhancer	Mirror
HAUSMANNITE		Attractor	Transformer
Hawk's Eye	QUARTZ polymorph of Crocidolite	Seeker/Simplifier	Transformer
HEDENBERGITE		Guardian/Dreamholder	Harmonizer
Heliodor	BERYL	Seeker/Simplifier	Energizer
Heliotrope	Bloodstone Chalcedony QUARTZ	Seeker/Simplifier	Transformer

Continued on next page

Common Name or MINERAL	MINERAL	Crystal Matrix	Earth Power
Hemachate	Red Jasper Chalcedony QUARTZ	Seeker/Simplifier	Transformer
HEMATITE		Seeker/Simplifier	Transformer
HEMIMORPHITE		Dispeller/Restorer	Unifier
HENMILITE		Barrier	Builder
Hessonite (Garnet)		Enhancer	Strengthener
Heterosite	PURPURITE	Dispeller/Restorer	Buffer
HEULANDITE		Guardian/Dreamholder	Filter
Hickoryite	Rhyolite (a rock)	mixed	mixed
Hiddenite	SPODUMENE	Guardian/Dreamholder	Harmonizer
Holly Blue	Chalcedony QUARTZ	Seeker/Simplifier	Transformer
Holly Blue Agate	Agate Chalcedony QUARTZ	Seeker/Simplifier	Transformer
HOPEITE		Dispeller/Restorer	Buffer
HORNBLENDE		Guardian/Dreamholder	Harmonizer
Hornstone	Chert QUARTZ	Seeker/Simplifier	Transformer
Hot Pink Topaz	Heat-Treated TOPAZ	Dispeller/Restorer	Strengthener
HOWLITE		Guardian/Dreamholder	Harmonizer
HUBEITE		Barrier	Unifier
HUBNERITE		Guardian/Dreamholder	Transformer
HUMITE		Dispeller/Restorer	Strengthener
HUREAULITE		Guardian/Dreamholder	Buffer
HYDROBORACITE		Guardian/Dreamholder	Builder
HYDROMAGNESITE		Guardian/Dreamholder	Builder
Hydroxylapatite	APATITE	Seeker/Simplifier	Buffer
HYDROZINCITE		Guardian/Dreamholder	Builder
Hypersthene	ENSTATITE	Dispeller/Restorer	Harmonizer
Ice Stone	White Chert QUARTZ	Seeker/Simplifier	Transformer
Iceland Spar (Calcite)	CALCITE	Seeker/Simplifier	Builder
Idocrase	VESUVIANITE	Attractor	Unifier
ILMENITE		Seeker/Simplifier	Transformer
ILVAITE		Dispeller/Restorer	Unifier
Imperial Garnet	SPESSARTINE	Enhancer	Strengthener
Imperial Jasper	Green/Yellow Jasper QUARTZ	Seeker/Simplifier	Transformer
Indian Star Ruby	CORUNDUM	Seeker/Simplifier	Transformer
Indicolite Tourmaline	Blue ELBAITE	Seeker/Simplifier	Energizer
Indigolite	TOURMALINE	Seeker/Simplifier	Energizer
INESITE		Barrier	Harmonizer

Common Name or MINERAL	MINERAL	Crystal Matrix	Earth Power
Infinite	Serpentine (ANTIGORITE)	Guardian/Dreamholder	Bonder
Iolanthite	Banded Red Jasper QUARTZ	Seeker/Simplifier	Transformer
Iolite	CORDIERITE	Dispeller/Restorer	Energizer
Iris Agate	Agate Chalcedony QUARTZ	Seeker/Simplifier	Transformer
IRON		Enhancer	Purifier
Iron Pyrite	PYRITE	Enhancer	Mirror
Jade	Nephrite ACTINOLITE, or JADEITE	Guardian/Dreamholder	Harmonizer
JADEITE		Guardian/Dreamholder	Harmonizer
JAMESONITE		Guardian/Dreamholder	Mirror
JAROSITE		Seeker/Simplifier	Solidifier
Jasp-Agate	Jasper QUARTZ	Seeker/Simplifier	Transformer
Jasper	Jasper QUARTZ	Seeker/Simplifier	Transformer
Jasper Breccia	Jasper QUARTZ	Seeker/Simplifier	Transformer
Jasperine	Jasper QUARTZ	Seeker/Simplifier	Transformer
Jasponyx	Agate Chalcedony QUARTZ	Seeker/Simplifier	Transformer
JENNITE		Barrier	Unifier
Jet	Coal	none	none
JORDANITE		Guardian/Dreamholder	Mirror
Joshua Tree Agate	Agate Chalcedony QUARTZ	Seeker/Simplifier	Transformer
Kämmererite	CLINOCHLORE	Guardian/Dreamholder	Bonder
KAOLINITE		Guardian/Dreamholder	Bonder
KERNITE		Guardian/Dreamholder	Builder
Kidney Ore	HEMATITE	Seeker/Simplifier	Transformer
Kidney Stones	JADEITE	Guardian/Dreamholder	Harmonizer
KINOITE		Guardian/Dreamholder	Strengthener
Kinradite	Jasper QUARTZ	Seeker/Simplifier	Transformer
Knaufite	VOLBORTHITE	Guardian/Dreamholder	Buffer
KORNERUPINE		Dispeller/Restorer	Strengthener
Koroit Opal	OPAL	mixed	mixed
Kosmochlor Jade	Mawsitsit (a rock)	mixed	mixed
Kunzite	SPODUMENE	Guardian/Dreamholder	Harmonizer
KYANITE		Barrier	Strengthener
LABRADORITE		Barrier	Filter
Lantana	Agate Chalcedony QUARTZ	Seeker/Simplifier	Transformer
Lapis Lazuli	LAZURITE (mostly), PYRITE, CALCITE	Enhancer	Filter

Continued on next page

Common Name or MINERAL	MINERAL	Crystal Matrix	Earth Power
Larimar	PECTOLITE	Seeker/Simplifier	Harmonizer
Larvikite	a Granite rock	mixed	mixed
Lavenderine	LEPIDOLITE	Guardian/Dreamholder	Bonder
LAZULITE		Guardian/Dreamholder	Buffer
LAZURITE		Enhancer	Filter
Lazurquartz	Blue Chalcedony QUARTZ	Seeker/Simplifier	Transformer
LEGRANDITE		Guardian/Dreamholder	Buffer
LEIFITE		Seeker/Simplifier	Filter
Lemon Chrysoprase	Chrysoprase Chalcedony QUARTZ	Seeker/Simplifier	Transformer
Lemon Jade	Serpentine	Guardian/Dreamholder	Bonder
Lemon Yellow Citrine	QUARTZ	Seeker/Simplifier	Transformer
Leolite	Agate Chalcedony QUARTZ	Seeker/Simplifier	Transformer
Leopard Jasper	Jasper Chalcedony QUARTZ	Seeker/Simplifier	Transformer
Leopardskin Jasper	Orange/Tan Jasper QUARTZ	Seeker/Simplifier	Transformer
LEPIDACHROSITE	found in QUARTZ	Dispeller/Restorer	Transformer
LEPIDOLITE		Guardian/Dreamholder	Bonder
LEUCITE		Enhancer	Filter
LIBETHENITE		Dispeller/Restorer	Buffer
Light Ruby Silver	PROUSTITE	Seeker/Simplifier	Mirror
Lignite	Coal	mixed	mixed
Limestone	a rock	mixed	mixed
Limonite	a rock	none	none
LINARITE		Guardian/Dreamholder	Solidifier
Linerite	LINARITE	Guardian/Dreamholder	Solidifier
Lingam	Jasper QUARTZ	Seeker/Simplifier	Transformer
London Blue Topaz	Irradiated TOPAZ	Dispeller/Restorer	Strengthener
Lorimar	PECTOLITE	Seeker/Simplifier	Harmonizer
Lucky Strike Thundereggs	Agate Chalcedony QUARTZ	Seeker/Simplifier	Transformer
LUDLAMITE		Guardian/Dreamholder	Solidifier
Lydian Stone	BASANITE	Seeker/Simplifier	Transformer
Madagascar Mariposite	Yellow Chalcedony QUARTZ	Seeker/Simplifier	Transformer
Madeira Citrine	QUARTZ	Seeker/Simplifier	Transformer
MAGNESITE		Seeker/Simplifier	Builder
MAGNETITE (Iron Oxide)		Enhancer	Transformer
Mahogany Obsidian	glass	mixed	mixed
MALACHITE		Guardian/Dreamholder	Builder

Common Name or MINERAL	MINERAL	Crystal Matrix	Earth Power
Malaya Garnet	Mixed GARNET	Enhancer	Strengthener
Man Yü	Red Carnelian Chalcedony QUARTZ	Seeker/Simplifier	Transformer
Mandarin Garnet	Mixed GARNET	Enhancer	Strengthener
MANGANESE (Mn)	only lab grown (not natural)	mixed	mixed
MANGANITE		Guardian/Dreamholder	Transformer
MANGANOTANTALITE		Dispeller/Restorer	Transformer
Marble	a rock	mixed	mixed
MARCASITE		Enhancer	Mirror
Marra Mamba	Jasper QUARTZ (Tiger Iron)	Seeker/Simplifier	Transformer
Maury Mt. Moss Agate	Agate Chalcedony QUARTZ	Seeker/Simplifier	Transformer
Mawsitsit	a rock	mixed	mixed
McDermitt Thundereggs	Agate Chalcedony QUARTZ	Seeker/Simplifier	Transformer
Mecca Stone	Carnelian Chalcedony QUARTZ	Seeker/Simplifier	Transformer
Melanite	ANDRADITE	Enhancer	Strengthener
Merelani Mint Garnet	ALMANDINE (mostly)	Enhancer	Strengthener
MESOLITE		Guardian/Dreamholder	Filter
Mexican Black Opal	amorphous (not a crystal structure)	mixed	mixed
Mexican Cherry Opal	amorphous (not a crystal structure)	mixed	mixed
Mexican Fire Opal	amorphous (not a crystal structure)	mixed	mixed
Mexican Jelly Opal	amorphous (not a crystal structure)	mixed	mixed
Mexican Matrix Opal	amorphous (not a crystal structure)	mixed	mixed
MICROCLINE		Barrier	Filter
MIMETITE		Seeker/Simplifier	Buffer
Mohave Blue	Violet Chalcedony QUARTZ	Seeker/Simplifier	Transformer
MOISSANITE	synthetic only	mixed	mixed
Mojave Moonstone	Blue Chalcedony QUARTZ	Seeker/Simplifier	Transformer
Moldavite (Tektite)	glass	mixed	mixed
MONAZITE		Guardian/Dreamholder	Buffer
Montana Moss Agate	Agate Chalcedony QUARTZ	Seeker/Simplifier	Transformer
MONTEBRASITE		Barrier	Buffer
Moonstone	ORTHOCLASE/ALBITE	Guardian/Dreamholder/Barrier	Filter

Continued on next page

Common Name or MINERAL	MINERAL	Crystal Matrix	Earth Power
Moqui Marbles	HEMATITE and Sandstone	mixed	mixed
Morganite	BERYL	Seeker/Simplifier	Energizer
Morlop	Jasper QUARTZ	Seeker/Simplifier	Transformer
Morrisonite	Jasper QUARTZ	Seeker/Simplifier	Transformer
Mosaic Agate	Agate Chalcedony QUARTZ	Seeker/Simplifier	Transformer
Moss Agate	Agate Chalcedony QUARTZ	Seeker/Simplifier	Transformer
Moss Jasper	Jasper QUARTZ	Seeker/Simplifier	Transformer
MOTTRAMITE		Dispeller/Restorer	Solidifier
Moukaite	Pink Jasper QUARTZ	Seeker/Simplifier	Transformer
Mozambique Garnet	Mixed GARNET	Enhancer	Strengthener
Mozarkite	multicolored Chert QUARTZ	Seeker/Simplifier	Transformer
Mtorolite	Dark Green Jasper QUARTZ	Seeker/Simplifier	Transformer
Munjina Stone	Agate Chalcedony QUARTZ	Seeker/Simplifier	Transformer
MUSCOVITE		Guardian/Dreamholder	Bonder
Myrickite	Red Chalcedony QUARTZ with CINNABAR	Seeker/Simplifier	Transformer
Mystic Fire Topaz	Coated Topaz (not all natural)	none	none
NATROLITE		Dispeller/Restorer	Filter
Nebula Stone	a rock	a rock	a rock
Neon Quartz	Irradiated QUARTZ	Seeker/Simplifier	Transformer
Nephrite (Jade)	ACTINOLITE	Guardian/Dreamholder	Harmonizer
NÉPOUITE		Dispeller/Restorer	Bonder
NEPTUNITE		Guardian/Dreamholder	Harmonizer
Niccolite	NICKELINE	Seeker/Simplifier	Mirror
NICKEL (the element Nickel)	only lab grown (not natural)	mixed	mixed
Nickel Bloom	ANNABERGITE	Guardian/Dreamholder	Buffer
NICKELINE		Seeker/Simplifier	Mirror
Norwegian Pearl Granite	a Granite rock	mixed	mixed
Novaculite	White Chert QUARTZ	Seeker/Simplifier	Transformer
Nunderite	EPIDOTE in QUARTZ	Seeker/Simplifier	Transformer
Nunkirchner Jasper	Brown Jasper QUARTZ	Seeker/Simplifier	Transformer
Nuumite	ANTHOPHYLLITE	Dispeller/Restorer	Harmonizer
Obsidian	glass	mixed	mixed
Ocean Jasper	Jasper QUARTZ	Seeker/Simplifier	Transformer
Odontolite	fossil	mixed	mixed
OKENITE		Barrier	Harmonizer

Common Name or MINERAL	MINERAL	Crystal Matrix	Earth Power
OLIGOCLASE		Barrier	Filter
OLIVINE (usually FORSTERITE)	a mineral group	Seeker/Simplifier	Transformer
Onyx	Jasper QUARTZ	Seeker/Simplifier	Transformer
Oolitic Chert	Chert QUARTZ	Seeker/Simplifier	Transformer
Oolitic Hematite	HEMATITE	Seeker/Simplifier	Transformer
Oolitic Jasper	Jasper QUARTZ	Seeker/Simplifier	Transformer
Opal	amorphous (not a crystal structure)	mixed	mixed
Opal Butte Thundereggs	Agate Chalcedony QUARTZ	Seeker/Simplifier	Transformer
Ora Verde Quartz	Irradiated QUARTZ	Seeker/Simplifier	Transformer
Orange Beryl	BERYL	Seeker/Simplifier	Energizer
Orange Chalcedony	Chalcedony QUARTZ	Seeker/Simplifier	Transformer
Orange Sapphire	CORUNDUM	Seeker/Simplifier	Transformer
Orange Tourmaline	TOURMALINE	Seeker/Simplifier	Transformer
Orbicular Jasper	Jasper QUARTZ	Seeker/Simplifier	Transformer
Oregon Jade	Plasma Chalcedony QUARTZ	Seeker/Simplifier	Transformer
Oregonite	Jasper Chalcedony QUARTZ	Seeker/Simplifier	Transformer
ORPIMENT		Guardian/Dreamholder	Mirror
ORTHOCLASE		Guardian/Dreamholder	Filter
Owyhee Picture Jasper	Jasper QUARTZ	Seeker/Simplifier	Transformer
Padparadscha Sapphire	CORUNDUM	Seeker/Simplifier	Transformer
PALYGORSKITE		Guardian/Dreamholder	Filter
PAPAGOITE		Guardian/Dreamholder	Energizer
PARADAMITE		Barrier	Buffer
Paradise Jasper	Red Jasper QUARTZ	Seeker/Simplifier	Transformer
Paraiba Tourmaline	TOURMALINE	Seeker/Simplifier	Energizer
PARAVAUXITE		Barrier	Buffer
Pastelite	Pink/Green Jasper QUARTZ	Seeker/Simplifier	Transformer
Peach Aventurine	QUARTZ	Seeker/Simplifier	Transformer
Peach Beryl	BERYL	Seeker/Simplifier	Energizer
Peach Moonstone	ORTHOCLASE/ALBITE	Guardian/Dreamholder/Barrier	Filter
Peacock Copper	BORNITE	Enhancer	Mirror
Peacock Ore	BORNITE	Enhancer	Mirror
Peacock Topaz	TOPAZ	Dispeller/Restorer	Strengthener
PECTOLITE		Seeker/Simplifier	Harmonizer

Continued on next page

Common Name or MINERAL	MINERAL	Crystal Matrix	Earth Power
PENTAGONITE		Dispeller/Restorer	Bonder
PERICLASE		Enhancer	Transformer
Peridot	FORSTERITE	Dispeller/Restorer	Strengthener
Peridotite	a rock	mixed	mixed
Peristerite	ALBITE	Barrier	Filter
PEROVSKITE		Dispeller/Restorer	Transformer
Perthite	MICROCLINE	Barrier	Filter
Peruvian Blue Opal	OPAL—amorphous (not a crystal)	mixed	mixed
PETALITE		Guardian/Dreamholder	Bonder
Petersite	QUARTZ	Seeker/Simplifier	Transformer
Petrified Wood	Jasper QUARTZ	Seeker/Simplifier	Transformer
PHENAKITE		Seeker/Simplifier	Strengthener
PHILLIPSITE		Guardian/Dreamholder	Filter
PHLOGOPITE		Guardian/Dreamholder	Bonder
Phonolite	a rock	mixed	mixed
PHOSGENITE		Attractor	Builder
PHOSPHOPHYLLITE		Guardian/Dreamholder	Buffer
Phosphorite	a rock	mixed	mixed
Picture Jasper	Jasper QUARTZ	Seeker/Simplifier	Transformer
PIEDMONTITE		Guardian/Dreamholder	Unifier
Pietersite	Hawk's Eye Chalcedony QUARTZ	Seeker/Simplifier	Transformer
Pigeon Blood Agate	Carnelian Chalcedony QUARTZ	Seeker/Simplifier	Transformer
Pink Lazurine	synthetic QUARTZ	none	none
Pink Sapphire	CORUNDUM	Seeker/Simplifier	Transformer
Pink Spinel	SPINEL	Enhancer	Transformer
Pink Tourmaline	TOURMALINE	Seeker/Simplifier	Energizer
Pipestone	Catlinite (mostly Muscovite) (a rock)	mixed	mixed
Pisolitic Chert	Chert QUARTZ	Seeker/Simplifier	Transformer
PLANCHÉITE		Dispeller/Restorer	Harmonizer
Plasma	Chalcedony QUARTZ	Seeker/Simplifier	Transformer
PLATINUM		Enhancer	Purifier
PLATTNERITE		Attractor	Transformer
PLUMBOGUMMITE		Seeker/Simplifier	Buffer
Polianite	PYROLUSITE	Attractor	Transformer

Common Name or MINERAL	MINERAL	Crystal Matrix	Earth Power
Polka-dot Agate	Agate Chalcedony QUARTZ	Seeker/Simplifier	Transformer
Polka-dot Jasper	Jasper QUARTZ	Seeker/Simplifier	Transformer
POLYBASITE		Guardian/Dreamholder	Mirror
POLYHALITE		Barrier	Solidifier
POLYLITHIONITE		Guardian/Dreamholder	Bonder
Pony Butte Thundereggs	Agate Chalcedony QUARTZ	Seeker/Simplifier	Transformer
Poppy	Red/Orange/Yellow Jasper QUARTZ	Seeker/Simplifier	Transformer
Poppy Jasper	Jasper QUARTZ	Seeker/Simplifier	Transformer
Poppy stone	Jasper QUARTZ	Seeker/Simplifier	Transformer
POWELLITE		Attractor	Solidifier
Prase	Green QUARTZ	Seeker/Simplifier	Transformer
Prase Malachite	Green Chalcedony QUARTZ	Seeker/Simplifier	Transformer
Prasiolite	QUARTZ	Seeker/Simplifier	Transformer
Precious Topaz	TOPAZ	Dispeller/Restorer	Strengthener
PREHNITE		Dispeller/Restorer	Bonder
Preseli Bluestone	AUGITE (with feldspar)	Guardian/Dreamholder	Harmonizer
Priday Plume Agate	Agate Chalcedony QUARTZ	Seeker/Simplifier	Transformer
Priday Thundereggs	Agate Chalcedony QUARTZ	Seeker/Simplifier	Transformer
PROUSTITE		Seeker/Simplifier	Mirror
PSEUDOMALACHITE		Guardian/Dreamholder	Solidifier
Psilomelane	ROMANECHITE	Enhancer	Transformer
Pub Stone	a Granite rock	mixed	mixed
PUMPELLYITE	Chlorastrolite PUMPELLYITE	Guardian/Dreamholder	Unifier
Purple Garnet	ALMANDINE-PYROPE	Enhancer	Strengthener
Purple Jade	a rock	mixed	mixed
PURPURITE		Dispeller/Restorer	Buffer
PYRARGYRITE		Seeker/Simplifier	Mirror
PYRITE		Enhancer	Mirror
Pyrite Dollars	PYRITE	Enhancer	Mirror
Pyrite Suns	PYRITE	Enhancer	Mirror
PYROLUSITE		Attractor	Transformer
PYROMORPHITE		Seeker/Simplifier	Buffer
Pyrope Garnet	PYROPE	Enhancer	Strengthener
Pyrope-Almandine Garnet	ALMANDINE-PYROPE	Enhancer	Strengthener
PYROPHYLLITE		Guardian/Dreamholder	Bonder

Continued on next page

Common Name or MINERAL	MINERAL	Crystal Matrix	Earth Power
PYRRHOTITE		Enhancer	Mirror
QUARTZ		Seeker/Simplifier	Transformer
Queensland Garnet	ALMANDINE-PYROPE	Enhancer	Strengthener
Rainbow Moonstone	LABRADORITE	Barrier	Filter
Rainbow Obsidian	glass	mixed	mixed
Rainbow Topaz	Azotic Coated TOPAZ (not natural)	mixed	mixed
Rainforest Jasper	Jasper QUARTZ	Seeker/Simplifier	Transformer
REALGAR		Guardian	Mirror
Red Beryl	BERYL	Seeker/Simplifier	Energizer
Red Jasper	Jasper QUARTZ	Seeker/Simplifier	Transformer
Red Spinel	SPINEL	Enhancer	Transformer
RHODIZITE		Enhancer	Builder
RHODOCHROSITE		Seeker/Simplifier	Builder
Rhodolite	ALMANDINE-PYROPE	Enhancer	Strengthener
RHODONITE		Barrier	Harmonizer
Riband Jasper	Banded Jasper QUARTZ	Seeker/Simplifier	Transformer
Richardson's Thundereggs	Agate Chalcedony QUARTZ	Seeker/Simplifier	Transformer
RICHTERITE		Guardian/Dreamholder	Harmonizer
Ricolite	Serpentine and TALC	Guardian/Dreamholder	Bonder
RIEBECKITE		Guardian/Dreamholder	Harmonizer
ROCK CRYSTAL	QUARTZ	Seeker/Simplifier	Transformer
Rocky Butte Picture Jasper	Jasper QUARTZ	Seeker/Simplifier	Transformer
Rogueite	Green Jasper QUARTZ	Seeker/Simplifier	Transformer
ROMANECHITE		Enhancer	Transformer
ROSASITE		Guardian/Dreamholder	Builder
Rose Cat's Eye Quartz	QUARTZ	Seeker/Simplifier	Transformer
Rose de France Amethyst	QUARTZ	Seeker/Simplifier	Transformer
Rose Quartz	QUARTZ	Seeker/Simplifier	Transformer
ROSELITE		Guardian/Dreamholder	Buffer
Rubellite	ELBAITE TOURMALINE	Seeker/Simplifier	Energizer
Ruby	CORUNDUM	Seeker/Simplifier	Transformer
Ruin Agate	Agate Chalcedony QUARTZ	Seeker/Simplifier	Transformer
Russian Agate	Agate Chalcedony QUARTZ	Seeker/Simplifier	Transformer
Russian Jasper	Red-Flecked Jasper QUARTZ	Seeker/Simplifier	Transformer
Rutilated Quartz	QUARTZ	Seeker/Simplifier	Transformer
RUTILE		Attractor	Transformer

Common Name or MINERAL	MINERAL	Crystal Matrix	Earth Power
Saddle Mountain Fire Agate	Agate Chalcedony QUARTZ	Seeker/Simplifier	Transformer
Sagenite	QUARTZ	Seeker/Simplifier	Transformer
Saint Stephen's Stone	Bloodstone Chalcedony QUARTZ	Seeker/Simplifier	Transformer
SAL AMMONIAC		Enhancer	Brightener
SANBORNITE		Dispeller/Restorer	Bonder
Sandstone	a rock	mixed	mixed
SANIDINE		Guardian/Dreamholder	Filter
Sapphire	CORUNDUM	Seeker/Simplifier	Transformer
Sapphirine	Blue Chalcedony QUARTZ	Seeker/Simplifier	Transformer
Sard	Brown Chalcedony QUARTZ	Seeker/Simplifier	Transformer
Sardonyx	Chalcedony QUARTZ	Seeker/Simplifier	Transformer
Satin Spar	GYPSUM	Guardian/Dreamholder	Solidifier
SCAPOLITE		Attractor	Filter
Scenic Jasper	Tan Jasper QUARTZ	Seeker/Simplifier	Transformer
SCHEELITE		Attractor	Solidifier
Schizolite	PECTOLITE	Seeker/Simplifier	Harmonizer
SCHOLZITE		Dispeller/Restorer	Buffer
SCHORL	Black TOURMALINE	Seeker/Simplifier	Energizer
SCOLECITE		Guardian/Dreamholder	Filter
SCORODITE		Dispeller/Restorer	Buffer
SCORZALITE		Guardian/Dreamholder	Buffer
Sea Jasper	Jasper QUARTZ	Seeker/Simplifier	Transformer
Seftonite	Green Chalcedony QUARTZ	Seeker/Simplifier	Transformer
Selenite	GYPSUM	Guardian/Dreamholder	Solidifier
SENARMONTITE		Enhancer	Transformer
Septarian	Sandstone (a rock)	mixed	mixed
Serandite	PECTOLITE	Seeker/Simplifier	Harmonizer
Seraphinite	CLINOCHLORE	Guardian/Dreamholder	Bonder
Serpentine		Guardian/Dreamholder	Bonder
Serpentinite	a rock	mixed	mixed
Shale	a rock	mixed	mixed
Shaman Stones	HEMATITE and Sandstone	mixed	mixed
SHATTUCKITE		Dispeller/Restorer	Harmonizer
SIDERITE		Seeker/Simplifier	Builder
SILLIMANITE		Dispeller/Restorer	Strengthener

Continued on next page

Common Name or MINERAL	MINERAL	Crystal Matrix	Earth Power
SILVER (Ag)		Enhancer	Purifier
Silver Topaz	TOPAZ	Dispeller/Restorer	Strengthener
SINHALITE		Dispeller/Restorer	Builder
Sioux Falls Jasper	Jasper QUARTZ	Seeker/Simplifier	Transformer
SKUTTERUDITE		Enhancer	Mirror
Sky Blue Topaz	TOPAZ	Dispeller/Restorer	Strengthener
SMITHSONITE		Seeker/Simplifier	Builder
Smoky Quartz	QUARTZ	Seeker/Simplifier	Transformer
Snowflake Obsidian	glass	mixed	mixed
Soapstone	TALC	Guardian/Dreamholder	Bonder
SODALITE		Enhancer	Filter
SPANGOLITE		Seeker/Simplifier	Solidifier
Spectrolite	LABRADORITE	Barrier	Filter
Specularite	HEMATITE	Seeker/Simplifier	Transformer
SPESSARTINE		Enhancer	Strengthener
Spessartite	SPESSARTINE	Enhancer	Strengthener
SPHAEROCOBALTITE		Seeker/Simplifier	Builder
SPHALERITE		Enhancer	Mirror
Sphene	TITANITE	Guardian/Dreamholder	Strengthener
SPINEL		Enhancer	Transformer
Spirit Quartz	QUARTZ	Seeker/Simplifier	Transformer
SPODUMENE		Guardian/Dreamholder	Harmonizer
Star Malachite	Green Chalcedony QUARTZ	Seeker/Simplifier	Transformer
Star Quartz	QUARTZ	Seeker/Simplifier	Transformer
Star Ruby	CORUNDUM	Seeker/Simplifier	Transformer
STAUROLITE		Seeker/Simplifier	Transformer
Steins Pillar Thundereggs	Agate Chalcedony QUARTZ	Seeker/Simplifier	Transformer
STELLERITE		Guardian/Dreamholder	Filter
STEPHANITE		Dispeller/Restorer	Mirror
STIBICONITE		Enhancer	Transformer
STIBNITE		Dispeller/Restorer	Mirror
STICHTITE		Seeker/Simplifier	Builder
STILBITE		Enhancer	Filter
Stinking Water Plume Agate	Agate Chalcedony QUARTZ	Seeker/Simplifier	Transformer
Stone Yard	Jasper QUARTZ	Seeker/Simplifier	Transformer
STRENGITE		Dispeller/Restorer	Buffer
STRUNZITE		Barrier	Buffer

Common Name or MINERAL	MINERAL	Crystal Matrix	Earth Power
STURMANITE		Seeker/Simplifier	Solidifier
Succor Creek Thundereggs	Agate Chalcedony QUARTZ	Seeker/Simplifier	Transformer
SUGILITE		Seeker/Simplifier	Energizer
SULFUR (S)		Enhancer	Purifier
Sunset Agate	Agate Chalcedony QUARTZ	Seeker/Simplifier	Transformer
Sunstone	OLIGOCLASE Feldspar	Barrier	Filter
SUOLUNITE		Barrier	Unifier
Swiss Blue Topaz	Irradiated TOPAZ	Dispeller/Restorer	Strengthener
Swiss Lapis	Dyed-Blue Chalcedony QUARTZ	Seeker/Simplifier	Transformer
Syenite	a rock	mixed	mixed
Sylvine	SYLVITE	Enhancer	Brightener
SYLVITE		Enhancer	Brightener
TAAFFEITE		Seeker/Simplifier	Transformer
TALC		Guardian/Dreamholder	Bonder
Tanganyika Artstone	ZOISITE, with Ruby	Dispeller/Restorer	Unifier
TANTALITE		Dispeller/Restorer	Transformer
Tanzanite	ZOISITE	Dispeller/Restorer	Unifier
Tanzanite Topaz	TOPAZ	Dispeller/Restorer	Strengthener
Tarnowitzite	ARAGONITE	Dispeller/Restorer	Builder
Tawmawite	EPIDOTE	Guardian/Dreamholder	Harmonizer
Teal Topaz	TOPAZ	Dispeller/Restorer	Strengthener
Tektite	glass	mixed	mixed
Television Stone	ULEXITE	Barrier	Builder
TENNANTITE		Enhancer	Mirror
Teanaway Agate	Agate Chalcedony QUARTZ	Seeker/Simplifier	Transformer
TEPHROITE		Dispeller/Restorer	Strengthener
TETRAHEDRITE		Enhancer	Mirror
Thai Garnet	ALMANDINE	Enhancer	Strengthener
THAUMASITE		Seeker/Simplifier	Solidifier
THENARDITE		Dispeller/Restorer	Buffer
THOMSENOLITE		Guardian/Dreamholder	Brightener
THOMSONITE		Dispeller/Restorer	Filter
Tiger's Eye	Jasper QUARTZ	Seeker/Simplifier	Transformer
TINCALCONITE		Guardian/Dreamholder	Builder
TITANITE		Guardian/Dreamholder	Strengthener
Toothstone	fossil	mixed	mixed

Continued on next page

Common Name or MINERAL	MINERAL	Crystal Matrix	Earth Power
TOPAZ		Dispeller/Restorer	Strengthener
Topazolite	ANDRADITE	Enhancer	Strengthener
Tourmalinated Quartz	QUARTZ	Seeker/Simplifier	Strengthener
TOURMALINE	a mineral group	Seeker/Simplifier	Energizer
Trachyte	a rock	mixed	mixed
Tree Agate	Agate Chalcedony QUARTZ	Seeker/Simplifier	Transformer
TREMOLITE		Guardian/Dreamholder	Harmonizer
TRONA		Guardian/Dreamholder	Builder
Tsavorite	GROSSULAR	Enhancer	Strengthener
TSUMEBITE		Guardian/Dreamholder	Buffer
TUNDRITE		Barrier	Harmonizer
Turgite	HEMATITE	Seeker/Simplifier	Transformer
TURQUOISE		Barrier	Buffer
Turritella Agate	Agate Chalcedony QUARTZ	Seeker/Simplifier	Transformer
Turtleback	Chlorastrolite PUMPELLYITE	Guardian/Dreamholder	Unifier
Uigite	Chlorastrolite PUMPELLYITE	Guardian/Dreamholder	Unifier
ULEXITE		Barrier	Builder
Umbalite Garnet	ALMANDINE-PYROPE	Enhancer	Strengthener
Unakite	a rock	mixed	mixed
Utica Jewelstone	White-Banded Chert QUARTZ	Seeker/Simplifier	Transformer
UVAROVITE		Enhancer	Strengthener
UVITE	TOURMALINE	Seeker/Simplifier	Energizer
Vabanite	Red/Yellow Jasper QUARTZ	Seeker/Simplifier	Transformer
VALENTINITE		Dispeller/Restorer	Transformer
Valley View Thundereggs	Agate Chalcedony QUARTZ	Seeker/Simplifier	Transformer
VANADINITE		Seeker/Simplifier	Buffer
Variegated Jasper	Jasper QUARTZ	Seeker/Simplifier	Transformer
VARISCITE		Dispeller/Restorer	Buffer
VAUXITE		Barrier	Buffer
VERDELITE	TOURMALINE	Seeker/Simplifier	Energizer
VESUVIANITE		Attractor	Unifier
VESZELYITE		Guardian/Dreamholder	Buffer
VILLIAUMITE		Enhancer	Transformer
Violan	Blue DIOPSIDE	Guardian/Dreamholder	Harmonizer
Violet Sapphire	CORUNDUM	Seeker/Simplifier	Transformer

Common Name or MINERAL	MINERAL	Crystal Matrix	Earth Power
Violet Spinel	SPINEL	Enhancer	Transformer
Violite	Violet Chalcedony QUARTZ	Seeker/Simplifier	Transformer
VOLBORTHITE		Guardian/Dreamholder	Buffer
WARDITE		Attractor	Buffer
Water Sapphire (Iolite)	CORDIERITE	Dispeller/Restorer	Energizer
Watermelon Tourmaline	TOURMALINE	Seeker/Simplifier	Energizer
WAVELLITE		Dispeller/Restorer	Buffer
WENDWILSONITE		Guardian/Dreamholder	Buffer
WERNERITE	SCAPOLITE	Attractor	Filter
Whistler Springs Thundereggs	Agate Chalcedony QUARTZ	Seeker/Simplifier	Transformer
White Fir Springs Thundereggs	Jasper QUARTZ	Seeker/Simplifier	Transformer
White Sapphire	CORUNDUM	Seeker/Simplifier	Transformer
White Spinel	SPINEL	Enhancer	Transformer
White Topaz	TOPAZ	Dispeller/Restorer	Strengthener
WHITEITE		Guardian/Dreamholder	Buffer
Whiteskins	Agate Chalcedony QUARTZ	Seeker/Simplifier	Transformer
Wild Horse Jasper	Jasper QUARTZ	Seeker/Simplifier	Transformer
Wilkite	Multicolored Jasper QUARTZ	Seeker/Simplifier	Transformer
WILLEMITE		Seeker/Simplifier	Strengthener
Willow Creek Jasper	Jasper QUARTZ	Seeker/Simplifier	Transformer
Withamite	Red EPIDOTE	Guardian/Dreamholder	Harmonizer
WITHERITE		Dispeller/Restorer	Builder
WOLFEITE		Guardian/Dreamholder	Buffer
WOLFRAMITE		Guardian/Dreamholder	Solidifier
WOLLASTONITE		Barrier	Harmonizer
Wonderstone	Rhyolite (a rock)	mixed	mixed
WULFENITE		Attractor	Solidifier
XONOTLITE		Guardian/Dreamholder	Harmonizer
Xyloid Jasper	Jasper QUARTZ	Seeker/Simplifier	Transformer
Yellow Sapphire	CORUNDUM	Seeker/Simplifier	Transformer
Yellow Tourmaline	TOURMALINE	Seeker/Simplifier	Energizer
YUKSPORITE		Dispeller/Restorer	Harmonizer
Zebra Jasper	Jasper QUARTZ	Seeker/Simplifier	Transformer
ZINKENITE		Seeker/Simplifier	Mirror
ZOISITE		Dispeller/Restorer	Unifier
Zonite	Jasper QUARTZ	Seeker/Simplifier	Transformer

GLOSSARY

Amulet: A device worn to protect the wearer from some specific evil or malady. The term *amulet* seems to be derived from the Latin word *amuletum*, a "means of defense." Amulets are Barrier and Guardian talismans.

Arrangers: A secondary use of talismans from the isometric crystal system. These talismans have an internal structure that is perfectly arranged, and it holds the energy we need to help us arrange our life in a more orderly manner. When there is a need for arranging our paths through life, establishing equality or equilibrium, reducing chaos, aligning priorities, or just "squaring" things away, talismans made from crystals from this system are very powerful.

Autumnal Equinox: The first day of fall. Usually about September 23 each year in the Northern Hemisphere.

Balancers: A less common name for Buffers, talismans made from Class VII "phosphates." They have the chemical earth power to help promote stability, balance, and centering.

Barriers: Barriers are talismans made from minerals that form in the triclinic crystal system, possessing the form of a trapezium, a geometric figure with no right angles. This structure gives these talismans strength in all directions, allowing them to provide barriers to attack from all directions simultaneously. Their crystal structure gives Barrier talismans the crystal energy to form an effective amulet that can aid in defending against the misfortunes of this world.

Bonders: Bonders are talismans that are made from minerals that form in the Class VIII-5 "sheet silicates" group. These crystals are formed when silicate tetrahedrons connect in sheets, producing very cohesive minerals. They are very tough to cut. They are outstanding minerals that have the chemical earth power to make effective talismans when there is need to create something that is bound tightly. Like glue bonding wooden planks together, Bonder talismans are useful in cementing relationships and agreements.

Brighteners: Brighteners are talismans made from Class III "halides." They are often very brightly colored, among the brightest of the mineral kingdom. These crystals and minerals, including halite and fluorite, are prized for their ability to bring out the beauty in something. As talismans, the Brighteners have the chemical earth energy to help us in enhancing efforts that focus on the sensual aspects of life in which some aspect has become dull, tarnished, or dingy.

Buffers: Buffers are talismans made from Class VII "phosphate" minerals. These minerals are mostly derived from phosphoric acid, which forms compounds that buffer, balance, and neutralize both acids and alkalis. Other talismans from this class have similar chemistry. Buffers have the chemical earth power to help us when we need to promote stability, balance, and centering. Also sometimes called Balancers.

Builders: The Builders are talismans made from minerals of the Class V "carbonates" group. These are minerals that are rarely in their final form, but rather in a transitional state. The Builders have the chemical earth power that is needed in applications in which something new needs to be made from something old. Woodworkers, stoneworkers, artists, painters, and others involved in the creative arts benefit from these types of talismans. The Builder talismans can help artists and craftspersons to focus on the artistic outcome they are trying to achieve.

Cabochon: A cabochon is a fashioned talisman that usually has a convex shape on one side and is flat on the other, although any fashioning that does not involve faceting or tumbling is often considered to be "making a cabochon." They are often of oval shape, but irregular shapes are common.

Causal Duality: The principle of Causal Duality states that equal benefit comes from action toward a goal and inaction away from it. The causes of our success are to be found both in efforts to move forward and in the absence of efforts to move backward. Causal Duality is the key concept of the Seventh Secret of Talismans.

Circle of Bluestone: The circle of bluestone is a small ring carved from Preseli bluestone, the substance from which the Inner Ring of Stonehenge is made. It is used with Transport talismans on the equinoxes and solstices to unify talismans—combining their power with all other talismans. The power of the circle of bluestone is revealed in the Sixth Secret of Talismans.

Color Ray of Influence: Every mineral reflects some portion of the natural color spectrum. These reflections connect the crystal energy and earth power of the mineral to the human mind. The meanings of the color rays are determined from the Color Wheel of Influence and are discussed in the Third Secret of Talismans.

Color Wheel of Influence: The Great Talismanic Color Wheel of Influence shows the cycles of human life and the cycles of the earth combined within the color spectrum. It matches human activities, desires, and life events to the cycles of the earth and depicts the appropriate color ray of influence for a talisman. The use and application of the Color Wheel are revealed in the Third Secret of Talismans.

Dispellers: The Dispellers are talismans that form in the orthorhombic system with "diamond-shaped" internal crystal arrangements. They often appear as small multiple-diamond-shaped crystals like a multitude of arrowheads or pyramids. The diamond shape of their crystal lattice acts like a radiator, with sharp points from which the energy can flow easily outward. This outward flow of energy can carry with it the undesirable elements in our lives. Dispellers are talismans used when the need is to rid ourselves of these elements.

Dreamholders: A secondary power of the minerals that form in the monoclinic crystal system. These minerals often appear hazy, as if there is something veiled from our sight just beneath the surface. They are used to aid us in focusing our energy to hold on to our dreams.

Energizers: Energizers are talismans made from minerals that form in the Class VIII-3 "ring silicates" group. They have crystal lattices that contain three to twelve rings of silicate tetrahedrons. Energizers are talismans that can help us in many efforts to gain what we seek, enhance our lives, protect that which we value, and protect us from the undesirable elements of life on earth because they have the chemical Earth energy to augment our natural energy and drive.

Enhancers: These are the "building block" talismans from the isometric crystal system. Their internal structure of blocks builds up perfect crystal lattices that can help us focus our efforts to build on our successes and enhance our lives. Whereas the Seekers and Simplifiers system produces crystals and minerals that aid in new beginnings, the Enhancers aid us in building on our successes and achievements.

Faceting: Faceting is a process of grinding flat surfaces on a crystal to give it a shape.

Filters: Filters are talismans that are made from minerals that form in the Class VIII-6 "framework silicates" group. They are formed by three-dimensional grids of tetrahedrons of silicates that very much look and act like filters. They absorb certain things and allow others to pass. They filter energy, allowing positive charges to flow and blocking negative ones when properly used and aligned. The feldspars are common Filters, and they have a wide variety of uses in the talismanic world.

Guardians: Guardians are talismans made from the minerals of the monoclinic crystal system that have an internal structure composed of parallelograms. The parallel structure of their crystalline lattice gives Guardian talismans their power to protect us in the physical world and in the spiritual one. Guardians are amulets that focus our energy and help us use the Life Force to protect that which we value.

Harmonizers: The Harmonizers are talismans that form in the Class VIII-4 "chain and band silicates" group. They contain silicate tetrahedrons bound together in a long chain. They distribute energy in a balanced, long-term way, promoting harmony. For efforts aimed at smoothing a path through difficulties, or aiding in promoting a harmonious relationship with a larger group, like a family, then a Harmonizer brings us the chemical earth power we need.

Mirrors: These talismans are made from minerals from the Class II "sulfides." They are usually volcanic in origin. They are normally opaque and have a metallic sheen or luster to them. This mirrorlike surface is an outward manifestation of the power of these talismans to reflect what is normally hidden. These minerals have the chemical earth power to help us in knowing ourselves, as they help reveal to us things that we didn't consciously realize.

Personal Talisman: These are usually fashioned in some manner because they are meant to be carried or worn. They are usually made from the harder minerals that respond well to the cutting, grinding, and polishing involved in fashioning. Personal talismans are usually faceted, made into cabochons, tumbled, or carved.

Purifiers: The Purifiers are talismans made from minerals from the Class I "natural elements." These pure elemental minerals have the chemical earth power to aid us when we have unambiguously righteous goals.

Resisters: An alternate name for Strengtheners, talismans made from Class VIII-1 "island silicates" minerals.

Restorers: A secondary power of the talismans that form in the orthorhombic crystal system. These crystals are used to put things right again after they are out of balance. If we are worry free, then become plagued by doubt, these crystals help us to focus and magnify our energy to rid ourselves of the doubt and restore ourselves to the worry-free state. For example, if we are working in a great job, then lose it for some reason, these crystals and minerals can help us restore our lives as productive members of the working community.

Seekers: Talismans from the hexagonal crystal system. They are powerful, numerous, and very useful talismans for aiding us in successfully starting a new effort. The Seeker talismans help us to discover new opportunities and to set out to achieve new goals. These are the fresh-start talismans, the talismans of new beginnings and new discoveries.

Simplifiers: A secondary use of talismans from the hexagonal crystal system. In addition to their use as Seekers, talismans from this crystal system can be used effectively when the need is to simplify a life or situation. With their triangular crystal energy matrices they bring us the attributes of simplicity, tranquility, minimal effort, mastery of the path of least resistance, pragmatism, practicality, indulgence, rest, relaxation, and peace.

Solidifiers: The Solidifiers are talismans made from Class VI "sulfates," which are crystals that result from the action of sulfuric acid. Sulfuric acid is a very dense, very stable liquid. Solidifiers have the chemical earth power to aid us when the need is to solidify a relationship or a new habit. They are used to add permanence to anything that is temporary.

Specimen Talisman: Specimen talismans are not fashioned but rather are left in the condition in which they were found in or on the earth. They also can be large, fashioned talismans that are not usually carried during use.

Strengtheners: Strengtheners are talismans made from Class VIII "island silicates." They are formed when tetrahedrons of silicate form islands between the metal ions of the compound. This class of minerals is made of very compact materials that are strong, resistant, and unyielding. They provide us with the chemical Earth energy to resist temptations and distractions from our goals.

Summer Solstice: The first day of summer. Usually about June 21 in the Northern Hemisphere.

Talisman: A talisman is an object, often a crystal or gemstone, that has the ability to focus and amplify a person's power to achieve his or her desires. Whatever the desire or need, the correct talisman, used properly, can focus and amplify people's power to get what they want, protect what they have, and help guard and defend them from harm and trouble.

Telesma: A place where talismans are made. *Telesma* is the Middle Greek word for "consecrated object" from which the English, Spanish, and French word *talisman* is derived. So, too, a telesma is a source of talismans. In a way, it is a workshop, but it is much more. A telesma is a mineralogical laboratory, a metaphysical library, an artist's studio, and a center of learning. It is a place where the power of the natural Life Force of this planet is combined with the power of the human mind. A telesma is truly a magical place.

Touchstones: Touchstones are small talismans used with a circle of bluestone on the equinoxes and solstices to unify talismans—combining their power with all other talismans.

Transformers: Transformers are talismans that are made from Class IV "oxides," which form as less stable chemical compositions become more stable ones when they come into contact with oxygen. The transformative powers of these stones and crystals are legendary. Transformers are an extremely important class of talismans. Efforts to change ourselves, our situations, our prospects, our health, our relationships, and our outlook can all be improved by using a Transformer talisman.

Unifiers: Unifiers are talismans made from the Class VIII-2 "group silicates." Unifiers contain silicate molecules bound in pairs or small groups. Unifiers have the chemical earth power to aid us in group efforts. If you are the leader of a small group and seek to ensure it works well together, accomplishes its goals, and continues to be effective, a Unifier will be a big help to you. Unifiers are also very useful for efforts that require instilling allegiance or loyalty.

Vernal Equinox: The beginning of spring. Usually about March 20 in the Northern Hemisphere.

Winter Solstice: The first day of winter. Usually about December 21 in the Northern Hemisphere.

SUGGESTED READING

Andrews, Ted. *How to Heal with Color.* St. Paul, MN: Llewellyn Worldwide, 2003.

Ball, Philip. *Bright Earth: Art and the Invention of Color.* Chicago, IL: University of Chicago Press, 2001.

Buckland, Ray. *Practical Color Magick.* St. Paul, MN: Llewellyn Worldwide, 1997.

Crow, W. B. *Precious Stones: Their Occult Power & Hidden Significance.* New York: Samuel Weiser, Inc., 1968.

Cunningham, Scott. *Cunningham's Encyclopedia of Crystal, Gem & Metal Magic.* St Paul, MN: Llewellyn Worldwide, 1994.

Deatsman, Colleen. *Energy for Life.* Woodbury, MN: Llewellyn Worldwide, 2006.

Dunwich, Gerina. *Dunwich's Guide to Gemstone Sorcery: Using Stones for Spells, Amulets, Rituals, and Divination.* Franklin Lakes, NJ: New Page Books, 2003.

Elsbeth, Marguerite. *Crystal Medicine.* St. Paul, MN: Llewellyn Worldwide, 2004.

Farrell, Nick. *Making Talismans: Living Entities of Power.* St. Paul, MN: Llewellyn Worldwide, 2001.

Fernie, William T. *The Occult and Curative Powers of Precious Stones.* Blauvelt, NY: Rudolf Steiner Publications, 1973.

Finlay, Victoria. *Color: A Natural History of the Palette.* New York: Random House, 2002.

Gage, John. *Color and Meaning: Art, Science, and Symbolism.* Berkeley CA: University of California Press, 1999.

Gienger, Michael. *Crystal Power, Crystal Healing: The Complete Handbook.* London: Cassell Illustrated, 2002.

Goethe, Johann Wolfgang von. *Theory of Colours*. Translated by Charles Eastlake. Cambridge, MA: MIT Press, 1970.

Gonzalez-Wippler, Migene. *The Complete Book of Amulets & Talismans*. St. Paul, MN: Llewellyn Worldwide, 1991.

Hall, Judy. *The Encyclopedia of Crystals*. Gloucester, MA: Fair Winds, 2006.

Hawkins, Gerald S., and John B. White. *Stonehenge Decoded*. New York: Dell Publishing, 1965.

Henes, Donna. *Celestially Auspicious Occasions: Seasons, Cycles, & Celebrations*. New York: Berkley Publishing, 1996.

Howard, Michael. *The Sacred Ring: The Pagan Origins of British Folk Festivals and Customs*. Freshfields, Berks, UK: Capall Bann Publishing, 1995.

Kaehr, Shelley. *Gemstone Journeys*. Dallas, TX: Out of This World Productions, 2002.

Knuth, Bruce G. *Gems in Myth, Legend, and Lore*. Thornton, CO: Jewelers Press, 1999.

Kunz, George Fredrick. *The Curious Lore of Precious Stones*. New York: Dover Publications, 1971.

Matthews, Caitlin. *The Celtic Spirit*. San Francisco, CA: HarperSanFrancisco, 1999.

McColman, Carl. *The Complete Idiot's Guide to Celtic Wisdom*. New York: Alpha Books, 2003.

Mella, Dorothee. *Stone Power*. New York: Warner Books, 1988.

Northcote, Lady Rosalind. *The Book of Herb Lore*. New York: Dover Books, 1971.

Raphaell, Katrina. *Crystal Enlightenment*. New York: Aurora Press, 1985.

Scoble, Gretchen, and Ann Field. *The Meaning of Herbs, Myth, Language, and Lore*. San Francisco, CA: Chronicle Books, 2001.

Seleem, Ramses. *The Illustrated Egyptian Book of the Dead*. New York: Sterling Press, 2001.

Watkins, Alfred. *The Old Straight Track: The Classic Book on Ley Lines*. London: Abacus, 2005.

Webster, Richard. *Amulets & Talismans for Beginners: How to Choose, Make & Use Magical Objects*. St. Paul MN: Llewellyn Worldwide, 2004.

Zolar. *Zolar's Magick of Color: Use the Power of Color to Transform Your Luck, Prosperity, or Romance*. New York: Fireside, 1994.

INDEX

Mineral species are listed in BLOCK CAPITALS. Pages A-1 through A-28 refer to the plates of the color insert.

To Write to the Author

If you wish to contact the author or would like more information about this book, please write to the author in care of Llewellyn Worldwide and we will forward your request. Both the author and publisher appreciate hearing from you and learning of your enjoyment of this book and how it has helped you. Llewellyn Worldwide cannot guarantee that every letter written to the author can be answered, but all will be forwarded. Please write to:

Henry M. Mason
c/o Llewellyn Worldwide
2143 Wooddale Drive, Dept. 978-0-7387-1144-7
Woodbury, MN 55125-2989, U.S.A.
Please enclose a self-addressed stamped envelope for reply,
or $1.00 to cover costs. If outside U.S.A., enclose
international postal reply coupon.

Many of Llewellyn's authors have websites with additional information and resources. For more information, please visit our website at:

www.llewellyn.com

Color Plates

Note: Tables 1-6 are not all-inclusive, but they provide listings of the more common and readily available minerals.

Table 1: Seeker and Simplifier Talismans

Used for acquiring that which we do not possess yet desire: new achievements and new goals.

	I	II	III	IV	V	VI
	Elements	*Sulfides*	*Halides*	*Oxides*	*Carbonates*	*Sulfates*
	Purifiers	Mirrors	Brighteners	Transformers	Builders	Solidifiers
Light Blue *Acceptance*		Covellite		Sapphire, Chalcedony (Quartz), Blue Lace Agate	Calcite	Connellite, Spangolite
Blue *Trust*		Covellite		Sapphire, Hawk's Eye (Quartz) Aventurine (Quartz), Blue Lace Agate, Chalcedony		Connellite, Spangolite
Dark Blue *Respect, Compassion*		Covellite		Sapphire		Connellite, Spangolite
Light Turquoise *Harmony*					Smithsonite	Spangolite
Turquoise *Discovery, Balance*					Smithsonite	Spangolite
Dark Turquoise *Flexibility*					Smithsonite	Spangolite
Light Green *Spiritual Development*				Green Sapphire, Moss Agate, Bloodstone, Chrysoprase, Seftonite (Chalcedony)	Gaspeite, Smithsonite, Calcite	
Green *Growth, Renewal*				Green Sapphire, Moss Agate, Bloodstone, Aventurine (Quartz)	Smithsonite, Calcite	Spangolite
Dark Green *Physical Growth, Safety*				Green Sapphire, Moss Agate (Quartz), Bloodstone (Quartz), Aventurine (Quartz), Plasma (Quartz), Zincite	Siderite	Spangolite
Light Olive *Perseverance*				Green Sapphire, Chalcedony	Smithsonite, Calcite	
Olive *Awakening*				Green Sapphire, Chalcedony	Gaspeite	
Dark Olive *Learning*				Green Sapphire, Chalcedony		
Light Yellow *Awareness*				Yellow Sapphire, Citrine	Calcite	
Yellow *Enlightenment*				Yellow Sapphire, Citrine		Ettringite, Sturmanite
Dark Yellow *Clarity*				Yellow Sapphire, Citrine	Smithsonite	Jarosite
Light Gold *Happiness*				Citrine, Spirit Quartz	Smithsonite	
Gold *Enthusiasm, Exuberance*				Pink Sapphire, Rose Quartz, Carnelian (Quartz), Pink Chalcedony (Quartz), Zincite	Smithsonite, Calcite, Bastnasite	
Dark Gold *Power*				Citrine	Smithsonite, Bastnasite	Jarosite
Light Orange *Friendship*				Orange Sapphire	Calcite, Ankerite	
Orange *Joy*				Orange Sapphire	Smithsonite, Ankerite	

VII	VIII-1	VIII-2	VIII-3	VIII-4	VIII-5	VIII-6
Phosphates	*Nesosilicates or Orthosilicates*	*Sorosilicates*	*Cyclosilicates*	*Inosilicates*	*Phyllosilicates*	*Tectosilicates*
Buffers	**Strengtheners**	**Unifiers**	**Energizers**	**Harmonizers**	**Bonders**	**Filters**
Apatite	Willemite		Aquamarine, Indicolite			Afghanite
Apatite		Vesuvianite	Aquamarine, Indicolite, Benitoite			Afghanite
Apatite			Dioptase, Indicolite (Elbaite), Dark Blue Beryl (Irradiated)			Afghanite
Apatite			Aquamarine, Indicolite			
Apatite, Chalcophyllite			Aquamarine, Indicolite			
Apatite			Dioptase			
Apatite, Pyromorphite, Chalcophyllite						
Apatite, Pyromorphite, Chalcophyllite	Willemite		Verdelite (Tourmaline), Emerald			
Apatite, Pyromorphite, Chalcophyllite, Agardite			Dioptase, Emerald, Elbaite			
Apatite, Pyromorphite, Plumbogummite	Willemite	Idocrase	Heliodor, Tourmaline			
Apatite, Pyromorphite, Mimetite, Plumbogummite		Idocrase	Heliodor, Tourmaline			
Agardite, Plumbogummite		Idocrase	Heliodor, Tourmaline			
	Willemite		Heliodor, Tourmaline			
Apatite, Mimetite	Phenakite	Vesuvianite	Heliodor, Tourmaline			
Mimetite			Heliodor, Eudialyte			
			Golden Beryl			
Apatite			Golden Beryl			
Pyromorphite			Golden Beryl			
Vanadinite			Tourmaline, Orange Beryl, Eudialyte	Rhodonite		
Vanadinite			Elbaite (Tourmaline), Orange Beryl, Eudialyte	Rhodonite		Gmelinite

Continued on next page

	I	II	III	IV	V	VI
	Elements	*Sulfides*	*Halides*	*Oxides*	*Carbonates*	*Sulfates*
	Purifiers	Mirrors	Brighteners	Transformers	Builders	Solidifiers
Dark Orange *Belonging*				Carnelian	Cobaltian Calcite, Ankerite	
Light Scarlet *Dedication*		Proustite		Agate	Cobaltian Calcite	
Scarlet *Strength*		Proustite, Cinnabar		Carnelian	Cobaltian Calcite	
Dark Scarlet *Vitality*		Proustite		Agate	Cobaltian Calcite	
Pink *Love, Commitment*		Cinnabar, Nickeline		Pink Sapphire, Rose Quartz, Carnelian (Quartz), Pink Chalcedony (Quartz)	Mangano (Calcite), Rhodochrosite, Sphaerocobaltite, Cobaltian Dolomite, Magnesite, Stichtite	
Red *Energy, Courage, Drive, Action*		Proustite		Ruby Jasper (Quartz), Myrickite (Chalcedony)	Rhodochrosite, Sphaerocobaltite, Calcite, Cobaltian Dolomite	
Dark Red *Passion, Devotion*		Proustite, Pyrrhotite, Nickeline, Pyrargyrite		Hematite, Ruby Jasper, Sardonyx	Siderite, Rhodochrosite, Sphaerocobaltite	
Light Amethyst *Self-Knowledge*				Amethyst, Taaffeite, Purple Sapphire	Dolomite, Stichtite	
Amethyst *Creativity, Vision*				Amethyst, Taaffeite, Purple Sapphire	Rhodochrosite, Calcite, Cobaltian Dolomite, Stichtite	
Dark Amethyst *Insight*				Amethyst, Taaffeite, Purple Sapphire	Cobaltian Calcite	
Lavender *Luxury, Imagination*				Amethyst, Taaffeite, Spirit Quartz	Smithsonite, Stichtite	
Violet *Intuition*				Amethyst, Taaffeite, Purple Sapphire	Smithsonite, Stichtite	
Dark Violet *Dreams, Magic*				Amethyst, Taaffeite		
Light Indigo *Virtue*				Chalcedony, Spirit Quartz,	Cobaltian Dolomite, Stichtite	
Indigo *Wisdom*		Covellite		Chalcedony		
Dark Indigo *Truth*		Covellite		Chalcedony		
White *Illumination*				Rock Crystal, Azeztulite (Quartz), Herkimer Diamonds (Quartz), Jasper Chalcedony	Calcite, Smithsonite, Magnesite, Ankerite	Hanksite, Thaumasite
Silver *Reflection*	Antimony			Agate, Specularite (Hematite)		Alunite
Brown *Earth, Center, Stability*		Pyrrhotite, Cinnabar, Millerite		Corundum, Smoky Quartz, Picture Jasper, Aventurine (Quartz), Tiger Iron (Jasper, Hematite, and Tiger's Eye)	Calcite, Siderite, Bastnasite, Ankerite	Alunite, Jarosite
Black *Power, Mystery, Security*	Graphite	Covellite, Pyrargyrite, Zinkenite		Basanite (Jasper), Onyx, Black Star Sapphire, Hematite, Ilmenite		

VII	VIII-1	VIII-2	VIII-3	VIII-4	VIII-5	VIII-6
Phosphates	*Nesosilicates or Orthosilicates*	*Sorosilicates*	*Cyclosilicates*	*Inosilicates*	*Phyllosilicates*	*Tectosilicates*
Buffers	**Strengtheners**	**Unifiers**	**Energizers**	**Harmonizers**	**Bonders**	**Filters**
Vanadinite			Tourmaline	Rhodonite		Gmelinite
Vanadinite				Rhodonite		
Vanadinite			Tourmaline	Rhodonite		
Vanadinite			Eudialyte	Rhodonite		
			Morganite (Beryl), Rubellite (Elbaite), Eudialyte	Rhodonite, Schizolite (Pectolite)		Gmelinite
Apatite, Vanadinite			Bixbite (Red Beryl), Rubellite (Elbaite Tourmaline)	Rhodonite		
			Eudialyte	Rhodonite		
			Eudialyte, Sugilite			
			Eudialyte, Sugilite			
			Eudialyte, Sugilite			
Apatite			Tourmaline, Eudialyte			
Apatite		Vesuvianite	Tourmaline, Eudialyte, Strunzite			
		Vesuvianite	Tourmaline, Sugilite			
			Eudialyte			
Apatite			Tourmaline, Eudialyte			
			Eudialyte			
	Phenakite, Willemite		Goshenite	Pectolite		Chabazite, Leifite
Pyromorphite	Willemite		Dravite, Buergerite	Schizolite (Pectolite)		
			Schorl, Aphrizite (Tourmaline)			

Table 2: Enhancer and Arranger Talismans

Used for improving that which we have and value; also used for adding organization and order to our lives.

	I	II	III	IV	V	VI
	Element	*Sulfides*	*Halides*	*Oxides*	*Carbonates*	*Sulfates*
	Purifiers	**Mirrors**	**Brighteners**	**Transformers**	**Builders**	**Solidifiers**
Light Blue *Acceptance*	Diamond		Halite, Fluorite			
Blue *Trust*	Diamond		Fluorite	Spinel		
Dark Blue *Respect, Compassion*				Spinel		
Light Turquoise *Harmony*						
Turquoise *Discovery, Balance*						
Dark Turquoise *Flexibility*						
Light Green *Spiritual Development*			Fluorite			
Green *Growth, Renewal*			Fluorite	Spinel		
Dark Green *Physical Growth, Safety*		Sphalerite	Fluorite	Gahnite		
Light Olive *Perseverance*				Periclase		
Olive *Awakening*			Fluorite	Periclase		
Dark Olive *Learning*		Sphalerite				
Light Yellow *Awareness*	Diamond		Halite, Sylvite	Stibiconite		
Yellow *Enlightenment*	Diamond		Fluorite	Stibiconite		
Dark Yellow *Clarity*	Copper	Pyrite Sphalerite		Stibiconite		
Light Gold *Happiness*	Gold		Fluorite	Stibiconite		
Gold *Enthusiasm, Exuberance*	Gold, Copper	Pyrite		Stibiconite		
Dark Gold *Power*	Gold	Pyrrhotite	Fluorite			
Light Orange *Friendship*						
Orange *Joy*						
Dark Orange *Belonging*						
Light Scarlet *Dedication*						

VII	VIII-1	VIII-2	VIII-3	VIII-4	VIII-5	VIII-6
Phosphates	*Nesosilicates or Orthosilicates*	*Sorosilicates*	*Cyclosilicates*	*Inosilicates*	*Phyllosilicates*	*Tectosilicates*
Buffers	Strengtheners	Unifiers	Energizers	Harmonizers	Bonders	Filters
						Sodalite
						Lazurite, Lapis Lazuli
						Lazurite, Lapis Lazuli
	Tsavorite (Grossular, Garnet), Merelani Mint Garnet					Sodalite
	Uvarovite, Tsavorite, Demantoid, Andradite, Uvite					
	Uvarovite, Tsavorite					
	Demantoid (Andradite Garnet)					
	Grossular, Garnet					
	Grossular, Garnet					
	Grossular, Topazolite (Andradite Garnet)					
	Grossular, Garnet					
	Grossular, Garnet					
	Hessonite (Grossular, Garnet), Spessartine					
	Spessartine, Grossular, Garnet					
	Spessartine, Hessonite (Grossular, Garnet)					
	Spessartine, Grossular, Pyrope (Garnet)					
	Almandine, Grossular					

Continued on next page

Table 2: Enhancer and Arranger Talismans (continued)

	I	II	III	IV	V	VI
	Element	*Sulfides*	*Halides*	*Oxides*	*Carbonates*	*Sulfates*
	Purifiers	Mirrors	Brighteners	Transformers	Builders	Solidifiers
Scarlet *Strength*				Cuprite, Villiaumite		
Dark Scarlet *Vitality*				Cuprite		
Pink *Love, Commitment*	Copper, Diamond		Halite, Fluorite, Villiaumite	Spinel		
Red *Energy, Courage, Drive, Action*			Villiaumite	Cuprite, Spinel		
Dark Red *Passion, Devotion*		Sphalerite	Sylvite, Villiaumite	Cuprite		
Light Amethyst *Self-Knowledge*			Halite	Spinel		
Amethyst *Creativity, Vision*				Spinel		
Dark Amethyst *Insight*			Halite	Spinel		
Lavender *Luxury, Imagination*			Halite	Spinel		
Violet *Intuition*			Fluorite	Spinel		
Dark Violet *Dreams, Magic*			Halite			
Light Indigo *Virtue*			Fluorite			
Indigo *Wisdom*			Fluorite, Halite			
Dark Indigo *Truth*						
White *Illumination*	Diamond, Ballas Crystals	Skutterudite	Halite, Sal Ammoniac, Sylvite	Senarmontite	Rhodizite	
Silver *Reflection*	Silver, Platinum, Iron	Gersdorffite, Boulangerite, Galena, Skutterudite		Senarmontite		
Brown *Earth, Center, Stability*	Diamond, Copper	Sphalerite, Bornite, Pyrrhotite	Fluorite, Sylvite	Spinel, Stibiconite		
Black *Power, Mystery, Security*	Iron	Sphalerite, Argentite, Bornite, Marcasite (Pyrite), Hauerite, Tetrahedrite, Tennantite	Fluorite	Spinel, Bixbyite, Franklinite, Magnetite, Romanechite		

VII	VIII-1	VIII-2	VIII-3	VIII-4	VIII-5	VIII-6
Phosphates	*Nesosilicates or Orthosilicates*	*Sorosilicates*	*Cyclosilicates*	*Inosilicates*	*Phyllosilicates*	*Tectosilicates*
Buffers	Strengtheners	Unifiers	Energizers	Harmonizers	Bonders	Filters
	Spessartine, Grossular, Garnet					
	Almandine, Grossular, Pyrope					
	Spessartine, Garnet, Pyrope					Hackmanite (Sodalite)
	Rhodolite, Grossular, Spessartine					
	Almandine, Rhodolite, Grossular, Spessartine					
	Pyrope, Garnet					
	Rhodolite					
	Pyrope, Garnet					Lazurite
	Umbalite, Garnet					
	Umbalite, Garnet					Lazurite
	Umbalite, Garnet					
	Umbalite, Garnet					Lazurite
						Analcime, Leucite
	Almandine, Pyrope, Hessonite					
	Melanite (Andradite Garnet), Uvite					

Table 3: Guardian and Dreamholder Talismans

Used for protecting what we value: our possessions and our dreams.

	I	II	III	IV	V	VI
	Element	*Sulfides*	*Halides*	*Oxides*	*Carbonates*	*Sulfates*
	Purifiers	Mirrors	Brighteners	Transformers	Builders	Solidifiers
Light Blue *Acceptance*					Azurite	Selenite (Gypsum)
Blue *Trust*					Azurite	Linarite
Dark Blue *Respect, Compassion*					Azurite	
Light Turquoise *Harmony*					Rosasite	
Turquoise *Discovery, Balance*					Rosasite	Selenite (Gypsum)
Dark Turquoise *Flexibility*					Rosasite	
Light Green *Spiritual Development*				Gibbsite	Rosasite, Malachite	Selenite (Gypsum), Arthurite, Chenevixite, Ludlamite
Green *Growth, Renewal*					Rosasite, Malachite	Brochantite, Arthurite, Ludlamite
Dark Green *Physical Growth, Safety*					Rosasite, Malachite	Brochantite, Arthurite, Chenevixite, Ludlamite, Pseudomalachite
Light Olive *Perseverance*						Chenevixite
Olive *Awakening*						Chenevixite
Dark Olive *Learning*						Chenevixite
Light Yellow *Awareness*		Orpiment				
Yellow *Enlightenment*		Orpiment				Selenite (Gypsum)
Dark Yellow *Clarity*		Orpiment				
Light Gold *Happiness*		Orpiment				Selenite (Gypsum)
Gold *Enthusiasm, Exuberance*		Orpiment				Selenite (Gypsum)
Dark Gold *Power*		Orpiment				Selenite (Gypsum)
Light Orange *Friendship*		Pararealgar, Orpiment				Crocoite

VII	VIII-1	VIII-2	VIII-3	VIII-4	VIII-5	VIII-6
Phosphates	*Nesosilicates or Orthosilicates*	*Sorosilicates*	*Cyclosilicates*	*Inosilicates*	*Phyllosilicates*	*Tectosilicates*
Buffers	**Strengtheners**	**Unifiers**	**Energizers**	**Harmonizers**	**Bonders**	**Filters**
Guanacoite, Veszelyite	Kinoite		Papagoite	Violan (Diopside)	Polylithionite	Azulicite (Sanidine)
Lazulite, Veszelyite			Papagoite	Jadeite, Violan (Diopside)		Azulicite (Sanidine)
Lazulite, Vivianite, Clinoclase, Guanacoite, Scorzalite	Kinoite		Papagoite	Preseli Bluestone, Richterite, Riebeckite	Euclase	
Guanacoite, Phosphophyllite					Euclase, Chrysocolla	
Guanacoite, Phosphophyllite					Euclase, Chrysocolla	
Clinoclase, Guanacoite, Phosphophyllite					Euclase, Chrysocolla	
Annabergite	Datolite			Jadeite, Hiddenite (Spodumene), Diopside, Nephrite Jade (Actinolite), Tremolite	Talc, Fuchsite (Muscovite), Chrysotile (Serpentine)	Stilbite, Moonstone (Orthoclase)
Vivianite, Arthurite, Tsumebite, Veszelyite, Bayldonite	Datolite, Sphene	Chlorastrolite (Pumpellyite)		Nephrite Jade (Actinolite), Diopside, Jadeite, Tremolite	Chrysotile (Serpentine)	Stilbite
Vivianite, Atelestite, Bayldonite		Chlorastrolite (Pumpellyite)		Nephrite Jade (Actinolite), Augite, Diopside, Aegirine, Cat's Eye Diopside, Hedenbergite, Tremolite	Antigorite (Serpentine), Seraphinite (Clinochlore Chlorite)	Stilbite
Brazilianite, Volborthite, Tsumebite, Veszelyite	Titanite			Diopside		Heulandite, Stilbite
Brazilianite, Volborthite, Tsumebite, Veszelyite	Titanite, Bakerite, Datolite			Diopside		Heulandite, Stilbite
Brazilianite, Volborthite, Tsumebite, Veszelyite	Titanite			Diopside, Epidote, Hedenbergite		Heulandite, Stilbite
	Boltwoodite				Polylithionite	Sanidine
Brazilianite, Carnotite	Boltwoodite, Clinohumite				Muscovite	Stilbite
Legrandite	Boltwoodite					
Legrandite						
Legrandite						Stilbite, Sanidine
Legrandite						Stilbite
Legrandite						

Continued on next page

Table 3: Guardian and Dreamholder Talismans (continued)

	I	II	III	IV	V	VI
	Element	*Sulfides*	*Halides*	*Oxides*	*Carbonates*	*Sulfates*
	Purifiers	Mirrors	Brighteners	Transformers	Builders	Solidifiers
Orange *Joy*		Pararealgar, Orpiment				Crocoite
Dark Orange *Belonging*		Pararealgar, Orpiment				Crocoite
Light Scarlet *Dedication*		Realgar				Crocoite
Scarlet *Strength*		Realgar				Crocoite
Dark Scarlet *Vitality*		Realgar				Crocoite
Pink *Love, Commitment*						
Red *Energy, Courage, Drive, Action*		Realgar, Polybasite				
Dark Red *Passion, Devotion*		Realgar				
Light Amethyst *Self-Knowledge*						
Amethyst *Creativity, Vision*						
Dark Amethyst *Insight*						
Lavender *Luxury, Imagination*						Creedite
Violet *Intuition*						
Dark Violet *Dreams, Magic*						
Light Indigo *Virtue*						Creedite
Indigo *Wisdom*						
Dark Indigo *Truth*						
White *Illumination*			Thomsenolite	Gibbsite	Artinite, Borax, Colemanite, Gaylussite, Hydroboracite, Hydromagnesite, Hydrozincite, Kernite, Tincalconite, Trona	Selenite, Alabaster (Gypsum), Creedite, Glauberite
Silver *Reflection*	Silver	Arsenopyrite				
Brown *Earth, Center, Stability*			Cryolite	Samarskite, Hubnerite		Desert Rose (Selenite [Gypsum])
Black *Power, Mystery, Security*		Jamesonite, Jordanite, Polybasite		Merlinite (Drusy Psilomelane), Manganite		Ferberite, Wolframite

VII	VIII-1	VIII-2	VIII-3	VIII-4	VIII-5	VIII-6
Phosphates	*Nesosilicates or Orthosilicates*	*Sorosilicates*	*Cyclosilicates*	*Inosilicates*	*Phyllosilicates*	*Tectosilicates*
Buffers	Strengtheners	Unifiers	Energizers	Harmonizers	Bonders	Filters
Legrandite	Clinohumite					
		Piemontite				
Rosalite		Piemontite			Muscovite, Kämmererite	
Hureaulite, Rosalite, Wendwilsonite	Datolite	Piemontite		Kunsite (Spodumene), Xonotlite	Talc, Lepidolite, Polylithionite	Epistilbite
Rosalite, Wendwilsonite	Clinohumite	Piemontite				Stilbite
Erythrite, Rosalite, Wendwilsonite		Piemontite				
Rosalite				Kunsite (Spodumene), Charoite	Lepidolite	Palygorskite
Rosalite				Kunsite (Spodumene)	Lepidolite	
Erythrite, Rosalite				Kunsite (Spodumene), Charoite	Lepidolite, Kämmererite (Clinochlore)	
				Jadeite, Charoite	Kämmererite (Clinochlore), Chlorite	
				Kunsite (Spodumene), Charoite	Lepidolite, Kämmererite (Clinochlore)	
				Violane (Diopside), Charoite	Kämmererite (Clinochlore), Chlorite	
				Charoite		
				Charoite	Kämmererite (Clinochlore), Chlorite	
				Charoite	Euclase	
Beryllonite, Churchite	Titanite, Bakerite, Datolite			Jadeite, Eudidymite, Howlite, Tremolite	Kaolinite, Talc, Polylithionite, Pyrophyllite, Petalite	Moonstone (Orthoclase), Stilbite, Petalite, Epistilbite, Goosecreekite, Mesolite, Palygorskite, Phillipsite, Scolecite, Stellerite
					Muscovite, Polylithionite	
Dufrenite, Monazite, Arrojadite, Whiteite, Wolfeite	Clinohumite, Sphene			Edenite	Muscovite, Pyrophyllite	Sanidine
	Allanite, Gadolinite			Aegirine, Augite, Fluorrichterite, Hedenbergite, Hornblende, Neptunite, Arfvedsonite	Biotite, Phlogopite	

Table 4: Dispeller and Restorer Talismans

Used for ridding ourselves of undesirable traits and attributes.
Select based on the results desired after the undesired elements are gone.

	I	II	III	IV	V	VI
	Element	*Sulfides*	*Halides*	*Oxides*	*Carbonates*	*Sulfates*
	Purifiers	Mirrors	Brighteners	Transformers	Builders	Solidifiers
Light Blue *Acceptance*						Barite, Celestine, Caledonite
Blue *Trust*						Celestine, Caledonite
Dark Blue *Respect, Compassion*					Aragonite	Caledonite, Celestine
Light Turquoise *Harmony*				Boracite	Aragonite, Cerussite	Caledonite
Turquoise *Discovery, Balance*				Boracite	Aragonite	Caledonite
Dark Turquoise *Flexibility*		Marcasite	Atacamite	Boracite	Aragonite	Caledonite
Light Green *Spiritual Development*	Sulfur			Alexandrite	Aragonite	Barite, Anglesite, Antlerite
Green *Growth, Renewal*				Alexandrite	Boracite	Antlerite, Mottramite
Dark Green *Physical Growth, Safety*			Atacamite	Alexandrite	Boracite	Antlerite, Cornetite, Mottramite
Light Olive *Perseverance*				Cat's Eye, Chrysoberyl	Aragonite, Strontianite	
Olive *Awakening*				Cat's Eye, Chrysoberyl	Aurichalcite	
Dark Olive *Learning*				Cat's Eye, Chrysoberyl	Strontianite	
Light Yellow *Awareness*				Diaspore		Barite, Anglesite
Yellow *Enlightenment*	Sulfur					Anglesite
Dark Yellow *Clarity*	Sulfur					Barite, Anglesite
Light Gold *Happiness*					Aragonite	Barite, Anglesite
Gold *Enthusiasm, Exuberance*		Marcasite			Aragonite	Barite, Anglesite
Dark Gold *Power*						Barite, Anglesite
Light Orange *Friendship*						Barite, Anglesite
Orange *Joy*						Barite, Anglesite
Dark Orange *Belonging*						Barite, Anglesite

VII	VIII-1	VIII-2	VIII-3	VIII-4	VIII-5	VIII-6
Phosphates	*Nesosilicates or Orthosilicates*	*Sorosilicates*	*Cyclosilicates*	*Inosilicates*	*Phyllosilicates*	*Tectosilicates*
Buffers	**Strengtheners**	**Unifiers**	**Energizers**	**Harmonizers**	**Bonders**	**Filters**
	Topaz	Tanzanite (Zoisite)	Iolite (Cordierite), Chrysocolla	Shattuckite	Cavansite, Pentagonite	
Cornetite	Topaz, Dumortierite	Tanzanite (Zoisite)	Iolite	Shattuckite	Cavansite, Pentagonite	
Cornetite	Topaz	Tanzanite (Zoisite)	Iolite, Cordierite	Shattuckite	Cavansite, Pentagonite	
	Topaz	Hemimorphite	Chrysocolla	Shattuckite, Planchéite	Cavansite, Pentagonite	
	Topaz	Hemimorphite		Shattuckite, Planchéite	Cavansite, Pentagonite	
Cornetite	Topaz	Hemimorphite		Shattuckite, Planchéite	Cavansite, Pentagonite	
Wavellite, Adamite, Variscite, Conichalcite	Topaz	Zoisite		Sanbornite	Prehnite, Népouite	
Wavellite, Adamite, Austinite, Conichalcite, Duftite, Scorodite	Topaz, Sillimanite	Zoisite			Prehnite	
Wavellite, Adamite, Conichalcite, Duftite, Scorodite, Libethenite	Topaz, Kornerupine	Zoisite, Anyolite (Zoisite, Ruby)		Nuumite (Anthophyllite), Cat's Eye Enstatite	Prehnite, Elpidite	
Wavellite, Adamite, Duftite	Topaz, Peridot (Forsterite Olivine)		Prehnite			
Wavellite, Adamite, Duftite	Topaz, Peridot (Forsterite Olivine)					
Wavellite, Olivenite, Adamite, Duftite	Fayalite, Topaz, Peridot (Forsterite Olivine)		Prehnite			
	Topaz, Humite, Kornerupine		Prehnite			Danburite, Thomsonite
	Topaz, Humite, Sillimanite		Prehnite			Danburite, Thomsonite
Childrenite	Topaz, Humite		Prehnite			Danburite
	Topaz, Andalusite					Danburite
	Topaz		Prehnite			Danburite
	Topaz, Andalusite			Bronzite (Enstatite)		
	Topaz					
	Topaz					Stellerite
	Topaz					

Continued on next page

Table 4: Dispeller and Restorer Talismans (continued)

	I	II	III	IV	V	VI
	Element	*Sulfides*	*Halides*	*Oxides*	*Carbonates*	*Sulfates*
	Purifiers	Mirrors	Brighteners	Transformers	Builders	Solidifiers
Light Scarlet *Dedication*						
Scarlet *Strength*						
Dark Scarlet *Vitality*						
Pink *Love, Commitment*				Alexandrite, Lepidocrocite		Desert Rose (Barite)
Red *Energy, Courage, Drive, Action*				Alexandrite, Lepidocrocite		Barite
Dark Red *Passion, Devotion*				Alexandrite, Lepidocrocite		
Light Amethyst *Self-Knowledge*				Alexandrite, Lepidocrocite		
Amethyst *Creativity, Vision*				Alexandrite, Lepidocrocite		
Dark Amethyst *Insight*				Alexandrite, Lepidocrocite		
Lavender *Luxury, Imagination*						
Violet *Intuition*				Diaspore		
Dark Violet *Dreams, Magic*						
Light Indigo *Virtue*						
Indigo *Wisdom*						
Dark Indigo *Truth*						
White *Illumination*				Valentinite	Aragonite, Witherite, Cerussite, Hambergite, Witherite	Anglesite, Anhydrite
Silver *Reflection*		Stibnite, Cobaltite, Bournonite, Enargite				
Brown *Earth, Center, Stability*	Sulfur	Berthierite		Valentinite, Manganotantalite	Aragonite, Sinhalite	Desert Rose (Barite)
Black *Power, Mystery, Security*		Stephanite, Bournonite, Enargite		Brookite, Columbite, Goethite, Perovskite, Tantalite, Manganotantalite		

VII	VIII-1	VIII-2	VIII-3	VIII-4	VIII-5	VIII-6
Phosphates	*Nesosilicates or Orthosilicates*	*Sorosilicates*	*Cyclosilicates*	*Inosilicates*	*Phyllosilicates*	*Tectosilicates*
Buffers	Strengtheners	Unifiers	Energizers	Harmonizers	Bonders	Filters
	Topaz					
Carminite	Topaz, Poldervaartite					
Eosphorite, Carminite	Topaz				Elpidite	
Eosphorite, Strengite	Topaz, Chiastolite (Andalusite), Kornerupine	Thulite (Zoisite)		Yuksporite		
Carminite	Topaz	Thulite (Zoisite)				Thomsonite
Strengite, Carminite	Topaz	Thulite (Zoisite)				
Strengite	Topaz					Danburite
Strengite	Topaz					Danburite
Strengite	Topaz, Dumortierite					
Strengite	Topaz	Tanzanite				
Strengite	Topaz	Tanzanite				
Purpurite	Topaz, Dumortierite	Tanzanite				
		Tanzanite				
Purpurite		Tanzanite				
		Tanzanite	Iolite (Cordierite),			
Wavellite, Variscite, Scholzite, Thenardite	Chrysanthemum Stone (Andalusite), Tephroite	Bertrandite, Danburite		Anthophyllite, Epididymite	Elpidite, Sanbornite	Natrolite, Thomsonite
Childrenite, Descloizite, Eosphorite, Hopeite	Chiastolite (Cross), Staurolite (Fairy Cross), Kornerupine, Sillimanite			Anthophyllite, Bronzite (Enstatite)		Stellerite
Descloizite		Ilvaite				

Table 5: Barrier Talismans

Used to protect us from undesirable elements in life.
Select based on the desired outcome.

	I	II	III	IV	V	VI
	Element	*Sulfides*	*Halides*	*Oxides*	*Carbonates*	*Sulfates*
	Purifiers	Mirrors	Brighteners	Transformers	Builders	Solidifiers
Light Blue *Acceptance*					Henmilite	Chalcanthite
Blue *Trust*					Henmilite	Chalcanthite
Dark Blue *Respect, Compassion*					Henmilite	Chalcanthite
Light Turquoise *Harmony*						
Turquoise *Discovery, Balance*						
Dark Turquoise *Flexibility*						
Light Green *Spiritual Development*						
Green *Growth, Renewal*						
Dark Green *Physical Growth, Safety*						
Light Olive *Perseverance*						Copiapite, Emmonsite
Olive *Awakening*						Copiapite, Emmonsite
Dark Olive *Learning*						Copiapite, Emmonsite
Light Yellow *Awareness*						Copiapite
Yellow *Enlightenment*						Copiapite
Dark Yellow *Clarity*						Copiapite
Light Gold *Happiness*						Copiapite
Gold *Enthusiasm, Exuberance*						Copiapite
Dark Gold *Power*						Copiapite
Light Orange *Friendship*						Copiapite
Orange *Joy*						Copiapite
Dark Orange *Belonging*						
Light Scarlet *Dedication*						

VII	VIII-1	VIII-2	VIII-3	VIII-4	VIII-5	VIII-6
Phosphates	*Nesosilicates or Orthosilicates*	*Sorosilicates*	*Cyclosilicates*	*Inosilicates*	*Phyllosilicates*	*Tectosilicates*
Buffers	**Strengtheners**	**Unifiers**	**Energizers**	**Harmonizers**	**Bonders**	**Filters**
Amblygonite, Vauxite, Ceruléite	Kyanite		Axinite	Larimar (or Lorimar) (Pectolite)		Labradorite, Moonstone (Albite)
Vauxite, Ceruléite	Kyanite					Labradorite, Moonstone (Albite)
Turquoise, Vauxite, Ceruléite	Kyanite					Labradorite, Moonstone (Albite)
Turquoise, Gormanite					Ajoite	Labradorite, Amazonite
Turquoise, Gormanite				Larimar (or Lorimar) (Pectolite)	Ajoite	Labradorite, Amazonite
Turquoise, Gormanite					Ajoite	Labradorite, Amazonite
Turquoise, Amblygonite, Anapaite, Paravauxite					Gyrolite	Labradorite, Amazonite, Perthite
Turquoise, Amblygonite, Anapaite						Labradorite, Amazonite, Perthite
Turquoise, Amblygonite, Anapaite	Kyanite			Babingtonite		Labradorite, Amazonite, Perthite
				Tundrite		
Turquoise				Tundrite		
				Tundrite		
Amblygonite, Montebrasite, Paradamite			Axinite			Oligoclase
Strunzite						
			Axinite			Bytownite
			Axinite			
			Axinite			Bytownite
			Axinite	Tundrite	Astrophyllite	
				Inesite		
				Inesite		
				Inesite		
				Rhodonite		Sunstone

Continued on next page

Table 5: Barrier Talismans (continued)

	I	II	III	IV	V	VI
	Element	*Sulfides*	*Halides*	*Oxides*	*Carbonates*	*Sulfates*
	Purifiers	Mirrors	Brighteners	Transformers	Builders	Solidifiers
Scarlet *Strength*						
Dark Scarlet *Vitality*						
Pink *Love, Commitment*						Polyhalite
Red *Energy, Courage, Drive, Action*						
Dark Red *Passion, Devotion*						
Light Amethyst *Self-Knowledge*						
Amethyst *Creativity, Vision*						
Dark Amethyst *Insight*						
Lavender *Luxury, Imagination*						
Violet *Intuition*						
Dark Violet *Dreams, Magic*					Henmilite	
Light Indigo *Virtue*					Henmilite	
Indigo *Wisdom*					Henmilite	
Dark Indigo *Truth*					Henmilite	
White *Illumination*					Ulexite	Polyhalite
Silver *Reflection*						
Brown *Earth, Center, Stability*		Franckeite				
Black *Power, Mystery, Security*						

VII	VIII-1	VIII-2	VIII-3	VIII-4	VIII-5	VIII-6
Phosphates	*Nesosilicates or Orthosilicates*	*Sorosilicates*	*Cyclosilicates*	*Inosilicates*	*Phyllosilicates*	*Tectosilicates*
Buffers	Strengtheners	Unifiers	Energizers	Harmonizers	Bonders	Filters
				Rhodonite, Bustamite		Sunstone
				Rhodonite		Sunstone, Andesine
				Rhodonite, Inesite		Inesite
				Rhodonite		Sunstone
				Rhodonite		Sunstone, Andesine
				Rhodonite		
Amblygonite				Rhodonite		
				Rhodonite		
		Suolunite				
		Suolunite				
		Suolunite				
		Suolunite				
Amblygonite, Montebrasite		Jennite		Okenite, Wollastonite	Gyrolite	Albite, Analcime, Andesine
Strunzite	Bultfonteinite	Hubeite		Bustamite	Gyrolite	Oligoclase
				Babingtonite		

Table 6: Attractor Talismans

Used to augment Seekers and Enhancers to bring us what we seek.

	I	II	III	IV	V	VI
	Element	*Sulfides*	*Halides*	*Oxides*	*Carbonates*	*Sulfates*
	Purifiers	Mirrors	Brighteners	Transformers	Builders	Solidifiers
Light Blue *Acceptance*						
Blue *Trust*			Boleite, Diaboleite			Powellite
Dark Blue *Respect, Compassion*			Boleite, Diaboleite			
Light Turquoise *Harmony*						
Turquoise *Discovery, Balance*						
Dark Turquoise *Flexibility*						
Light Green *Spiritual Development*						
Green *Growth, Renewal*						
Dark Green *Physical Growth, Safety*						
Light Olive *Perseverance*						
Olive *Awakening*						
Dark Olive *Learning*				Anatase		
Light Yellow *Awareness*					Phosgenite	Wulfenite
Yellow *Enlightenment*			Calomel			Wulfenite, Powellite
Dark Yellow *Clarity*						Wulfenite, Scheelite
Light Gold *Happiness*		Chalcopyrite		Rutile		Wulfenite
Gold *Enthusiasm, Exuberance*		Chalcopyrite		Rutile		Wulfenite
Dark Gold *Power*		Chalcopyrite		Rutile		Wulfenite, Scheelite
Light Orange *Friendship*						Wulfenite
Orange *Joy*						Wulfenite
Dark Orange *Belonging*						Wulfenite
Light Scarlet *Dedication*						Wulfenite
Scarlet *Strength*						Wulfenite

VII	VIII-1	VIII-2	VIII-3	VIII-4	VIII-5	VIII-6
Phosphates	*Nesosilicates or Orthosilicates*	*Sorosilicates*	*Cyclosilicates*	*Inosilicates*	*Phyllosilicates*	*Tectosilicates*
Buffers	Strengtheners	Unifiers	Energizers	Harmonizers	Bonders	Filters
		Vesuvianite			Carletonite	Scapolite
		Vesuvianite				
		Vesuvianite			Carletonite	
		Vesuvianite			Apophyllite	
		Vesuvianite				
		Vesuvianite				
Wardite		Idocrase (Vesuvianite)			Apophyllite	
		Idocrase (Vesuvianite)				
		Idocrase (Vesuvianite)			Apophyllite	
Torbernite						
						Scapolite
					Apophyllite	Scapolite
		Vesuvianite				Scapolite
		Vesuvianite				Scapolite
		Vesuvianite				Scapolite
		Vesuvianite				Scapolite
					Apophyllite	
		Vesuvianite				

Continued on next page

Table 6: Attractor Talismans (continued)

	I	II	III	IV	V	VI
	Element	Sulfides	Halides	Oxides	Carbonates	Sulfates
	Purifiers	Mirrors	Brighteners	Transformers	Builders	Solidifiers
Dark Scarlet *Vitality*						Wulfenite
Pink *Love, Commitment*						
Red *Energy, Courage, Drive, Action*						Wulfenite
Dark Red *Passion, Devotion*		Sphalerite				Wulfenite
Light Amethyst *Self-Knowledge*		Chalcopyrite				
Amethyst *Creativity, Vision*						
Dark Amethyst *Insight*		Chalcopyrite				
Lavender *Luxury, Imagination*		Chalcopyrite				
Violet *Intuition*		Chalcopyrite				
Dark Violet *Dreams, Magic*		Chalcopyrite				
Light Indigo *Virtue*		Chalcopyrite				
Indigo *Wisdom*		Chalcopyrite				
Dark Indigo *Truth*		Chalcopyrite				
White *Illumination*			Calomel		Phosgenite	Wulfenite, Scheelite
Silver *Reflection*				Hausmannite		Wulfenite, Powellite
Brown *Earth, Center, Stability*		Sphalerite		Anatase, Periclase	Sinhalite, Phosgenite	Powellite, Scheelite
Black *Power, Mystery, Security*		Sphalerite		Anatase, Rutile, Cassiterite, Pyrolusite, Hausmannite, Plattnerite		

VII	VIII-1	VIII-2	VIII-3	VIII-4	VIII-5	VIII-6
Phosphates	*Nesosilicates or Orthosilicates*	*Sorosilicates*	*Cyclosilicates*	*Inosilicates*	*Phyllosilicates*	*Tectosilicates*
Buffers	**Strengtheners**	**Unifiers**	**Energizers**	**Harmonizers**	**Bonders**	**Filters**
					Apophyllite	Scapolite
		Vesuvianite				
					Apophyllite	Scapolite
Wardite		Hardystonite				
Wardite						

The Great Talismanic Color Wheel of Influence

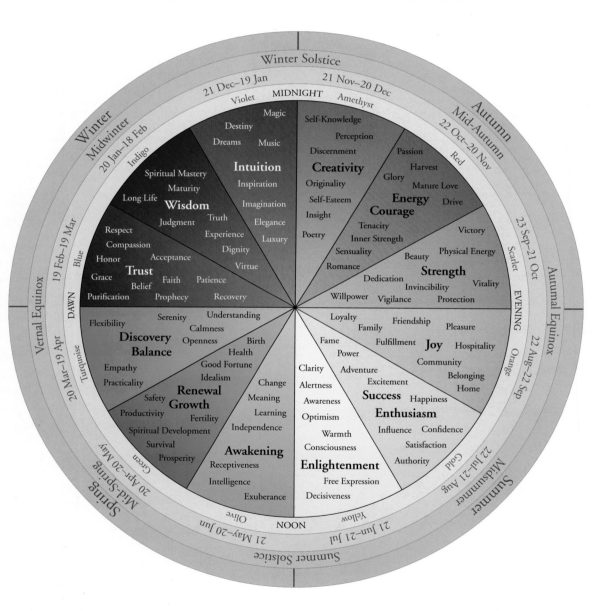

Winter Solstice

21 Dec–19 Jan · MIDNIGHT · 21 Nov–20 Dec

Violet · Amethyst

Winter · Midwinter · 20 Jan–18 Feb · Indigo

Autumn · Mid-Autumn · 22 Oct–20 Nov · Red

Intuition
Magic
Destiny
Dreams
Music
Inspiration
Imagination
Elegance
Luxury

Creativity
Self-Knowledge
Perception
Discernment
Originality
Self-Esteem
Insight
Poetry

Energy Courage
Passion
Harvest
Glory
Mature Love
Drive
Tenacity
Inner Strength
Sensuality
Romance

Wisdom
Spiritual Mastery
Maturity
Long Life
Truth
Judgment
Experience
Dignity
Virtue

Trust
Respect
Compassion
Honor
Grace
Acceptance
Belief
Faith
Patience
Purification
Prophecy
Recovery

Strength
Victory
Physical Energy
Beauty
Dedication
Vitality
Invincibility
Willpower
Vigilance
Protection

Vernal Equinox · 19 Feb–19 Mar · Blue · DAWN

23 Sep–21 Oct · Scarlet · EVENING · Autumnal Equinox

Discovery Balance
Understanding
Serenity
Calmness
Flexibility
Openness
Birth
Health
Empathy
Good Fortune
Practicality
Idealism

Renewal Growth
Change
Meaning
Learning
Independence
Safety
Productivity
Fertility
Spiritual Development
Survival
Prosperity

Awakening
Receptiveness
Intelligence
Exuberance

Joy
Loyalty
Family
Friendship
Pleasure
Fame
Fulfillment
Hospitality
Power
Community
Adventure
Belonging
Home

Success Enthusiasm
Clarity
Alertness
Awareness
Optimism
Warmth
Consciousness
Excitement
Happiness
Influence
Confidence
Satisfaction
Authority

Enlightenment
Free Expression
Decisiveness

20 Mar–19 Apr · Turquoise · 20 Apr–20 May · Green

Spring · Mid-Spring · 21 May–20 Jun · Olive

Summer · Midsummer · 22 Jul–21 Aug · Gold

22 Aug–22 Sep · Orange · Autumnal Equinox

NOON · Yellow · 21 Jun–21 Jul

Summer Solstice

Crystal Structures

Hexagonal
Example:
Quartz

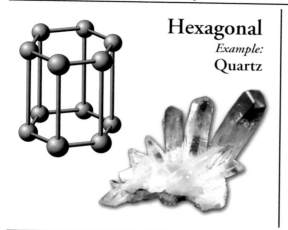

Isometric
Example:
Pyrite

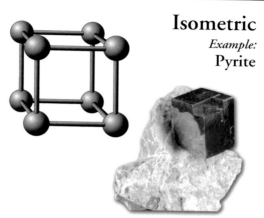

Monoclinic
Example:
Epidote

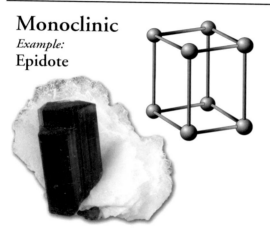

Tetragonal
Example:
Rutile

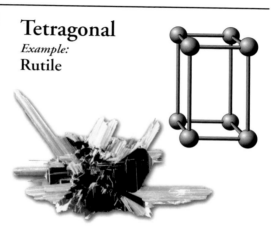

Triclinic
Example:
Inesite

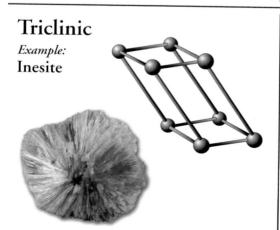

Orthorhombic
Example:
Cavansite

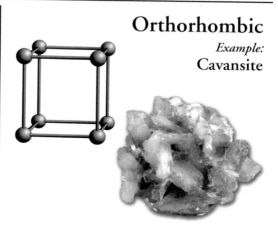

Prepared Crystal Talismans

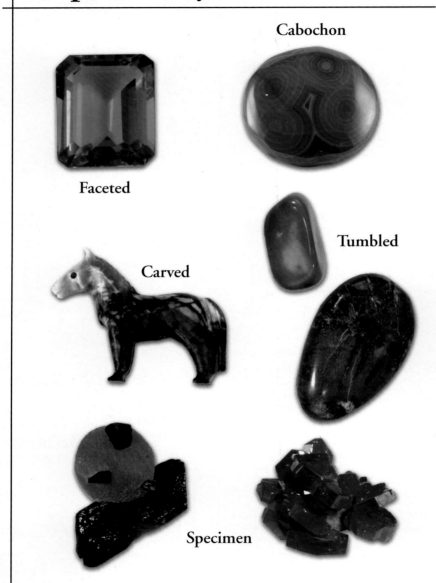

Cabochon

Faceted

Tumbled

Carved

Specimen